C-4626   CAREER EXAMINATION SERIES

This is your
PASSBOOK for...

Deputy Sheriff I

Test Preparation Study Guide
Questions & Answers

COPYRIGHT NOTICE

This book is SOLELY intended for, is sold ONLY to, and its use is RESTRICTED to individual, bona fide applicants or candidates who qualify by virtue of having seriously filed applications for appropriate license, certificate, professional and/or promotional advancement, higher school matriculation, scholarship, or other legitimate requirements of education and/or governmental authorities.

This book is NOT intended for use, class instruction, tutoring, training, duplication, copying, reprinting, excerption, or adaptation, etc., by:

1) Other publishers
2) Proprietors and/or Instructors of "Coaching" and/or Preparatory Courses
3) Personnel and/or Training Divisions of commercial, industrial, and governmental organizations
4) Schools, colleges, or universities and/or their departments and staffs, including teachers and other personnel
5) Testing Agencies or Bureaus
6) Study groups which seek by the purchase of a single volume to copy and/or duplicate and/or adapt this material for use by the group as a whole without having purchased individual volumes for each of the members of the group
7) Et al.

Such persons would be in violation of appropriate Federal and State statutes.

PROVISION OF LICENSING AGREEMENTS – Recognized educational, commercial, industrial, and governmental institutions and organizations, and others legitimately engaged in educational pursuits, including training, testing, and measurement activities, may address request for a licensing agreement to the copyright owners, who will determine whether, and under what conditions, including fees and charges, the materials in this book may be used them. In other words, a licensing facility exists for the legitimate use of the material in this book on other than an individual basis. However, it is asseverated and affirmed here that the material in this book CANNOT be used without the receipt of the express permission of such a licensing agreement from the Publishers. Inquiries re licensing should be addressed to the company, attention rights and permissions department.

All rights reserved, including the right of reproduction in whole or in part, in any form or by any means, electronic or mechanical, including photocopying, recording, or by any information storage and retrieval system, without permission in writing from the Publisher.

Copyright © 2024 by
National Learning Corporation

212 Michael Drive, Syosset, NY 11791
(516) 921-8888 • www.passbooks.com
E-mail: info@passbooks.com

PASSBOOK® SERIES

THE *PASSBOOK® SERIES* has been created to prepare applicants and candidates for the ultimate academic battlefield – the examination room.

At some time in our lives, each and every one of us may be required to take an examination – for validation, matriculation, admission, qualification, registration, certification, or licensure.

Based on the assumption that every applicant or candidate has met the basic formal educational standards, has taken the required number of courses, and read the necessary texts, the *PASSBOOK® SERIES* furnishes the one special preparation which may assure passing with confidence, instead of failing with insecurity. Examination questions – together with answers – are furnished as the basic vehicle for study so that the mysteries of the examination and its compounding difficulties may be eliminated or diminished by a sure method.

This book is meant to help you pass your examination provided that you qualify and are serious in your objective.

The entire field is reviewed through the huge store of content information which is succinctly presented through a provocative and challenging approach – the question-and-answer method.

A climate of success is established by furnishing the correct answers at the end of each test.

You soon learn to recognize types of questions, forms of questions, and patterns of questioning. You may even begin to anticipate expected outcomes.

You perceive that many questions are repeated or adapted so that you can gain acute insights, which may enable you to score many sure points.

You learn how to confront new questions, or types of questions, and to attack them confidently and work out the correct answers.

You note objectives and emphases, and recognize pitfalls and dangers, so that you may make positive educational adjustments.

Moreover, you are kept fully informed in relation to new concepts, methods, practices, and directions in the field.

You discover that you are actually taking the examination all the time: you are preparing for the examination by "taking" an examination, not by reading extraneous and/or supererogatory textbooks.

In short, this PASSBOOK®, used directedly, should be an important factor in helping you to pass your test.

DEPUTY SHERIFF I

DUTIES

An employee in this class enforces State laws, including Civil, Penal and Vehicle and Traffic Law. The employee makes arrests, transports prisoners, serves legal processes, patrols highways and secures court detention facilities. Routine assignments and special orders are received from superior officers who review work methods and results through reports, inspections and discussions. Does related work as required.

SCOPE OF THE EXAMINATION

The written test will cover knowledge, skills, and/or abilities in such areas as:
1. Understanding and applying laws, rules and procedures in law enforcement;
2. Understanding and interpreting written material; and
3. Preparation of written material and reports.

HOW TO TAKE A TEST

I. YOU MUST PASS AN EXAMINATION

A. WHAT EVERY CANDIDATE SHOULD KNOW

Examination applicants often ask us for help in preparing for the written test. What can I study in advance? What kinds of questions will be asked? How will the test be given? How will the papers be graded?

As an applicant for a civil service examination, you may be wondering about some of these things. Our purpose here is to suggest effective methods of advance study and to describe civil service examinations.

Your chances for success on this examination can be increased if you know how to prepare. Those "pre-examination jitters" can be reduced if you know what to expect. You can even experience an adventure in good citizenship if you know why civil service exams are given.

B. WHY ARE CIVIL SERVICE EXAMINATIONS GIVEN?

Civil service examinations are important to you in two ways. As a citizen, you want public jobs filled by employees who know how to do their work. As a job seeker, you want a fair chance to compete for that job on an equal footing with other candidates. The best-known means of accomplishing this two-fold goal is the competitive examination.

Exams are widely publicized throughout the nation. They may be administered for jobs in federal, state, city, municipal, town or village governments or agencies.

Any citizen may apply, with some limitations, such as the age or residence of applicants. Your experience and education may be reviewed to see whether you meet the requirements for the particular examination. When these requirements exist, they are reasonable and applied consistently to all applicants. Thus, a competitive examination may cause you some uneasiness now, but it is your privilege and safeguard.

C. HOW ARE CIVIL SERVICE EXAMS DEVELOPED?

Examinations are carefully written by trained technicians who are specialists in the field known as "psychological measurement," in consultation with recognized authorities in the field of work that the test will cover. These experts recommend the subject matter areas or skills to be tested; only those knowledges or skills important to your success on the job are included. The most reliable books and source materials available are used as references. Together, the experts and technicians judge the difficulty level of the questions.

Test technicians know how to phrase questions so that the problem is clearly stated. Their ethics do not permit "trick" or "catch" questions. Questions may have been tried out on sample groups, or subjected to statistical analysis, to determine their usefulness.

Written tests are often used in combination with performance tests, ratings of training and experience, and oral interviews. All of these measures combine to form the best-known means of finding the right person for the right job.

II. HOW TO PASS THE WRITTEN TEST

A. NATURE OF THE EXAMINATION

To prepare intelligently for civil service examinations, you should know how they differ from school examinations you have taken. In school you were assigned certain definite pages to read or subjects to cover. The examination questions were quite detailed and usually emphasized memory. Civil service exams, on the other hand, try to discover your present ability to perform the duties of a position, plus your potentiality to learn these duties. In other words, a civil service exam attempts to predict how successful you will be. Questions cover such a broad area that they cannot be as minute and detailed as school exam questions.

In the public service similar kinds of work, or positions, are grouped together in one "class." This process is known as *position-classification*. All the positions in a class are paid according to the salary range for that class. One class title covers all of these positions, and they are all tested by the same examination.

B. FOUR BASIC STEPS

1) Study the announcement

How, then, can you know what subjects to study? Our best answer is: "Learn as much as possible about the class of positions for which you've applied." The exam will test the knowledge, skills and abilities needed to do the work.

Your most valuable source of information about the position you want is the official exam announcement. This announcement lists the training and experience qualifications. Check these standards and apply only if you come reasonably close to meeting them.

The brief description of the position in the examination announcement offers some clues to the subjects which will be tested. Think about the job itself. Review the duties in your mind. Can you perform them, or are there some in which you are rusty? Fill in the blank spots in your preparation.

Many jurisdictions preview the written test in the exam announcement by including a section called "Knowledge and Abilities Required," "Scope of the Examination," or some similar heading. Here you will find out specifically what fields will be tested.

2) Review your own background

Once you learn in general what the position is all about, and what you need to know to do the work, ask yourself which subjects you already know fairly well and which need improvement. You may wonder whether to concentrate on improving your strong areas or on building some background in your fields of weakness. When the announcement has specified "some knowledge" or "considerable knowledge," or has used adjectives like "beginning principles of..." or "advanced ... methods," you can get a clue as to the number and difficulty of questions to be asked in any given field. More questions, and hence broader coverage, would be included for those subjects which are more important in the work. Now weigh your strengths and weaknesses against the job requirements and prepare accordingly.

3) Determine the level of the position

Another way to tell how intensively you should prepare is to understand the level of the job for which you are applying. Is it the entering level? In other words, is this the position in which beginners in a field of work are hired? Or is it an intermediate or advanced level? Sometimes this is indicated by such words as "Junior" or "Senior" in the class title. Other jurisdictions use Roman numerals to designate the level – Clerk I, Clerk II, for example. The word "Supervisor" sometimes appears in the title. If the level is not indicated by the title, check the description of duties. Will you be working under very close supervision, or will you have responsibility for independent decisions in this work?

4) Choose appropriate study materials

Now that you know the subjects to be examined and the relative amount of each subject to be covered, you can choose suitable study materials. For beginning level jobs, or even advanced ones, if you have a pronounced weakness in some aspect of your training, read a modern, standard textbook in that field. Be sure it is up to date and has general coverage. Such books are normally available at your library, and the librarian will be glad to help you locate one. For entry-level positions, questions of appropriate difficulty are chosen – neither highly advanced questions, nor those too simple. Such questions require careful thought but not advanced training.

If the position for which you are applying is technical or advanced, you will read more advanced, specialized material. If you are already familiar with the basic principles of your field, elementary textbooks would waste your time. Concentrate on advanced textbooks and technical periodicals. Think through the concepts and review difficult problems in your field.

These are all general sources. You can get more ideas on your own initiative, following these leads. For example, training manuals and publications of the government agency which employs workers in your field can be useful, particularly for technical and professional positions. A letter or visit to the government department involved may result in more specific study suggestions, and certainly will provide you with a more definite idea of the exact nature of the position you are seeking.

III. KINDS OF TESTS

Tests are used for purposes other than measuring knowledge and ability to perform specified duties. For some positions, it is equally important to test ability to make adjustments to new situations or to profit from training. In others, basic mental abilities not dependent on information are essential. Questions which test these things may not appear as pertinent to the duties of the position as those which test for knowledge and information. Yet they are often highly important parts of a fair examination. For very general questions, it is almost impossible to help you direct your study efforts. What we can do is to point out some of the more common of these general abilities needed in public service positions and describe some typical questions.

1) General information

Broad, general information has been found useful for predicting job success in some kinds of work. This is tested in a variety of ways, from vocabulary lists to questions about current events. Basic background in some field of work, such as sociology or economics, may be sampled in a group of questions. Often these are principles which have become familiar to most persons through exposure rather than through formal training. It is difficult to advise you how to study for these questions; being alert to the world around you is our best suggestion.

2) Verbal ability

An example of an ability needed in many positions is verbal or language ability. Verbal ability is, in brief, the ability to use and understand words. Vocabulary and grammar tests are typical measures of this ability. Reading comprehension or paragraph interpretation questions are common in many kinds of civil service tests. You are given a paragraph of written material and asked to find its central meaning.

3) Numerical ability
Number skills can be tested by the familiar arithmetic problem, by checking paired lists of numbers to see which are alike and which are different, or by interpreting charts and graphs. In the latter test, a graph may be printed in the test booklet which you are asked to use as the basis for answering questions.

4) Observation
A popular test for law-enforcement positions is the observation test. A picture is shown to you for several minutes, then taken away. Questions about the picture test your ability to observe both details and larger elements.

5) Following directions
In many positions in the public service, the employee must be able to carry out written instructions dependably and accurately. You may be given a chart with several columns, each column listing a variety of information. The questions require you to carry out directions involving the information given in the chart.

6) Skills and aptitudes
Performance tests effectively measure some manual skills and aptitudes. When the skill is one in which you are trained, such as typing or shorthand, you can practice. These tests are often very much like those given in business school or high school courses. For many of the other skills and aptitudes, however, no short-time preparation can be made. Skills and abilities natural to you or that you have developed throughout your lifetime are being tested.

Many of the general questions just described provide all the data needed to answer the questions and ask you to use your reasoning ability to find the answers. Your best preparation for these tests, as well as for tests of facts and ideas, is to be at your physical and mental best. You, no doubt, have your own methods of getting into an exam-taking mood and keeping "in shape." The next section lists some ideas on this subject.

IV. KINDS OF QUESTIONS

Only rarely is the "essay" question, which you answer in narrative form, used in civil service tests. Civil service tests are usually of the short-answer type. Full instructions for answering these questions will be given to you at the examination. But in case this is your first experience with short-answer questions and separate answer sheets, here is what you need to know:

1) Multiple-choice Questions
Most popular of the short-answer questions is the "multiple choice" or "best answer" question. It can be used, for example, to test for factual knowledge, ability to solve problems or judgment in meeting situations found at work.
A multiple-choice question is normally one of three types—
- It can begin with an incomplete statement followed by several possible endings. You are to find the one ending which *best* completes the statement, although some of the others may not be entirely wrong.
- It can also be a complete statement in the form of a question which is answered by choosing one of the statements listed.

- It can be in the form of a problem – again you select the best answer.

Here is an example of a multiple-choice question with a discussion which should give you some clues as to the method for choosing the right answer:

When an employee has a complaint about his assignment, the action which will *best* help him overcome his difficulty is to
- A. discuss his difficulty with his coworkers
- B. take the problem to the head of the organization
- C. take the problem to the person who gave him the assignment
- D. say nothing to anyone about his complaint

In answering this question, you should study each of the choices to find which is best. Consider choice "A" – Certainly an employee may discuss his complaint with fellow employees, but no change or improvement can result, and the complaint remains unresolved. Choice "B" is a poor choice since the head of the organization probably does not know what assignment you have been given, and taking your problem to him is known as "going over the head" of the supervisor. The supervisor, or person who made the assignment, is the person who can clarify it or correct any injustice. Choice "C" is, therefore, correct. To say nothing, as in choice "D," is unwise. Supervisors have and interest in knowing the problems employees are facing, and the employee is seeking a solution to his problem.

2) True/False Questions

The "true/false" or "right/wrong" form of question is sometimes used. Here a complete statement is given. Your job is to decide whether the statement is right or wrong.

SAMPLE: A roaming cell-phone call to a nearby city costs less than a non-roaming call to a distant city.

This statement is wrong, or false, since roaming calls are more expensive.

This is not a complete list of all possible question forms, although most of the others are variations of these common types. You will always get complete directions for answering questions. Be sure you understand *how* to mark your answers – ask questions until you do.

V. RECORDING YOUR ANSWERS

Computer terminals are used more and more today for many different kinds of exams.

For an examination with very few applicants, you may be told to record your answers in the test booklet itself. Separate answer sheets are much more common. If this separate answer sheet is to be scored by machine – and this is often the case – it is highly important that you mark your answers correctly in order to get credit.

An electronic scoring machine is often used in civil service offices because of the speed with which papers can be scored. Machine-scored answer sheets must be marked with a pencil, which will be given to you. This pencil has a high graphite content which responds to the electronic scoring machine. As a matter of fact, stray dots may register as answers, so do not let your pencil rest on the answer sheet while you are pondering the correct answer. Also, if your pencil lead breaks or is otherwise defective, ask for another.

Since the answer sheet will be dropped in a slot in the scoring machine, be careful not to bend the corners or get the paper crumpled.

The answer sheet normally has five vertical columns of numbers, with 30 numbers to a column. These numbers correspond to the question numbers in your test booklet. After each number, going across the page are four or five pairs of dotted lines. These short dotted lines have small letters or numbers above them. The first two pairs may also have a "T" or "F" above the letters. This indicates that the first two pairs only are to be used if the questions are of the true-false type. If the questions are multiple choice, disregard the "T" and "F" and pay attention only to the small letters or numbers.

Answer your questions in the manner of the sample that follows:

32. The largest city in the United States is
    A. Washington, D.C.
    B. New York City
    C. Chicago
    D. Detroit
    E. San Francisco

1) Choose the answer you think is best. (New York City is the largest, so "B" is correct.)
2) Find the row of dotted lines numbered the same as the question you are answering. (Find row number 32)
3) Find the pair of dotted lines corresponding to the answer. (Find the pair of lines under the mark "B.")
4) Make a solid black mark between the dotted lines.

VI. BEFORE THE TEST

Common sense will help you find procedures to follow to get ready for an examination. Too many of us, however, overlook these sensible measures. Indeed, nervousness and fatigue have been found to be the most serious reasons why applicants fail to do their best on civil service tests. Here is a list of reminders:

- Begin your preparation early – Don't wait until the last minute to go scurrying around for books and materials or to find out what the position is all about.
- Prepare continuously – An hour a night for a week is better than an all-night cram session. This has been definitely established. What is more, a night a week for a month will return better dividends than crowding your study into a shorter period of time.
- Locate the place of the exam – You have been sent a notice telling you when and where to report for the examination. If the location is in a different town or otherwise unfamiliar to you, it would be well to inquire the best route and learn something about the building.
- Relax the night before the test – Allow your mind to rest. Do not study at all that night. Plan some mild recreation or diversion; then go to bed early and get a good night's sleep.
- Get up early enough to make a leisurely trip to the place for the test – This way unforeseen events, traffic snarls, unfamiliar buildings, etc. will not upset you.
- Dress comfortably – A written test is not a fashion show. You will be known by number and not by name, so wear something comfortable.

- Leave excess paraphernalia at home – Shopping bags and odd bundles will get in your way. You need bring only the items mentioned in the official notice you received; usually everything you need is provided. Do not bring reference books to the exam. They will only confuse those last minutes and be taken away from you when in the test room.
- Arrive somewhat ahead of time – If because of transportation schedules you must get there very early, bring a newspaper or magazine to take your mind off yourself while waiting.
- Locate the examination room – When you have found the proper room, you will be directed to the seat or part of the room where you will sit. Sometimes you are given a sheet of instructions to read while you are waiting. Do not fill out any forms until you are told to do so; just read them and be prepared.
- Relax and prepare to listen to the instructions
- If you have any physical problem that may keep you from doing your best, be sure to tell the test administrator. If you are sick or in poor health, you really cannot do your best on the exam. You can come back and take the test some other time.

VII. AT THE TEST

The day of the test is here and you have the test booklet in your hand. The temptation to get going is very strong. Caution! There is more to success than knowing the right answers. You must know how to identify your papers and understand variations in the type of short-answer question used in this particular examination. Follow these suggestions for maximum results from your efforts:

1) Cooperate with the monitor
The test administrator has a duty to create a situation in which you can be as much at ease as possible. He will give instructions, tell you when to begin, check to see that you are marking your answer sheet correctly, and so on. He is not there to guard you, although he will see that your competitors do not take unfair advantage. He wants to help you do your best.

2) Listen to all instructions
Don't jump the gun! Wait until you understand all directions. In most civil service tests you get more time than you need to answer the questions. So don't be in a hurry. Read each word of instructions until you clearly understand the meaning. Study the examples, listen to all announcements and follow directions. Ask questions if you do not understand what to do.

3) Identify your papers
Civil service exams are usually identified by number only. You will be assigned a number; you must not put your name on your test papers. Be sure to copy your number correctly. Since more than one exam may be given, copy your exact examination title.

4) Plan your time
Unless you are told that a test is a "speed" or "rate of work" test, speed itself is usually not important. Time enough to answer all the questions will be provided, but this does not mean that you have all day. An overall time limit has been set. Divide the total time (in minutes) by the number of questions to determine the approximate time you have for each question.

5) Do not linger over difficult questions

If you come across a difficult question, mark it with a paper clip (useful to have along) and come back to it when you have been through the booklet. One caution if you do this – be sure to skip a number on your answer sheet as well. Check often to be sure that you have not lost your place and that you are marking in the row numbered the same as the question you are answering.

6) Read the questions

Be sure you know what the question asks! Many capable people are unsuccessful because they failed to *read* the questions correctly.

7) Answer all questions

Unless you have been instructed that a penalty will be deducted for incorrect answers, it is better to guess than to omit a question.

8) Speed tests

It is often better NOT to guess on speed tests. It has been found that on timed tests people are tempted to spend the last few seconds before time is called in marking answers at random – without even reading them – in the hope of picking up a few extra points. To discourage this practice, the instructions may warn you that your score will be "corrected" for guessing. That is, a penalty will be applied. The incorrect answers will be deducted from the correct ones, or some other penalty formula will be used.

9) Review your answers

If you finish before time is called, go back to the questions you guessed or omitted to give them further thought. Review other answers if you have time.

10) Return your test materials

If you are ready to leave before others have finished or time is called, take ALL your materials to the monitor and leave quietly. Never take any test material with you. The monitor can discover whose papers are not complete, and taking a test booklet may be grounds for disqualification.

VIII. EXAMINATION TECHNIQUES

1) Read the general instructions carefully. These are usually printed on the first page of the exam booklet. As a rule, these instructions refer to the timing of the examination; the fact that you should not start work until the signal and must stop work at a signal, etc. If there are any *special* instructions, such as a choice of questions to be answered, make sure that you note this instruction carefully.

2) When you are ready to start work on the examination, that is as soon as the signal has been given, read the instructions to each question booklet, underline any key words or phrases, such as *least, best, outline, describe* and the like. In this way you will tend to answer as requested rather than discover on reviewing your paper that you *listed without describing*, that you selected the *worst* choice rather than the *best* choice, etc.

3) If the examination is of the objective or multiple-choice type – that is, each question will also give a series of possible answers: A, B, C or D, and you are called upon to select the best answer and write the letter next to that answer on your answer paper – it is advisable to start answering each question in turn. There may be anywhere from 50 to 100 such questions in the three or four hours allotted and you can see how much time would be taken if you read through all the questions before beginning to answer any. Furthermore, if you come across a question or group of questions which you know would be difficult to answer, it would undoubtedly affect your handling of all the other questions.

4) If the examination is of the essay type and contains but a few questions, it is a moot point as to whether you should read all the questions before starting to answer any one. Of course, if you are given a choice – say five out of seven and the like – then it is essential to read all the questions so you can eliminate the two that are most difficult. If, however, you are asked to answer all the questions, there may be danger in trying to answer the easiest one first because you may find that you will spend too much time on it. The best technique is to answer the first question, then proceed to the second, etc.

5) Time your answers. Before the exam begins, write down the time it started, then add the time allowed for the examination and write down the time it must be completed, then divide the time available somewhat as follows:
   - If 3-1/2 hours are allowed, that would be 210 minutes. If you have 80 objective-type questions, that would be an average of 2-1/2 minutes per question. Allow yourself no more than 2 minutes per question, or a total of 160 minutes, which will permit about 50 minutes to review.
   - If for the time allotment of 210 minutes there are 7 essay questions to answer, that would average about 30 minutes a question. Give yourself only 25 minutes per question so that you have about 35 minutes to review.

6) The most important instruction is to *read each question* and make sure you know what is wanted. The second most important instruction is to *time yourself properly* so that you answer every question. The third most important instruction is to *answer every question*. Guess if you have to but include something for each question. Remember that you will receive no credit for a blank and will probably receive some credit if you write something in answer to an essay question. If you guess a letter – say "B" for a multiple-choice question – you may have guessed right. If you leave a blank as an answer to a multiple-choice question, the examiners may respect your feelings but it will not add a point to your score. Some exams may penalize you for wrong answers, so in such cases *only*, you may not want to guess unless you have some basis for your answer.

7) Suggestions
   a. Objective-type questions
      1. Examine the question booklet for proper sequence of pages and questions
      2. Read all instructions carefully
      3. Skip any question which seems too difficult; return to it after all other questions have been answered
      4. Apportion your time properly; do not spend too much time on any single question or group of questions

5. Note and underline key words – *all, most, fewest, least, best, worst, same, opposite,* etc.
6. Pay particular attention to negatives
7. Note unusual option, e.g., unduly long, short, complex, different or similar in content to the body of the question
8. Observe the use of "hedging" words – *probably, may, most likely,* etc.
9. Make sure that your answer is put next to the same number as the question
10. Do not second-guess unless you have good reason to believe the second answer is definitely more correct
11. Cross out original answer if you decide another answer is more accurate; do not erase until you are ready to hand your paper in
12. Answer all questions; guess unless instructed otherwise
13. Leave time for review

   b. Essay questions
   1. Read each question carefully
   2. Determine exactly what is wanted. Underline key words or phrases.
   3. Decide on outline or paragraph answer
   4. Include many different points and elements unless asked to develop any one or two points or elements
   5. Show impartiality by giving pros and cons unless directed to select one side only
   6. Make and write down any assumptions you find necessary to answer the questions
   7. Watch your English, grammar, punctuation and choice of words
   8. Time your answers; don't crowd material

8) Answering the essay question

Most essay questions can be answered by framing the specific response around several key words or ideas. Here are a few such key words or ideas:

M's: manpower, materials, methods, money, management
P's: purpose, program, policy, plan, procedure, practice, problems, pitfalls, personnel, public relations

   a. Six basic steps in handling problems:
   1. Preliminary plan and background development
   2. Collect information, data and facts
   3. Analyze and interpret information, data and facts
   4. Analyze and develop solutions as well as make recommendations
   5. Prepare report and sell recommendations
   6. Install recommendations and follow up effectiveness

   b. Pitfalls to avoid
   1. *Taking things for granted* – A statement of the situation does not necessarily imply that each of the elements is necessarily true; for example, a complaint may be invalid and biased so that all that can be taken for granted is that a complaint has been registered

2. *Considering only one side of a situation* – Wherever possible, indicate several alternatives and then point out the reasons you selected the best one
3. *Failing to indicate follow up* – Whenever your answer indicates action on your part, make certain that you will take proper follow-up action to see how successful your recommendations, procedures or actions turn out to be
4. *Taking too long in answering any single question* – Remember to time your answers properly

IX. AFTER THE TEST

Scoring procedures differ in detail among civil service jurisdictions although the general principles are the same. Whether the papers are hand-scored or graded by machine we have described, they are nearly always graded by number. That is, the person who marks the paper knows only the number – never the name – of the applicant. Not until all the papers have been graded will they be matched with names. If other tests, such as training and experience or oral interview ratings have been given, scores will be combined. Different parts of the examination usually have different weights. For example, the written test might count 60 percent of the final grade, and a rating of training and experience 40 percent. In many jurisdictions, veterans will have a certain number of points added to their grades.

After the final grade has been determined, the names are placed in grade order and an eligible list is established. There are various methods for resolving ties between those who get the same final grade – probably the most common is to place first the name of the person whose application was received first. Job offers are made from the eligible list in the order the names appear on it. You will be notified of your grade and your rank as soon as all these computations have been made. This will be done as rapidly as possible.

People who are found to meet the requirements in the announcement are called "eligibles." Their names are put on a list of eligible candidates. An eligible's chances of getting a job depend on how high he stands on this list and how fast agencies are filling jobs from the list.

When a job is to be filled from a list of eligibles, the agency asks for the names of people on the list of eligibles for that job. When the civil service commission receives this request, it sends to the agency the names of the three people highest on this list. Or, if the job to be filled has specialized requirements, the office sends the agency the names of the top three persons who meet these requirements from the general list.

The appointing officer makes a choice from among the three people whose names were sent to him. If the selected person accepts the appointment, the names of the others are put back on the list to be considered for future openings.

That is the rule in hiring from all kinds of eligible lists, whether they are for typist, carpenter, chemist, or something else. For every vacancy, the appointing officer has his choice of any one of the top three eligibles on the list. This explains why the person whose name is on top of the list sometimes does not get an appointment when some of the persons lower on the list do. If the appointing officer chooses the second or third eligible, the No. 1 eligible does not get a job at once, but stays on the list until he is appointed or the list is terminated.

X. HOW TO PASS THE INTERVIEW TEST

The examination for which you applied requires an oral interview test. You have already taken the written test and you are now being called for the interview test – the final part of the formal examination.

You may think that it is not possible to prepare for an interview test and that there are no procedures to follow during an interview. Our purpose is to point out some things you can do in advance that will help you and some good rules to follow and pitfalls to avoid while you are being interviewed.

What is an interview supposed to test?

The written examination is designed to test the technical knowledge and competence of the candidate; the oral is designed to evaluate intangible qualities, not readily measured otherwise, and to establish a list showing the relative fitness of each candidate – as measured against his competitors – for the position sought. Scoring is not on the basis of "right" and "wrong," but on a sliding scale of values ranging from "not passable" to "outstanding." As a matter of fact, it is possible to achieve a relatively low score without a single "incorrect" answer because of evident weakness in the qualities being measured.

Occasionally, an examination may consist entirely of an oral test – either an individual or a group oral. In such cases, information is sought concerning the technical knowledges and abilities of the candidate, since there has been no written examination for this purpose. More commonly, however, an oral test is used to supplement a written examination.

Who conducts interviews?

The composition of oral boards varies among different jurisdictions. In nearly all, a representative of the personnel department serves as chairman. One of the members of the board may be a representative of the department in which the candidate would work. In some cases, "outside experts" are used, and, frequently, a businessman or some other representative of the general public is asked to serve. Labor and management or other special groups may be represented. The aim is to secure the services of experts in the appropriate field.

However the board is composed, it is a good idea (and not at all improper or unethical) to ascertain in advance of the interview who the members are and what groups they represent. When you are introduced to them, you will have some idea of their backgrounds and interests, and at least you will not stutter and stammer over their names.

What should be done before the interview?

While knowledge about the board members is useful and takes some of the surprise element out of the interview, there is other preparation which is more substantive. It *is* possible to prepare for an oral interview – in several ways:

1) Keep a copy of your application and review it carefully before the interview

This may be the only document before the oral board, and the starting point of the interview. Know what education and experience you have listed there, and the sequence and dates of all of it. Sometimes the board will ask you to review the highlights of your experience for them; you should not have to hem and haw doing it.

2) Study the class specification and the examination announcement

Usually, the oral board has one or both of these to guide them. The qualities, characteristics or knowledges required by the position sought are stated in these documents. They offer valuable clues as to the nature of the oral interview. For example, if the job involves supervisory responsibilities, the announcement will usually indicate that knowledge of modern supervisory methods and the qualifications of the candidate as a supervisor will be tested. If so, you can expect such questions, frequently in the form of a hypothetical situation which you are expected to solve. NEVER go into an oral without knowledge of the duties and responsibilities of the job you seek.

3) Think through each qualification required

Try to visualize the kind of questions you would ask if you were a board member. How well could you answer them? Try especially to appraise your own knowledge and background in each area, *measured against the job sought*, and identify any areas in which you are weak. Be critical and realistic – do not flatter yourself.

4) Do some general reading in areas in which you feel you may be weak

For example, if the job involves supervision and your past experience has NOT, some general reading in supervisory methods and practices, particularly in the field of human relations, might be useful. Do NOT study agency procedures or detailed manuals. The oral board will be testing your understanding and capacity, not your memory.

5) Get a good night's sleep and watch your general health and mental attitude

You will want a clear head at the interview. Take care of a cold or any other minor ailment, and of course, no hangovers.

What should be done on the day of the interview?

Now comes the day of the interview itself. Give yourself plenty of time to get there. Plan to arrive somewhat ahead of the scheduled time, particularly if your appointment is in the fore part of the day. If a previous candidate fails to appear, the board might be ready for you a bit early. By early afternoon an oral board is almost invariably behind schedule if there are many candidates, and you may have to wait. Take along a book or magazine to read, or your application to review, but leave any extraneous material in the waiting room when you go in for your interview. In any event, relax and compose yourself.

The matter of dress is important. The board is forming impressions about you – from your experience, your manners, your attitude, and your appearance. Give your personal appearance careful attention. Dress your best, but not your flashiest. Choose conservative, appropriate clothing, and be sure it is immaculate. This is a business interview, and your appearance should indicate that you regard it as such. Besides, being well groomed and properly dressed will help boost your confidence.

Sooner or later, someone will call your name and escort you into the interview room. *This is it.* From here on you are on your own. It is too late for any more preparation. But remember, you asked for this opportunity to prove your fitness, and you are here because your request was granted.

What happens when you go in?

The usual sequence of events will be as follows: The clerk (who is often the board stenographer) will introduce you to the chairman of the oral board, who will introduce you to the other members of the board. Acknowledge the introductions before you sit down. Do not be surprised if you find a microphone facing you or a stenotypist sitting by. Oral interviews are usually recorded in the event of an appeal or other review.

Usually the chairman of the board will open the interview by reviewing the highlights of your education and work experience from your application – primarily for the benefit of the other members of the board, as well as to get the material into the record. Do not interrupt or comment unless there is an error or significant misinterpretation; if that is the case, do not hesitate. But do not quibble about insignificant matters. Also, he will usually ask you some question about your education, experience or your present job – partly to get you to start talking and to establish the interviewing "rapport." He may start the actual questioning, or turn it over to one of the other members. Frequently, each member undertakes the questioning on a particular area, one in which he is perhaps most competent, so you can expect each member to participate in the examination. Because time is limited, you may also expect some rather abrupt switches in the direction the questioning takes, so do not be upset by it. Normally, a board member will not pursue a single line of questioning unless he discovers a particular strength or weakness.

After each member has participated, the chairman will usually ask whether any member has any further questions, then will ask you if you have anything you wish to add. Unless you are expecting this question, it may floor you. Worse, it may start you off on an extended, extemporaneous speech. The board is not usually seeking more information. The question is principally to offer you a last opportunity to present further qualifications or to indicate that you have nothing to add. So, if you feel that a significant qualification or characteristic has been overlooked, it is proper to point it out in a sentence or so. Do not compliment the board on the thoroughness of their examination – they have been sketchy, and you know it. If you wish, merely say, "No thank you, I have nothing further to add." This is a point where you can "talk yourself out" of a good impression or fail to present an important bit of information. Remember, *you close the interview yourself*.

The chairman will then say, "That is all, Mr. _____, thank you." Do not be startled; the interview is over, and quicker than you think. Thank him, gather your belongings and take your leave. Save your sigh of relief for the other side of the door.

How to put your best foot forward
Throughout this entire process, you may feel that the board individually and collectively is trying to pierce your defenses, seek out your hidden weaknesses and embarrass and confuse you. Actually, this is not true. They are obliged to make an appraisal of your qualifications for the job you are seeking, and they want to see you in your best light. Remember, they must interview all candidates and a non-cooperative candidate may become a failure in spite of their best efforts to bring out his qualifications. Here are 15 suggestions that will help you:

1) Be natural – Keep your attitude confident, not cocky
If you are not confident that you can do the job, do not expect the board to be. Do not apologize for your weaknesses, try to bring out your strong points. The board is interested in a positive, not negative, presentation. Cockiness will antagonize any board member and make him wonder if you are covering up a weakness by a false show of strength.

2) Get comfortable, but don't lounge or sprawl
Sit erectly but not stiffly. A careless posture may lead the board to conclude that you are careless in other things, or at least that you are not impressed by the importance of the occasion. Either conclusion is natural, even if incorrect. Do not fuss with your clothing, a pencil or an ashtray. Your hands may occasionally be useful to emphasize a point; do not let them become a point of distraction.

3) Do not wisecrack or make small talk
This is a serious situation, and your attitude should show that you consider it as such. Further, the time of the board is limited – they do not want to waste it, and neither should you.

4) Do not exaggerate your experience or abilities

In the first place, from information in the application or other interviews and sources, the board may know more about you than you think. Secondly, you probably will not get away with it. An experienced board is rather adept at spotting such a situation, so do not take the chance.

5) If you know a board member, do not make a point of it, yet do not hide it

Certainly you are not fooling him, and probably not the other members of the board. Do not try to take advantage of your acquaintanceship – it will probably do you little good.

6) Do not dominate the interview

Let the board do that. They will give you the clues – do not assume that you have to do all the talking. Realize that the board has a number of questions to ask you, and do not try to take up all the interview time by showing off your extensive knowledge of the answer to the first one.

7) Be attentive

You only have 20 minutes or so, and you should keep your attention at its sharpest throughout. When a member is addressing a problem or question to you, give him your undivided attention. Address your reply principally to him, but do not exclude the other board members.

8) Do not interrupt

A board member may be stating a problem for you to analyze. He will ask you a question when the time comes. Let him state the problem, and wait for the question.

9) Make sure you understand the question

Do not try to answer until you are sure what the question is. If it is not clear, restate it in your own words or ask the board member to clarify it for you. However, do not haggle about minor elements.

10) Reply promptly but not hastily

A common entry on oral board rating sheets is "candidate responded readily," or "candidate hesitated in replies." Respond as promptly and quickly as you can, but do not jump to a hasty, ill-considered answer.

11) Do not be peremptory in your answers

A brief answer is proper – but do not fire your answer back. That is a losing game from your point of view. The board member can probably ask questions much faster than you can answer them.

12) Do not try to create the answer you think the board member wants

He is interested in what kind of mind you have and how it works – not in playing games. Furthermore, he can usually spot this practice and will actually grade you down on it.

13) Do not switch sides in your reply merely to agree with a board member

Frequently, a member will take a contrary position merely to draw you out and to see if you are willing and able to defend your point of view. Do not start a debate, yet do not surrender a good position. If a position is worth taking, it is worth defending.

14) Do not be afraid to admit an error in judgment if you are shown to be wrong

The board knows that you are forced to reply without any opportunity for careful consideration. Your answer may be demonstrably wrong. If so, admit it and get on with the interview.

15) Do not dwell at length on your present job

The opening question may relate to your present assignment. Answer the question but do not go into an extended discussion. You are being examined for a *new* job, not your present one. As a matter of fact, try to phrase ALL your answers in terms of the job for which you are being examined.

Basis of Rating

Probably you will forget most of these "do's" and "don'ts" when you walk into the oral interview room. Even remembering them all will not ensure you a passing grade. Perhaps you did not have the qualifications in the first place. But remembering them will help you to put your best foot forward, without treading on the toes of the board members.

Rumor and popular opinion to the contrary notwithstanding, an oral board wants you to make the best appearance possible. They know you are under pressure – but they also want to see how you respond to it as a guide to what your reaction would be under the pressures of the job you seek. They will be influenced by the degree of poise you display, the personal traits you show and the manner in which you respond.

ABOUT THIS BOOK

This book contains tests divided into Examination Sections. Go through each test, answering every question in the margin. We have also attached a sample answer sheet at the back of the book that can be removed and used. At the end of each test look at the answer key and check your answers. On the ones you got wrong, look at the right answer choice and learn. Do not fill in the answers first. Do not memorize the questions and answers, but understand the answer and principles involved. On your test, the questions will likely be different from the samples. Questions are changed and new ones added. If you understand these past questions you should have success with any changes that arise. Tests may consist of several types of questions. We have additional books on each subject should more study be advisable or necessary for you. Finally, the more you study, the better prepared you will be. This book is intended to be the last thing you study before you walk into the examination room. Prior study of relevant texts is also recommended. NLC publishes some of these in our Fundamental Series. Knowledge and good sense are important factors in passing your exam. Good luck also helps. So now study this Passbook, absorb the material contained within and take that knowledge into the examination. Then do your best to pass that exam.

EXAMINATION SECTION

EXAMINATION SECTION
TEST 1

DIRECTIONS: Each question or incomplete statement is followed by several suggested answers or completions. Select the one that BEST answers the question or completes the statement. *PRINT THE LETTER OF THE CORRECT ANSWER IN THE SPACE AT THE RIGHT.*

1. Physical and mental health are essential to the officer. According to this statement, the officer MUST be

   A. as wise as he is strong
   B. smarter than most people
   C. sound in mind and body
   D. stronger than the average criminal

2. Teamwork is the basis of successful law enforcement. The factor stressed by this statement is

   A. cooperation   B. determination
   C. initiative   D. pride

3. Legal procedure is a means, not an end. Its function is merely to accomplish the enforcement of legal rights. A litigant has no vested interest in the observance of the rules of procedure as such. All that he should be entitled to demand is that he be given an opportunity for a fair and impartial trial of his case. He should not be permitted to invoke the aid of technical rules merely to embarrass his adversary.
   According to this paragraph, it is MOST correct to state that

   A. observance of the rules of procedure guarantees a fair trial
   B. embarrassment of an adversary through technical rules does not make a fair trial
   C. a litigant is not interested in the observance of rules of procedure
   D. technical rules must not be used in a trial

4. One theory states that all criminal behavior is taught by a process of communication within small intimate groups. An individual engages in criminal behavior if the number of criminal patterns which he has acquired exceed the number of non-criminal patterns. This statement indicates that criminal behavior is

   A. learned   B. instinctive
   C. hereditary   D. reprehensible

5. The law enforcement staff of today requires training and mental qualities of a high order. The poorly or partially prepared staff member lowers the standard of work, retards his own earning power, and fails in a career meant to provide a livelihood and social improvement.
   According to this statement,

   A. an inefficient member of a law enforcement staff will still earn a good livelihood
   B. law enforcement officers move in good social circles
   C. many people fail in law enforcement careers
   D. persons of training and ability are essential to a law enforcement staff

6. In any state, no crime can occur unless there is a written law forbidding the act or the omission in question, and even though an act may not be exactly in harmony with public policy, such act is not a crime unless it is expressly forbidden by legislative enactment. According to the above statement,

    A. a crime is committed with reference to a particular law
    B. acts not in harmony with public policy should be forbidden by law
    C. non-criminal activity will promote public welfare
    D. legislative enactments frequently forbid actions in harmony with public policy

7. The unrestricted sale of firearms is one of the main causes of our shameful crime record. According to this statement, one of the causes of our crime record is

    A. development of firepower
    B. ease of securing weapons
    C. increased skill in using guns
    D. scientific perfection of firearms

8. Every person must be informed of the reason for his arrest unless he is arrested in the actual commission of a crime. Sufficient force to effect the arrest may be used, but the courts frown on brutal methods.
   According to this statement, a person does NOT have to be informed of the reason for his arrest if

    A. brutal force was not used in effecting it
    B. the courts will later turn the defendant loose
    C. the person arrested knows force will be used if necessary
    D. the reason for it is clearly evident from the circumstances

9. An important duty of an officer is to keep order in the court.
   On the basis of this statement, it is PROBABLY true that

    A. it is more important for an officer to be strong than it is for him to be smart
    B. people involved in court trials are noisy if not kept in check
    C. not every duty of an officer is important
    D. the maintenance of order is important for the proper conduct of court business

10. Ideally, a correctional system should include several types of institutions to provide different degrees of custody.
    On the basis of this statement, one could MOST reasonably say that

    A. as the number of institutions in a correctional system increases, the efficiency of the system increases
    B. the difference in degree of custody for the inmate depends on the types of institutions in a correctional system
    C. the greater the variety of institutions, the stricter the degree of custody that can be maintained
    D. the same type of correctional institution is not desirable for the custody of all prisoners

11. The enforced idleness of a large percentage of adult men and women in our prisons is one of the direct causes of the tensions which burst forth in riot and disorder.
On the basis of this statement, a good reason why inmates should perform daily work of some kind is that

    A. better morale and discipline can be maintained when inmates are kept busy
    B. daily work is an effective way of punishing inmates for the crimes they have committed
    C. law-abiding citizens must work, therefore, labor should also be required of inmates
    D. products of inmates' labor will in part pay the cost of their maintenance

12. With industry invading rural areas, the use of the automobile, and the speed of modern communications and transportation, the problems of neglect and delinquency are no longer peculiar to cities but an established feature of everyday life.
This statement implies MOST directly that

    A. delinquents are moving from cities to rural areas
    B. delinquency and neglect are found in rural areas
    C. delinquency is not as much of a problem in rural areas as in cities
    D. rural areas now surpass cities in industry

13. Young men from minority groups, if unable to find employment, become discouraged and hopeless because of their economic position and may finally resort to any means of supplying their wants.
The MOST reasonable of the following conclusions that may be drawn from this statement only is that

    A. discouragement sometimes leads to crime
    B. in general, young men from minority groups are criminals
    C. unemployment turns young men from crime
    D. young men from minority groups are seldom employed

14. To prevent crime, we must deal with the possible criminal long before he reaches the prison. Our aim should be not merely to reform the law breakers but to strike at the roots of crime: neglectful parents, bad companions, unsatisfactory homes, selfishness, disregard for the rights of others, and bad social conditions.
The above statement recommends

    A. abolition of prisons   B. better reformatories
    C. compulsory education   D. general social reform

15. There is evidence which shows that comic books which glorify the criminal and criminal acts have a distinct influence in producing young criminals.
According to this statement,

    A. comic books affect the development of criminal careers
    B. comic books specialize in reporting criminal acts
    C. young criminals read comic books exclusively
    D. young criminals should not be permitted to read comic books

16. Suppose a study shows that juvenile delinquents are equal in intelligence but three school grades behind juvenile non-delinquents.
    On the basis of this information only, it is MOST reasonable to say that

    A. a delinquent usually progresses to the educational limit set by his intelligence
    B. educational achievement depends on intelligence only
    C. educational achievement is closely associated with delinquency
    D. lack of intelligence is closely associated with delinquency

17. There is no proof today that the experience of a prison sentence makes a better citizen of an adult. On the contrary, there seems some evidence that the experience is an unwholesome one that frequently confirms the criminality of the inmate.
    From the above paragraph only, it may be BEST concluded that

    A. prison sentences tend to punish rather than rehabilitate
    B. all criminals should be given prison sentences
    C. we should abandon our penal institutions
    D. penal institutions are effective in rehabilitating criminals

18. Some courts are referred to as *criminal* courts while others are known as *civil* courts. This distinction in name is MOST probably based on the

    A. historical origin of the court
    B. link between the court and the police
    C. manner in which the judges are chosen
    D. type of cases tried there

19. Many children who are exposed to contacts and experiences of a delinquent nature become educated and trained in crime in the course of participating in the daily life of the neighborhood.
    From this statement only, we may reasonably conclude that

    A. delinquency passes from parent to child
    B. neighborhood influences are usually bad
    C. schools are training grounds for delinquents
    D. none of the above conclusions is reasonable

20. Old age insurance, for whose benefits a quarter of a million city employees may elect to become eligible, is one feature of the Social Security Act that is wholly administered by the Federal government.
    On the basis of this paragraph only, it may MOST reasonably be inferred that

    A. a quarter of a million city employees are drawing old age insurance
    B. a quarter of a million city employees have elected to become eligible for old age insurance
    C. the city has no part in administering Social Security old age insurance
    D. only the Federal government administers the Social Security Act

21. An officer's revolver is a defensive, and not offensive, weapon.
    On the basis of this statement only, an officer should BEST draw his revolver to

    A. fire at an unarmed burglar
    B. force a suspect to confess
    C. frighten a juvenile delinquent
    D. protect his own life

22. Prevention of crime is of greater value to the community than the punishment of crime. 22.____
    If this statement is accepted as true, GREATEST emphasis should be placed on

    A. malingering   B. medication
    C. imprisonment   D. rehabilitation

23. The criminal is rarely or never reformed. 23.____
    Acceptance of this statement as true would mean that GREATEST emphasis should
    be placed on

    A. imprisonment   B. parole
    C. probation   D. malingering

24. The MOST accurate of the following statements about persons convicted of crimes is 24.____
    that

    A. their criminal behavior is almost invariably the result of low intelligence
    B. they are almost invariably legally insane
    C. they are more likely to come from underprivileged groups than from other groups
    D. they have certain facial characteristics which distinguish them from non-criminals

25. Suppose a study shows that the I.Q. (Intelligence Quotient) of prison inmates is 95 as 25.____
    opposed to an I.Q. of 100 for a numerically equivalent civilian group.
    A claim, on the basis of this study, that criminals have a lower I.Q. than non-criminals
    would be

    A. *improper;* prison inmates are criminals who have been caught
    B. *proper;* the study was numerically well done
    C. *improper;* the sample was inadequate
    D. *proper;* even misdemeanors are sometimes penalized by prison sentences

Questions 26-45.

DIRECTIONS: Select the letter of the word or expression that MOST NEARLY expresses the
meaning of the capitalized word in the group.

26. ABDUCT 26.____

    A. lead   B. kidnap   C. sudden   D. worthless

27. BIAS 27.____

    A. ability   B. envy   C. prejudice   D. privilege

28. COERCE 28.____

    A. cancel   B. force   C. rescind   D. rugged

29. CONDONE 29.____

    A. combine   B. pardon   C. revive   D. spice

30. CONSISTENCY 30.____

    A. bravery   B. readiness   C. strain   D. uniformity

31. CREDENCE
    A. belief B. devotion C. resemblance D. tempo
32. CURRENT
    A. backward B. brave C. prevailing D. wary
33. CUSTODY
    A. advisement B. belligerence
    C. guardianship D. suspicion
34. DEBILITY
    A. deceitfulness B. decency
    C. strength D. weakness
35. DEPLETE
    A. beg B. empty C. excuse D. fold
36. ENUMERATE
    A. name one by one B. disappear
    C. get rid of D. pretend
37. FEIGN
    A. allow B. incur C. pretend D. weaken
38. INSTIGATE
    A. analyze B. coordinate C. oppose D. provoke
39. LIABLE
    A. careless B. growing C. mistaken D. responsible
40. PONDER
    A. attack B. heavy C. meditate D. solicit
41. PUGILIST
    A. farmer B. politician
    C. prize fighter D. stage actor
42. QUELL
    A. explode B. inform C. shake D. suppress
43. RECIPROCAL
    A. mutual B. organized C. redundant D. thoughtful
44. RUSE
    A. burn B. impolite C. rot D. trick

45. STEALTHY 45.____

   A. crazed   B. flowing   C. sly   D. wicked

Questions 46-50.

DIRECTIONS: Each of the sentences numbered 46 to 50 may be classified under one of the following four categories:
- A faulty because of incorrect grammar
- B faulty because of incorrect punctuation
- C faulty because of incorrect capitalization or incorrect spelling
- D correct

Examine each sentence carefully to determine under which of the above four options it is best classified. Then, in the corresponding space at the right, write the letter preceding the option which is the BEST of the four suggested above. Each faulty sentence contains but one type of error. Consider a sentence to be correct if it contains none of the types of errors mentioned, even though there may be other correct ways of expressing the same thought.

46. They told both he and I that the prisoner had escaped. 46.____

47. Any superior officer, who, disregards the just complaints of his subordinates, is remiss in the performance of his duty. 47.____

48. Only those members of the national organization who resided in the Middle west attended the conference in Chicago. 48.____

49. We told him to give the investigation assignment to whoever was available. 49.____

50. Please do not disappoint and embarass us by not appearing in court. 50.____

KEY (CORRECT ANSWERS)

1. C	11. A	21. D	31. A	41. C
2. A	12. B	22. D	32. C	42. D
3. B	13. A	23. A	33. C	43. A
4. A	14. D	24. C	34. D	44. D
5. D	15. A	25. A	35. B	45. C
6. A	16. C	26. B	36. A	46. A
7. B	17. A	27. C	37. C	47. B
8. D	18. D	28. B	38. D	48. C
9. D	19. D	29. B	39. D	49. D
10. D	20. C	30. D	40. C	50. C

TEST 2

DIRECTIONS: Each question or incomplete statement is followed by several suggested answers or completions. Select the one that BEST answers the question or completes the statement. *PRINT THE LETTER OF THE CORRECT ANSWER IN THE SPACE AT THE RIGHT.*

1. Suppose a man falls from a two-story high scaffold and is unconscious. You should   1.____

   A. call for medical assistance and avoid moving the man
   B. get someone to help you move him indoors to a bed
   C. have someone help you walk him around until he revives
   D. hold his head up and pour a stimulant down his throat

2. For proper first aid treatment, a person who has fainted should be   2.____

   A. doused with cold water and then warmly covered
   B. given artificial respiration until he is revived
   C. laid down with his head lower than the rest of his body
   D. slapped on the face until he is revived

3. If you are called on to give first aid to a person who is suffering from shock, you should   3.____

   A. apply cold towels   B. give him a stimulant
   C. keep him awake   D. wrap him warmly

4. Artificial respiration would NOT be proper first aid for a person suffering from   4.____

   A. drowning   B. electric shock
   C. external bleeding   D. suffocation

5. Suppose you are called on to give first aid to several victims of an accident. FIRST attention should be given to the one who is   5.____

   A. bleeding severely   B. groaning loudly
   C. unconscious   D. vomiting

6. If an officer's weekly salary is increased from $400.00 to $450.00, then the percent of increase is _____ percent.   6.____

   A. 10   B. 11 1/9   C. 12 1/2   D. 20

7. Suppose that one-half the officers in a department have served for more than ten years, and one-third have served for more than 15 years.
Then, the fraction of officers who have served between ten and fifteen years is   7.____

   A. 1/3   B. 1/5   C. 1/6   D. 1/12

8. In a city prison, there are four floors on which prisoners are housed. The top floor houses one-quarter of the inmates, the bottom floor houses one-sixth of the inmates, one-third are housed on the second floor. The rest of the inmates are housed on the third floor. If there are 90 inmates housed on the third floor, the total number of inmates housed on all four floors together is   8.____

   A. 270   B. 360   C. 450   D. 540

9. Suppose that ten percent of those who commit serious crimes are convicted and that fifteen percent of those convicted are sentenced for more than 3 years.
    The percentage of those committing serious crimes who are sentenced for more than 3 years is _____ percent.

    A. 15   B. 1.5   C. .15   D. .015

10. Assume that there are 1,100 employees in a city agency. Of these, 15 percent are officers, 80 percent of whom are attorneys; of the attorneys, two-fifths have been with the agency over five years.
    Then the number of officers who are attorneys and have over five years' experience with the agency is MOST NEARLY

    A. 45   B. 53   C. 132   D. 165

11. An employee who has 500 cartons of supplies to pack can pack them at the rate of 50 an hour. After this employee has worked for half an hour, he is jointed by another employee who can pack 45 cartons an hour.
    Assuming that both employees can maintain their respective rates of speed, the total number of hours required to pack all the cartons is

    A. 4 1/2   B. 5   C. 5 1/2   D. 6 1/2

12. Thirty-six officers can complete an assignment in 22 days. Assuming that all officers work at the same rate of speed, the number of officers that would be needed to complete this assignment in 12 days is

    A. 42   B. 54   C. 66   D. 72

Questions 13-15.

DIRECTIONS: Questions 13 through 15, inclusive, are to be answered on the basis of the table below. Data for certain categories have been omitted from the You are to calculate the missing numbers if needed to answer the questions.

	2007	2008	Numerical Increase
Correction Officers	1,226	1,347	
Court Officers		529	34
Deputy Sheriffs	38	40	
Supervisors			
	2,180	2,414	

13. The number in the *Supervisors* group in 2007 was MOST NEARLY

    A. 500   B. 475   C. 450   D. 425

14. The LARGEST percentage increase from 2007 to 2008 was in the group of

    A. Correction officers   B. Court officers
    C. Deputy sheriffs   D. Supervisors

15. In 2008, the ratio of the number of Correction Officers to the total of the other three categories of employees was MOST NEARLY

    A. 1:1   B. 2:1   C. 3:1   D. 4:1

16. A directed verdict is made by a court when

    A. the facts are not disputed
    B. the defendant's motion for a directed verdict has been denied
    C. there is no question of law involved
    D. neither party has moved for a directed verdict

17. Papers on appeal of a criminal case do NOT include one of the following:

    A. Summons
    B. Minutes of trial
    C. Complaint
    D. Intermediate motion papers

18. A pleading titled *Smith vs. Jones, et al.* indicates

    A. two plaintiffs
    B. two defendants
    C. more than two defendants
    D. unknown defendants

19. A District Attorney makes a *prima facie* case when

    A. there is proof of guilt beyond a reasonable doubt
    B. the evidence is sufficient to convict in the absence of rebutting evidence
    C. the prosecution presents more evidence than the defense
    D. the defendant fails to take the stand

20. A person is NOT qualified to act as a trial juror in a criminal action if he or she

    A. has been convicted previously of a misdemeanor
    B. is under 18 years of age
    C. has scruples against the death penalty
    D. does not own property of a value at least $500

21. A court clerk who falsifies a court record commits a(n)

    A. misdemeanor
    B. offense
    C. felony
    D. no crime, but automatically forfeits his tenure

22. Insolent and contemptuous behavior to a judge during a court of record proceeding is punishable as

    A. civil contempt
    B. criminal contempt
    C. disorderly conduct
    D. a disorderly person

23. Offering a bribe to a court clerk would not constitute a crime UNLESS the

    A. court clerk accepted the bribe
    B. bribe consisted of money
    C. bribe was given with intent to influence the court clerk in his official functions
    D. court was actually in session

24. A defendant comes to trial in the same court in which he had previously been defendant in a similar case.
    The court officer should

    A. tell him, *Knew we'd be seeing you again*
    B. tell newspaper reporters what he knows of the previous action

C. treat him the same as he would any other defendant
D. warn the judge that the man had previously been a defendant

25. Suppose in conversation with you, an attorney strongly criticizes a ruling of the judge, and you believe the attorney to be correct.
You should

   A. assure him you feel the same way
   B. tell him the judge knows the law
   C. tell him to ask for an exception
   D. refuse to discuss the matter

26. Suppose a doorman refuses to admit you to an apartment house in which you are attempting to serve a process on a tenant.
Of the following, the BEST action for you to take is to

   A. bribe the doorman to admit you
   B. discard the process since it cannot be served
   C. gain entrance by force
   D. report the matter to your superior

27. False arrest is an offense for which the deputy sheriff may be held liable.
Therefore, before making an arrest, the deputy sheriff should

   A. be sure a witness is present
   B. be sure it is legal
   C. seek assistance from a patrolman
   D. deputize a private citizen

28. An arrested person should not be transported upon a public conveyance such as a streetcar, subway, or bus, except in an extreme emergency.
The reason for this regulation is MOST probably the

   A. danger of escape   B. embarrassment to the prisoner
   C. expense involved   D. possible delays

29. Except in rare emergencies, a deputy should not attempt to make an arrest without a partner.
The BEST reason for this is that the partner may be needed to

   A. arbitrate the matter
   B. lend prestige to the sheriff's office
   C. overcome resistance
   D. provide company for the deputy

30. At the end of each month, the deputy sheriff must submit to his superior officer an activity report covering the status of his assignments and the extent of his activities in the service of process during the month.
It is MOST important that such report be

   A. accurate   B. brief
   C. grammatically correct   D. lengthy

31. Deputies are required to hold seized chattels for three days after service of the replevin papers. This means three full 24-hour days, exclusive of the day of service, and the property should not be turned over earlier than 12:01 A.M. on the fourth day. When one day of the period falls on a Sunday or a public holiday, that day is excluded and an additional day must be added to make up the three.
According to this statement only, if service of replevin papers is made on Thursday, June 23rd, the property should be turned over on

    A. Sunday, June 26th
    B. Monday, June 27th
    C. Tuesday, June 28th
    D. Wednesday, June 29th

32. Certain property is declared by law to be exempt from seizure to satisfy a debt because it is of importance to the comfort of the family, although of small money On the basis of this law, which of the following would you MOST expect to be exempt from seizure?

    A. Broadloom rug
    B. Dining table
    C. Marble statuette
    D. Modern painting

33. As a general rule, a deputy sheriff is justified in refusing to seize an article which differs from the description in the replevin papers, unless the difference is clearly unimportant in the light of other identifying facts. According to this statement, which of the following would a deputy sheriff BEST be justified in seizing where there is a difference from the description in the papers?
    A(n)

    A. automobile corresponding in make, year, model, and engine number, but differing in color
    B. sofa corresponding in upholstery material, color, width, and height, but differing in length
    C. television set corresponding in year, model, and size of screen, but differing in number of tubes required
    D. typewriter corresponding in year, model, size of type, and color, but differing in name of manufacturer

34. The legal aspect of the sheriff's duties is emphasized by his unique personal liability, not only for his own acts and omissions, but also for those of any deputy or employee in his office.
According to the foregoing quotation, it would be MOST correct to state that the sheriff

    A. and his employees have unique legal duties to perform
    B. is held responsible for actions taken by his subordinates
    C. is liable for the acts of his employees only under unique circumstances
    D. must personally serve many legal papers

35. Which one of the following descriptions of a defendant would help MOST in identifying him?

    A. Age - 31 years; weight - 168 pounds
    B. At time of escape was wearing gray hat, dark overcoat
    C. Deep scar running from left ear to chin
    D. Height - 5 feet, 9 inches; complexion - sallow

36. Which of the following could a deputy sheriff BEST accept as proof of a man's identity?   36._____

    A. A personal letter
    B. Automobile driver's license
    C. Automobile registration certificate
    D. Social security card

37. It was formerly the practice to require someone who knew the defendant by sight to   37._____
    accompany the deputy sheriff. It has been learned through experience that the value of
    such identification is over-rated.
    From this paragraph only, it may be BEST inferred that

    A. circumstantial evidence is not reliable
    B. identifications are sometimes inaccurate
    C. people are usually for the underdog
    D. testimony is often contradictory

38. The depositions must set forth the facts tending to establish that an illegal act was com-   38._____
    mitted and that the defendant is guilty.
    According to this statement only, the one of the following which need NOT be included
    in a deposition is evidence that establishes the

    A. fact that an illegal act was committed
    B. fact that defendant committed the illegal act
    C. guilt of the defendant
    D. method of commission of the illegal act

39. Each deputy sheriff should understand how his own work helps to accomplish the pur-   39._____
    pose of the entire agency.
    This statement means MOST NEARLY that the deputy sheriff should understand the

    A. efficiency of a small agency
    B. importance of his own job
    C. necessity for initiative
    D. value of a large organization

40. When X is accused of having cheated Y of a sum of money and Y is proven to have been   40._____
    deprived of the money, there is an additional requirement for a verdict against X.
    The additional requirement is to prove that

    A. the money was stolen from Y
    B. X had the money after Y had it
    C. X had the money before Y had it
    D. X cheated Y of the money

41. To gain a verdict against X in a trial, it was necessary to show that he could have been at   41._____
    Y Street at 5 P.M.
    It was proven that he was seen at Z Street at 4:45 P.M. The question that MUST be
    answered to show whether X is guilty is:

    A. How long does it take to get from Z Street to Y Street?
    B. In what sort of neighborhood is Z Street located?
    C. Was X acting suspiciously on the day in question?
    D. Who was with X when he was seen at Z Street at 4:45 P.M.?

42. The deputy sheriff must give the defendant reasonable time to secure the bail fixed in the process before confining him to jail.
    The CHIEF purpose of bail is to

    A. permit personnel to act as bondsmen
    B. permit the defendant his liberty while assuring his presence at the trial
    C. raise additional money for the general fund of the city treasury
    D. relieve the city of the necessity of bringing the defendant before a judge

43. When a jury is selected, the attorney for each side has a right to refuse to accept a certain number of prospective jurors without giving any reason therefor.
    The reason for this is MAINLY that

    A. attorneys can exclude persons likely to be biased even though no prejudice is admitted
    B. persons who will suffer economically by being summoned for jury duty can be excused forthwith
    C. relatives of the litigants can be excused, thus insuring a fair trial for each side
    D. there will be a greater number of people from which the jury can be selected, thus insuring better quality

44. Suppose a deputy sheriff, feeling that the verdict against a judgment debtor was unfair, permits him to escape.
    On the basis of this information only, it is safe to assume that the

    A. judge passing sentence was unduly harsh
    B. judgment debtor had possession of a large sum of money
    C. deputy sheriff was recently appointed
    D. deputy sheriff used poor judgment

45. A deputy sheriff shall not receive a gift from any defendant or other person on the defendant's behalf.
    The BEST explanation for this departmental rule is that

    A. acceptance of a gift has no significance
    B. favors may be expected in return
    C. gifts are only an expression of good will
    D. litigants cannot usually afford gifts

46. All concerned are MOST likely to recognize the deputy sheriff's authority and cooperate with him if he conveys by his manner a complete confidence that they will do so. According to this statement only, a deputy sheriff should display

    A. arrogance   B. agitation   C. assurance   D. excitement

47. Since he is a city employee, a deputy sheriff who refuses to waive immunity from prosecution when called on to testify in court automatically terminates his employment.
    From this statement only, it may be BEST inferred that

    A. a deputy sheriff is a city employee
    B. all city employees are deputy sheriffs
    C. city employees may be fired only for malfeasance
    D. deputy sheriffs who waive immunity may not be prosecuted

48. In one case, a mistrial was declared because the indictment used the pronoun *he* instead of *she*.
    The MOST useful information a deputy sheriff can derive from this statement is that

    A. accuracy is important
    B. mistrial is a legal term
    C. one must always use good grammar
    D. to misrepresent is felonious

49. It is desirable that a deputy sheriff acquire a knowledge of the procedures of the division to which he is assigned MAINLY because such knowledge will help him

    A. become familiar with anti-social behavior
    B. discharge his duties properly
    C. gain insight into causes of crime
    D. in any personal legal proceeding

50. It is a frequent misconception that deputy sheriffs can be recruited from those registers established for the recruitment of police officers or firefighters. While it is true that many common qualifications are found in all of these, specific standards for a sheriff's work are indicated, varying with the size, geographical location and policies of the office.
    According to this paragraph only, it may BEST be inferred that

    A. a successful deputy sheriff must have some qualifications not required of a policeman or fireman
    B. qualifications which make a successful patrolman will also make a successful fireman
    C. the same qualifications are required of a deputy sheriff regardless of the office to which he is assigned
    D. the successful deputy sheriff is required to be both more intelligent and stronger than a fireman

KEY (CORRECT ANSWERS

1. A	11. C	21. C	31. C	41. A
2. C	12. C	22. B	32. B	42. B
3. D	13. D	23. C	33. A	43. A
4. C	14. D	24. C	34. B	44. D
5. A	15. A	25. D	35. C	45. B
6. C	16. A	26. D	36. B	46. C
7. C	17. D	27. B	37. B	47. A
8. B	18. C	28. A	38. D	48. A
9. B	19. B	29. C	39. B	49. B
10. B	20. B	30. A	40. D	50. A

SOLUTIONS TO PROBLEMS

6. CORRECT ANSWER: C

$$\frac{50}{400} = \frac{1}{8} = 12\frac{1}{2}\%$$

7. CORRECT ANSWER: C

1/2 + 1/3 = 3/6 + 2/6 = 5/6

∴ 1 - 5/6 = 1/6

8. CORRECT ANSWER: B

1/4 + 1/6 + 1/3 = 3/12 + 2/12 + 4/12 = 9/12 = 3/4

∴ 1 - 3/4 = 1/4 (rest of inmates housed on the third floor) Since 90 = 1/4, therefore, 4/4 (or 1) = 360.

9. CORRECT ANSWER: B

.10 x .15 = .0150 = 1.5%

10. CORRECT ANSWER: B

Step (1)   1100
            x.15
            5500
            1100
            165.00 (peace officers)

Step (2)   165
            x .80
            132.00 (attorneys)

Step (3) 132 x 2/5 = 264/5 = 52.8 (peace officers who are attorneys and have over five years' experience with the agency)

11. CORRECT ANSWER: C

Since the first employee worked for 1/2 hour, he packed 25 cartons (50 ÷ 2). This leaves 475 cartons to be packed. This first employee packs at the rate of 50 an hour. The second employee, who joins him after 1/2 hour, packs at the rate of 45 an hour. 50 + 45 = 95 (rate of both employees together)

∴ 475 ÷ 95 = 5 hours (time it takes both employees together) 5 hours + 1/2 hour = 5 1/2 hours

12. CORRECT ANSWER: C

x : 36 = 22:12

12 × x = 36 × 22

12 x = 792

x = 66

EXAMINATION SECTION
TEST 1

DIRECTIONS: Each question or incomplete statement is followed by several suggested answers or completions. Select the one that BEST answers the question or completes the statement. *PRINT THE LETTER OF THE CORRECT ANSWER IN THE SPACE AT THE RIGHT.*

1. The delivery of an arrested person to his sureties, upon their giving security for his appearance at the time and place designated to submit to the jurisdiction and judgment of the court, is known as
   A. bail
   B. habeas corpus
   C. parole
   D. probation

2. Jones was charged with the murder of Smith. Brown, Jones' landlord, testified at the trial that Jones had in his home a well-equipped laboratory which contained all the necessary chemical for producing the poison which an autopsy showed caused Smith's death.
   Brown's testimony constitutes what is called _____ evidence.
   A. corroborative   B. opinion   C. hearsay   D. circumstantial

3. In addressing a class of recruits, a police lieutenant remarked: "Carelessness and failure are twins."
   The one of the following that MOST NEARLY expresses his meaning is
   A. negligence seldom accompanies success
   B. incomplete work is careless work
   C. conscientious work is never attended by failure
   D. a conscientious person never makes mistakes

4. In taking a statement from a person who has been shot by an assailant and is not expected to live, police are instructed to ask the person: "Do you believe you are about to die?"
   Of the following, the MOST probable reason for this question is
   A. the theory that a person about to die will tell the truth
   B. to determine if the victim is conscious and capable of making a statement
   C. to put the victim mentally at ease and more willing to talk
   D. that the statement could not be used in court if his mind was distraught by the fear of impending death

5. If, while you are on duty at a busy intersection, a pedestrian asks you for directions to a particular place, the BEST course of conduct is to
   A. ignore the question and continue directing operations
   B. tell the pedestrian to ask a patrolman on foot patrol
   C. answer the question in a brief, courteous manner
   D. leave your post only long enough to give clear and adequate directions

6. In lecturing on the law of arrest, a lieutenant remarked: "To go beyond is as bad as to fall short."
   The one of the following which MOST NEARLY expresses his meaning is
   A. never undertake the impossible   B. extremes are not desirable
   C. look before you leap   D. too much success is dangerous

7. Suppose you are an officer assigned to a patrol precinct. While you are in the vicinity of a school, your attention is called to a man who is selling small packages to school children. You are told that this man distributes similar packages to these same children daily and that he is suspected of dealing in narcotics.
   Of the following, the BEST action for you to take is to
   A. pretend to be an addict and attempt to purchase narcotics from him
   B. observe the man's action yourself for several days in order to obtain grounds for arrest
   C. stop and question one or more of the children after they have transacted business with the man
   D. stop and question the man as he leaves the children

8. In the event of a poison gas attack, civil defense authorities advise civilians to _____ door and windows and go to _____.
   A. open; upper floors   B. close; upper floors
   C. open; the basement   D. close; the basement

9. The procedure whereby a defendant is brought before a magistrate, informed of the charge against him, and asked how he pleads thereto, is called
   A. arraignment   B. indictment   C. presentment   D. inquisition

10. A written accusation of a crime presented by a grand jury is called a(n)
    A. commitment   B. arraignment   C. indictment   D. demurrer

11. The one of the following statements made by a prisoner that is correctly called an alibi is:
    A. "He struck me first."
    B. "I didn't intend to hurt him."
    C. "I was miles away from there at the time."
    D. "I don't remember what happened."

12. A person who, after the commission of a crime, conceals the defender with the intent that the latter may escape from arrest and trial, is called a(n)
    A. accessory   B. accomplice   C. confederate   D. associate

13. A sworn statement of fact is called a(n)
    A. affidavit   B. oath
    C. acknowledgment   D. subpoena

14. The right of trial by jury in the courts of the state is PRIMARILY safeguarded by a provision of
    A. the United States Constitution
    B. the constitution of the state
    C. a state statute
    D. a Federal statute

15. The task of protecting the President and his family is entrusted PRIMARILY to the
    A. Federal Bureau of Investigation
    B. United States Secret Service
    C. Central Intelligence Agency
    D. District of Columbia Police Department

16. The coordinating organization for the various Federal agencies engaged in intelligence activities is the
    A. Federal Bureau of Investigation
    B. Federal Security Agency
    C. Mutual Security Agency
    D. Central Intelligence Agency

17. A drug addict whose arm shows many scars from the injection of a hypodermic needle is MOST apt to be addicted to
    A. heroin   B. cocaine   C. opium   D. marijuana

18. All of the following drugs are derived from opium EXCEPT
    A. cocaine   B. heroin   C. morphine   D. codeine

19. In addition to cases of submersion, artificial respiration is a recommended first aid procedure for
    A. sunstroke
    B. chemical poisoning
    C. electric shock
    D. apoplexy

20. An injury to a muscle or tendon brought about by severe exertion and resulting in pain and stiffness is called a
    A. strain   B. sprain   C. bruise   D. fracture

21. Of the following kinds of wounds, the one in which there is the LEAST danger of infection is a(n) _____ wound.
    A. abrasive   B. punctured   C. lacerated   D. incised

22. When a person is found injured on the street, it is generally advisable, pending arrival of a physician, to help prevent fainting or shock by keeping the patient
    A. in a sitting position
    B. lying down with the head level
    C. lying down with the head raised
    D. standing on his feet

23. When an injured person appears to be suffering from shock, of the following, it is MOST essential to
    A. loosen his clothing
    B. keep him warm
    C. administer a stimulant
    D. place him in a prone position

24. In the sentence, "Malice was immanent in all his remarks," the word "immanent" means MOST NEARLY
    A. elevated   B. inherent   C. threatening   D. foreign

25. In the sentence, "The extant copies of the document were found in the safe," the word "extant" means MOST NEARLY
    A. existing   B. original   C. forged   D. duplicate

26. In the sentence, "The recruit was more complaisant after the captain spoke to him," the word "complaisant" means MOST NEARLY
    A. calm   B. affable   C. irritable   D. confident

27. In the sentence, "The man was captured under highly creditable circumstances," the word "creditable" means MOST NEARLY
    A. doubtful   B. believable   C. praiseworthy   D. unexpected

28. In the sentence, "His superior officers were more sagacious than he," the word "sagacious" means MOST NEARLY
    A. shrewd   B. obtuse   C. absurd   D. verbose

29. In the sentence, "He spoke with impunity," the word "impunity" means MOST NEARLY
    A. rashness   B. caution   C. without fear   D. immunity

30. In the sentence, "The new patrolman displayed unusual temerity during the emergency," the word "temerity" means MOST NEARLY
    A. fear   B. rashness   C. calmness   D. anxiety

31. In the sentence, "The portions of food were parsimoniously served," the word "parsimoniously" means MOST NEARLY
    A. stingily   B. piously   C. elaborately   D. generously

32. In the sentence, "Generally the speaker's remarks were sententious," the word "sententious" means MOST NEARLY
    A. verbose
    C. argumentative
    B. witty
    D. pithy

33. In the sentence, "The prisoner was fractious when brought to the station house," the word "fractious" means MOST NEARLY
    A. penitent   B. talkative   C. irascible   D. broken-hearted

34. In the sentence, "The judge was implacable when the attorney pleaded for leniency," the word "implacable" means MOST NEARLY
    A. inexorable
    C. inattentive
    B. disinterested
    D. indifferent

35. In the sentence, "The court ordered the mendacious statements stricken from the record," the word "mendacious" means MOST NEARLY
    A. begging   B. lying   C. threatening   D. lengthy

36. In the sentence, "The district attorney spoke in a strident voice," the word "strident" means MOST NEARLY
    A. loud
    B. harsh-sounding
    C. sing-song
    D. low

37. In the sentence, "The speaker had a predilection for long sentences," the word "predilection" means MOST NEARLY
    A. aversion
    B. talent
    C. propensity
    D. diffidence

38. In the sentence, "The candidate wants to file his application for preference before it is too late," the word "before" is used as a(n)
    A. preposition
    B. subordinating conjunction
    C. pronoun
    D. adverb

39. The one of the following sentences which is grammatically PREFERABLE to the others is:
    A. Our engineers will go over your blueprints so that you may have no problems in construction.
    B. For a long time he had been arguing that we, not he, are to blame for the confusion.
    C. I worked on this automobile for two hours and still cannot find out what is wrong with it.
    D. Accustomed to all kinds of hardships, fatigue seldom bothers veteran policemen.

40. The plural of
    A. turkey is turkies
    B. cargo is cargoes
    C. bankruptcy is bankruptcys
    D. son-in-law is son-in-laws

41. The abbreviation "viz." means MOST NEARLY
    A. namely
    B. for example
    C. the following
    D. see

42. In the sentence, "A man in a light-grey suit waited thirty-five minutes in the ante-room for the all-important document," the word IMPROPERLY hyphenated is
    A. light-grey
    B. thirty-five
    C. ante-room
    D. all-important

43. The MOST accurate of the following sentences is:
    A. The commissioner, as well as his deputy and various bureau heads, were present.
    B. A new organization of employers and employees have been formed.
    C. One or the other of these men have been selected.
    D. The number of pages in the book is enough to discourage a reader.

44. The MOST accurate of the following sentences is:
    A. Between you and me, I think he is the better man.
    B. He was believed to be me.
    C. Is it us that you wish to see?
    D. The winners are him and her.

45. In the sentence, "The committee favored submiting the amendment to the electorate," the MISSPELLED word is
    A. committee B. submiting C. amendment D. electorate

46. In the sentence, "He maliciously demurred to an ajournment of the proceedings," the MISSPELLED word is
    A. maliciously B. demurred C. ajournment D. proceedings

47. In the sentence, "His innocence at that time is irrelevent in view of his more recent villainous demeanor," the MISSPELLED word is
    A. innocence B. irrelevent C villainous D. demeanor

48. In the sentence, "The mischievous boys aggrevated the annoyance of their neighbor," the MISSPELLED word is
    A. mischievous B. aggrevated C. annoyance D. neighbor

49. In the sentence, "While his persiverance was commendable, his judgment was debatable, the MISSPELLED word is
    A. persiverance   B. commendable
    C. judgment   D. debatable

50. In the sentence, "He was hoping the appeal would facilitate his aquittal," the MISSPELLED word is
    A. hoping B. appeal C. facilitate D. aquittal

51. In the sentence, "It would be preferable for them to persue separate courses," the MISSPELLED word is
    A. preferable B. persue C. separate D. courses

52. In the sentence, "The litigant was complimented on his persistance and achievement," the MISSPELLED word is
    A. litigant   B. complimented
    C. persistance   D. achievement

53. In the sentence, "Ocassionally there are discrepancies in the descriptions of miscellaneous items," the MISSPELLED word is
    A. ocassionally   B. discrepancies
    C. descriptions   D. miscellaneous

54. In the sentence, "The councilmanic seargent-at-arms enforced the prohibition," the MISSPELLED word is
    A. councilmanic   B. seargent-at-arms
    C. enforced   D. prohibition

55. In the sentence, "The teacher had an ingenious device for mantaining attendance," the MISSPELLED word is
    A. ingenious B. device C. mantaining D. attendance

Questions 56-63.

DIRECTIONS: Questions 56 through 63 are to be answered on the basis of the following excerpt from a recorded annual report of the police department. This material should be read first and then referred to in answering these questions, which are to be answered SOLELY on the basis of the material herein contained.

LEGAL BUREAU

One of the more important functions of this bureau is to analyze and furnish the department with pertinent information concerning Federal and State statutes and Local Laws which affect the department, law enforcement or crime prevention. In addition, all measures introduced in the State Legislature and the City Council which may affect this department are carefully reviewed by members of the Legal Bureau and, where necessary, opinions and recommendations thereon are prepared.

Another important function of this office is the prosecution of cases in the Magistrate's Courts. This is accomplished by assignment of attorneys who are members of the Legal Bureau to appear in those cases which are deemed to raise issues of importance to the department or questions of law which require technical presentation to facilitate proper determination; and also in those cases where request is made for such appearances by a magistrate, some other official of the city, or a member of the force. Attorneys are regularly assigned to prosecute all cases in the Women's Court.

Proposed legislation was prepared and sponsored for introduction in the State Legislature and, at this writing, one of these proposals has already been enacted into law and five others are presently on the Governor's desk awaiting executive action. The new law prohibits the sale or possession of a hypodermic syringe or needle by an unauthorized person. The bureau's proposals awaiting executive action pertain to an amendment to the Code of Criminal Procedure prohibiting desk officers from taking bail in gambling cases or in cases mentioned in Section 552, Code of Criminal Procedure; including confidence men and swindlers as jostlers in the Penal Law; prohibiting the sale of switchblade knives of any size to children under 16 and bills extending the licensing period of gunsmiths.

The Legal Bureau has regularly cooperated with the Corporation Counsel and the District Attorneys in respect to matters affecting this department, and has continued to advise and represent the Police Athletic League, the Police Sports Association, the Police Relief Fund, and the Police Pension Fund.

The following is a statistical report of the activities of the bureau during the current year as compared with the previous year:

	Current Year	Previous Year
Memoranda of law prepared	68	83
Legal matters forwarded to corporation counsel	122	144
Letters requesting legal information	756	807
Letters requesting departmental records	139	111
Matters for publication	17	26
Court appearances of members of bureau	4,678	4,621
Conferences	94	103
Lectures at Police Academy	30	33
Reports on proposed legislation	194	255
Deciphering of codes	79	27
Expert testimony	31	16
Notices to court witnesses	55	81
Briefs prepared	22	18
Court papers prepared	258	--

56. One of the functions of the Legal Bureau is to
    A. review and make recommendations on proposed Federal laws affecting law enforcement
    B. prepare opinions on all measures introduced in the State Legislature and the City Council
    C. furnish the Police Department with pertinent information concerning all new Federal and State laws
    D. analyze all laws affecting the work of the Police Department

57. The one of the following that is NOT a function of the Legal Bureau is
    A. law enforcement and crime prevention
    B. prosecution of all cases in Women's Court
    C. advise and represent the Police Sports Association
    D. lecturing at the Police Academy

58. Members of the Legal Bureau frequently appear in Magistrate's Court for the purpose of
    A. defending members of the Police Force
    B. raising issues of importance to the Police Department
    C. prosecuting all offenders arrested by members of the Force
    D. facilitating proper determination of questions of law requiring technical presentation

59. The Legal Bureau sponsored a bill that would
    A. extend the licenses of gunsmiths
    B. prohibit the sale of switchblade knives to children of any size
    C. place confidence men and swindlers in the same category as jostlers in the Penal Law
    D. prohibit desk officers from admitting gamblers, confidence men, and swindlers to bail

9 (#1)

60. From the report, it is NOT reasonable to infer that
   A. fewer bills affecting the Police Department were introduced in the current year
   B. the preparation of court papers was a new activity assumed in the current year
   C. the Code of Criminal Procedure authorizes desk officers to accept bail in certain cases
   D. the penalty for jostling and swindling is the same

61. According to the statistical report, the activity showing the GREATEST percentage of decrease in the current year as compared to the previous year was
   A. matters for publication
   B. reports on proposed legislation
   C. notices to court witnesses
   D. memoranda of law prepared

62. According to the statistical report, the activity showing the GREATEST percentage of increase in the current year as compare with the previous year was
   A. court appearances of members of the bureau
   B. giving expert testimony
   C. deciphering of codes
   D. letters requesting departmental records

63. According to the report, the percentage of bills prepared and sponsored by the Legal Bureau which were passed by the State Legislature and sent to the Governor for approval was APPROXIMATELY
   A. 3.1%
   B. 2.6%
   C. .5%
   D. not capable of determination from the data given

64. A squad of officers assigned to enforce a new parking regulation in a particular area issued tag summonses on a particular day as follows: four officers issued 16 summonses each; three issued 19 each; one issued 22; seven issued 25 each; eleven issued 28 each; ten issued 30 each; two issued 36 each; one issued 41; and three issued 45 each.
   The average number of summonses issued by a member of this squad was MOST NEARLY
   A. 6.2   B. 17.2   C. 21.0   D. 27.9

65. A water storage tank is 75 feet long and 30 feet wide and has a depth of 6½ feet. Each cubic foot of the tank holds 9½ gallons.
   The TOTAL capacity of the tank is _____ gallons.
   A. 73,125½   B. 131,625   C. 138,937½   D. 146,250

66. The price of admission to a PAL entertainment were $2.50 each for adults and $1.00 for children; the turnstile at the entrance showed that 358 persons entered and the gate receipts were $626.50.
The number of children who attended was
A. 170   B. 175   C. 179   D. 183

67. A patrol car travels six times as fast as a bicycle.
If the patrol car goes 168 miles in two hours less time than the bicycle requires to go 42 miles, their respective rates of speed are _____ miles per hour.
A. 36 and 6   B. 42 and 7   C. 63 and 10½   D. 126 and 21

68. The radiator of an automobile already contains six quarts of a 10% solution of alcohol.
In order to make a mixture of 20% alcohol, it will be necessary to add _____ quarts of alcohol.
A. ¾   B. 1¾   C. 2½   D. 3

69. A man received an inheritance of $80,000 and wanted to invest it so that it would produce an annual income sufficient to pay his rent of $400 a month. In order to do this, he will have to receive interest or dividends at the rate of _____% per annum.
A. 3   B. 4   C. 5¾   D. 6

70. If the price of a bus ticket varies *directly* as the mileage involved, and a ticket to travel 135 miles costs $29.70, a ticket for a 30-mile trip will cost
A. $15.20   B. $13.40   C. $6.60   D. $2.20

71. A man owed a debt of $5,800. After a first payment of $100, he agreed to pay the balance by monthly payments in which each payment after this first would be $20 more than that of the preceding month.
If no interest charge is made, he will have to make, including the first payment, a total of _____ monthly payments.
A. 16   B. 20   C. 24   D. 28

72. The written test of a civil service examination has a weight of 30, the oral test a weight of 20, experience a weight of 20, and the physical test a weight of 30. A candidate received ratings of 76 on the written test, 84 on the oral, and 80 for experience.
In order to attain an average of 85 on the examination, his rating on the physical test must be
A. 86   B. 90   C. 94   D. 98

73. A family has an income of $3,200 per month. It spends 22% of this amount for rent, 36% for food, 16% for clothing, and 12% for additional household expenses. After meeting these expenses, 50% of the balance is deposited in the bank.
The amount deposited monthly is
A. $224.00   B. $366.00   C. $448.00   D. $520.00

11 (#1)

74. Upon retirement last July, an officer bought a farm of 64 acres for $18,000 per acre. He made a down payment of $612,000 and agreed to pay the balance in installments of $7,500 a month commencing on August 1, 2022.
Disregarding interest, he will make his LAST payment in
  A. July 2028
  B. August 2030
  C. January 2032
  D. April 2035

75. 40% of those who commit a particular crime are subsequently arrested and convicted. 75% of those committed receive sentences of 10 years or more. Assuming that those arrested for the first time serve less than 10 years, the percentage of those committing this crime who receive sentences of ten years or more is MOST NEARLY
  A. 20%   B. 30%   C. 40%   D. 50%

KEY (CORRECT ANSWERS)

1.	A	21.	D	41.	A	61.	A
2.	D	22.	B	42.	C	62.	C
3.	A	23.	B	43.	D	63.	D
4.	A	24.	B	44.	A	64.	D
5.	C	25.	A	45.	B	65.	C
6.	B	26.	B	46.	C	66.	C
7.	C	27.	C	47.	C	67.	B
8.	B	28.	A	48.	B	68.	A
9.	A	29.	D	49.	A	69.	D
10.	C	30.	B	50.	D	70.	C
11.	C	31.	A	51.	B	71.	B
12.	A	32.	D	52.	C	72.	D
13.	A	33.	C	53.	A	73.	A
14.	B	34.	A	54.	B	74.	A
15.	B	35.	B	55.	C	75.	B
16.	D	36.	B	56.	D		
17.	A	37.	C	57.	A		
18.	A	38.	B	58.	D		
19.	C	39.	A	59.	C		
20.	A	40.	B	60.	D		

EXAMINATION SECTION
TEST 1

DIRECTIONS: Each question or incomplete statement is followed by several suggested answers or completions. Select the one that BEST answers the question or completes the statement. *PRINT THE LETTER OF THE CORRECT ANSWER IN THE SPACE AT THE RIGHT.*

1. The basic purpose of patrol is to create a public impression of police presence everywhere so that potential offenders will think there is no opportunity for successful misconduct.
   In the assignment of police personnel, the type of police activity that MOST NEARLY realizes this purpose is
   A. traffic summons duty
   B. traffic duty
   C. patrol of all licensed premises
   D. patrol by the detective force
   E. radio motor patrol

   1._____

2. A patrolman, who is asked by a civilian about a legal matter, directs him to the appropriate court.
   Of the following information given by the patrolman, the item which is LEAST likely to be useful to the civilian is
   A. hours during which the court is in session
   B. location of the court
   C. name of the Magistrate sitting in this court
   D. location of the complaint clerk within the court building
   E. transportation directions necessary to get to the court

   2._____

3. An officer discovers two teenaged gangs, numbering about 50 boys, engaged in a free-for-all fight.
   The BEST immediate course for the officer to adopt is to
   A. call the station house for reinforcements
   B. fire over the heads of the boys and order them to disperse
   C. arrest the ringleaders
   D. call upon adult bystanders to assist him in restoring order
   E. attempt to stop the fight by using his club

   3._____

4. A radio motor patrol team arrives on the scene a few minutes after a pedestrian has been killed on a busy street by a hit-and-run driver.
   After obtaining a description of the car, the FIRST action the officer should take is to
   A. radio a description of the fleeing car to precinct headquarters
   B. try to overtake the fleeing car
   C. obtain complete statements from everyone at the scene
   D. call for an ambulance
   E. inspect the site of the accident for clues

   4._____

5. A police officer is approached by an obviously upset woman who reports that her husband is missing.
   The FIRST thing the officer should do is to
   A. check with the hospitals and the police station
   B. tell the woman to wait a few hours and call the police station if her husband has not returned by then
   C. obtain a description of the missing man so that an alarm can be broadcast
   D. ask the woman why she thinks her husband is missing
   E. make certain that the woman lives in his precinct

6. A violin is reported as missing from the home of Mrs. Brown.
   It would be LEAST important to the police, before making a routine check of pawnshops, to know that this violin
   A. is of a certain unusual shade of red
   B. has dimensions which are different from those of most violins
   C. has a well-known manufacturer's label stamped inside the violin
   D. has a hidden number given to the police by the owner
   E. has one tuning key with a chip mark on it in the shape of a triangle

7. In making his rounds, an officer should following the same route and schedule each time.
   The suggested procedure is
   A. *good*; a fixed routine enables the officer to proceed methodically and systematically
   B. *poor*; criminals can avoid observation by studying the officer's routine
   C. *good*; without a fixed routine, an officer may overlook some of his many duties
   D. *poor*; a fixed routine reduces an officer's alertness and initiative
   E. *good*; residents in the area covered will have more confidence in police efficiency

8. Police officers should call for ambulances to transport injured people to the hospital rather than use patrol cars for this purpose.
   Of the following, the MOST valid reason for this policy is that
   A. there is less danger of aggravating injuries
   B. patrol cars cannot be spared from police duty
   C. patrol cars are usually not equipped for giving emergency first aid
   D. medical assistance reaches the injured person sooner
   E. responsibility for treating injured people lies with the Department of Hospitals

9. A businessman requests advice concerning good practice in the use of a safe in his business office.
   The one of the following points which should be stressed MOST in the use of safes is that
   A. a safe should not be placed where it can be seen from the street
   B. the combination should be written down and carefully hidden in the office

C. a safe located in a dark place is more tempting to a burglar than one which is located in a well-lighted place
D. factors of size and weight alone determine the protection offered by a safe
E. the names of the manufacturer and the owner should be painted on the front of the safe

10. During a quarrel on a crowded city street, one man stabs another and flees. An officer arriving at the scene a short time later finds the victim unconscious, calls for an ambulance, and orders the crowd to leave.
His action was
    A. *bad*; there may have witnesses to the assault among the crowd
    B. *good*; it is proper first aid procedure to give an injured person room and air
    C. *bad*; the assailant is probably among the crowd
    D. *good*; a crowd may destroy needed evidence
    E. *bad*; it is poor public relations for the police to order people about needlessly

11. An officer walking his post at 3 A.M. notices heavy smoke coming out of a top floor window of a large apartment house.
Of the following, the action he should take FIRST is to
    A. make certain that there really is a fire
    B. enter the building and warn all the occupants of the apartment house
    C. attempt to extinguish the fire before it gets out of control
    D. call the Fire Department
    E. call precinct headquarters for Fire Department help

12. Two rival youth gangs have been involved in several minor classes. The youth officer working in their area believes that a serious clash will occur if steps are not taken to prevent it.
Of the following, the LEAST desirable action for the officer to take in his effort to head of trouble is to
    A. arrest the leaders of both groups as a warning
    B. warn the parents of the dangerous situation
    C. obtain the cooperation of religious and civic leaders in the community
    D. alert all social agencies working in that neighborhood
    E. report the situation to his superior

13. Police officers are instructed to pay particular attention to anyone apparently making repairs on an auto parked on a street.
The MOST important reason for this rule is that
    A. the auto may be parked illegally
    B. the person making the repairs may be obstructing traffic
    C. working on autos is prohibited on certain streets
    D. many people injure themselves while working on autos
    E. the person making the repairs may be stealing the auto

10.____

11.____

12.____

13.____

14. After making an arrest of a criminal, the officer is LEAST likely to request some kind of transportation if the
    A. prisoner is apparently a violent mental patient
    B. distance to be traveled is considerable
    C. prisoner is injured
    D. prisoner is in an alcoholic stupor
    E. prisoner talks of escaping

15. The Police Department, in an effort to prevent losses due to worthless checks, suggests to merchants that they place near the cash register a card stating that the merchant reserves the right to require positive identification and fingerprint from all persons who cash checks.
    This procedure is
    A. *poor*; the merchant's regular customers may be offended by compulsory fingerprinting
    B. *poor*; the taking of fingerprints would not deter the professional criminal
    C. *good*; the police criminal files may be enlarged by the addition of all fingerprints taken
    D. *poor*; this system could not work unless the fingerprinting was made mandatory
    E. *good*; the card might serve to discourage persons from attempting to cash worthless checks

16. A factory manager asks an officer to escort his payroll clerk to and from the local bank when payroll money is withdrawn. The officer knows that it is against departmental policy to provide payroll escort service.
    The officer should
    A. refuse and explain why he cannot do what is requested
    B. refer the manager to his precinct commander
    C. tell the manager that police officers have more important tasks
    D. advise the manager that he will provide this service if other duties do not interfere
    E. suggest that paychecks be issued to employees

17. A motorist who has been stopped by a motorcycle police officer for speeding acts rudely. He hints about his personal connections with high officials in the city government and demands the officer's name and shield number.
    The officer should
    A. arrest the motorist for threatening an officer in the performance of his duty
    B. give his name and shield number without comment
    C. ignore the question since his name and shield number will be on the summons he is about to issue
    D. give his name and shield number but add to the charges against the motorist
    E. ask the motorist why he wants the information and give it only if the answer is satisfactory

18. Tire skidmarks provide valuable information to policemen investigating automobile accidents.
    The MOST important information obtained from this source is the
    A. condition of the road at the time of the accident
    B. effectiveness of the automobile's brakes
    C. condition of the tires
    D. point at which the driver first saw the danger
    E. speed of the automobile at the time of the accident

19. An officer observes several youths in the act of looting a peanut-vending machine. The youths flee in several directions as he approaches, ignoring his order to halt. The officer then shoots at them, and they halt and are captured
    The officer's action was
    A. *right*; it was the most effective way of capturing the criminals
    B. *wrong*; extreme measures should not be taken in apprehending petty offenders
    C. *right*; provided that there was no danger of shooting innocent bystanders
    D. *wrong*; this is usually ineffective when more than one offender is involved
    E. *right*; it is particularly important to teach juvenile delinquents respect for the law

20. Before permitting automobiles involved in an accident to depart, an officer should take certain measures.
    Of the following, it is LEAST important that the officer make certain that
    A. both drivers are properly licensed
    B. the automobiles are in safe operating condition
    C. the drivers have exchanged names and license numbers
    D. the drivers are physically fit to drive
    E. he obtains the names and addresses of drivers and witnesses

21. A detective, following a tip that a notorious bank robber is to meet a woman in a certain restaurant, is seated in a booth from which he can observe people entering and leaving. While waiting, he notices a flashily dressed woman get up from a table and slip by the cashier without paying her check. The detective ignored the incident and continued watching for the wanted man.
    This course of action was
    A. *correct*; the woman probably forgot to pay her bill
    B. *incorrect*; he should have arrested the woman since a *bird in the hand is worth two in the bush*
    C. *correct*; it is not the duty of the police department to protect businessmen from loss due to their own negligence
    D. *incorrect*; he should have followed the woman since she may lead to the bank robber
    E. *correct*; the detective should not risk losing the bank robber by checking on this incident

22. All officers are required to maintain a record of their daily police activity in a memorandum book.
The LEAST likely reason for this requirement is to
   A. make it unnecessary for the officer to remember police incidents
   B. give supervisors information concerning the officer's daily work
   C. serve as a possible basis to refute unjustified complaints against the officer
   D. make a record of information that may have a bearing on a court action
   E. record any action which may later require an explanation

23. Police officers have a duty to take into custody any person who is actually or apparently mentally ill.
Of the following cases, the one LEAST likely to fall under this provision of the law is the
   A. quarrelsome person who makes unjustifiable accusations
   B. elderly man who appears confused and unable to dress or feed himself
   C. young man who sits on the sidewalk curb staring into space and, when questioned, gives meaningless answers
   D. man who shouts obscenities at strangers in the streets
   E. woman who accuses waiters of attempting to poison her

24. An officer should not take notes while first questioning a suspect.
Of the following, the MOST important reason for this procedure is that
   A. information obtained at this time will probably not be truthful
   B. unessential facts can be eliminated if statements are written late
   C. the physical reactions of the suspect during interrogation can be better observed
   D. the exact wording is of no importance
   E. the statement will be better organized if written later

25. An officer should know the occupations and habits of the people on his beat. In heavily populated districts, however, it is too much to ask that the officer know all the people on his beat.
If this statement is correct, the one of the following which would be the MOST practical course for an officer to follow is to
   A. concentrate on becoming acquainted with the oldest residents of the beat
   B. limit his attention to people who work as well as live in the district
   C. limit his attention to people with criminal records
   D. concentrate on becoming acquainted with key people such as janitors, bartenders, and local merchants
   E. concentrate on becoming acquainted with the newest residents of the beat

26. An officer off-duty but in uniform recognizes a stolen car parked outside of a tavern. He notices that the radiator of the car is warm, indicating recent use.
Of the following, the MOST practical course for the officer to follow is to
   A. enter the tavern and ask aloud for the driver of the car
   B. stand in a nearby doorway and watch the car

C. search for the officer on the beat and report the facts to him
D. telephone the station house as soon as he arrives home
E. enter the tavern and privately ask the bartender if he knows who owns the car

27. When a person is arrested, he is always asked whether he uses narcotics, regardless of the charge against him.
    Of the following, the MOST important reason for asking this question is that
    A. drug addicts can be induced to confess by withholding narcotics from them
    B. the theft of narcotics is becoming a serious police problem
    C. criminals are usually drug addicts
    D. many drug addicts commit crimes in order to obtain money for the purchase of narcotics
    E. it may be possible to convict the suspect of violation of the narcotics law

28. Of the following types of crimes, increased police vigilance would probably be LEAST successful in preventing
    A. murder
    B. burglary
    C. prostitution
    D. automobile thefts
    E. robbery

29. The Police Department has been hiring civilian women to direct traffic at school crossings.
    The MOST important reason for this policy is
    A. to stimulate civic interest in police problems
    B. to dramatize the traffic safety problem
    C. that women are more careful of the safety of children
    D. that young school children have more confidence in women who are mothers of their playmates
    E. to free policemen for regular patrol duty

30. Of the following, the fact that makes it MOST difficult to identify stolen cars is that
    A. thieves frequently damage stolen cars
    B. many cars are similar in appearance
    C. thieves frequently disguise stolen cars
    D. owners frequently don't report stolen cars which are covered by insurance
    E. owners frequently delay reporting the theft

31. When testifying in a criminal case, it is MOST important that a policeman endeavor to
    A. avoid technical terms which may be unfamiliar to the jury
    B. lean over backwards in order to be fair to the defendant
    C. assist the prosecutor even if some exaggeration is necessary
    D. avoid contradicting other prosecution witnesses
    E. confine his answers to the questions asked

32. When investigating a burglary, a policeman should obtain as complete descriptions as possible of articles of value which were stolen, but should list, without describing, stolen articles which are relatively valueless.
This suggested procedure is
   A. *poor*; what is valueless to one person may be of great value to another
   B. *good*; it enables the police to concentrate on recovering the most valuable articles
   C. *poor*; articles of little value frequently provide the only evidence connecting the suspect to the crime
   D. *good*; the listing of the inexpensive items is probably incomplete
   E. *poor*; the police should make the same effort to recover all stolen property, regardless of value

32.____

33. At 10 A.M. on a regular school day, an officer notices a boy about 11 years old wandering in the street. When asked the reason he is not in school, he replies that he attends school in the neighborhood, but that he felt sick that morning. The officer then took the boy to the principal of the school.
This method of handling the situation was
   A. *bad*; the officer should have obtained verification of the boy's illness
   B. *good*; the school authorities are best equipped to deal with the problem
   C. *bad*; the officer should have obtained the boy's name and address and reported the incident to the attendance officer
   D. *good*; seeing the truant boy escorted by an officer will deter other children from truancy
   E. *bad*; the principal of a school should not be saddled with a truancy problem

33.____

34. During an investigation of a robbery, an officer caught one of the witnesses contradicting himself on one point. Upon questioning, the witness readily admitted the contradiction.
The officer should conclude that
   A. the witness was truthful but emotionally disturbed by the experience
   B. all of the statements of the witness should be disregarded as untrustworthy
   C. the statements of the witness should be investigated carefully
   D. the witness was trying to protect the guilty person
   E. contradictions of this sort are inevitable

34.____

35. A woman was found dead by her estranged husband in the kitchen of a ground floor apartment. The husband stated that, although the apartment was full of gas and tightly closed, all the burners of the kitchen range were shut. The husband had gone to the apartment to get some clothes. When an officer arrived, the apartment was still heavy with gas fumes.
Of the following, the MOST likely explanation for these circumstances is that
   A. gas seeped into the apartment under the door from a defective gas furnace in the basement
   B. the husband has given false information to mislead the police

35.____

C. the woman changed her mind about committing suicide and shut off the jets just before she collapsed
D. a leak in the kitchen range had developed
E. the woman had died from some other cause than asphyxiation

36. An officer on post hears a cry for help from a woman in a car with two men. He approaches the car and is told by the woman that the men are kidnapping her. The men claim to be the woman's husband and doctor and state that they are taking her to a private mental hospital.
Of the following, the BEST course for the officer is to
    A. take all of them to the station house for further questioning
    B. permit the woman to depart and arrest the men
    C. call for an ambulance to take the woman to the nearest city mental hospital
    D. accompany the car to the private mental hospital
    E. permit the car to depart on the basis of the explanation

37. Social security cards are not acceptable proof of identification for police purposes.
Of the following, the MOST important reason for this rule is that the social security card
    A. is easily obtained
    B. states on its face *for social security purposes—not for identification*
    C. is frequently lost
    D. does not contain the address of the person
    E. does not contain a photograph, description, or fingerprints of the person

38. Many well-meaning people have proposed that officers in uniform not be permitted to arrest juveniles.
This proposal is
    A. *good*; the police are not equipped to handle juvenile offenders
    B. *bad*; juvenile offenders would lose respect for all law enforcement agencies
    C. *good*; offending juveniles should be segregated from hardened criminals
    D. *bad*; frequently it is the uniformed officer who first comes upon the youthful offender
    E. *good*; contact with the police would prevent any rehabilitative measures from being taken

39. An off-duty police officer was seated in a restaurant when two men entered, drew guns, and robbed the cashier. The officer made no effort to prevent the robbery or apprehend the criminals. Later he justified his conduct by stating that an officer when off-duty is a private citizen with the same duties and rights of all private citizens.
The officer's conduct was
    A. *wrong*; an officer must act to prevent crimes and apprehend criminals at all times
    B. *right*; he was out of uniform at the time of the robbery
    C. *wrong*; he had his gun with him at the time of the robbery

D. *right*; it would have been foolhardy for him to intervene when outnumbered by armed robbers
E. *wrong*; he should have obtained the necessary information and descriptions after the robbers left

40. Drivers with many convictions for traffic law violations sometimes try to conceal this record by cutting off the lower part of the operator's license and attaching to it clean section from a blank application form.
An officer who stops a driver and notices that his operator's license is torn and held together by transparent tape should FIRST
    A. verify the driver's explanation of the torn license
    B. examine both parts of the license to see if they match
    C. request additional proof of identity
    D. check the records of the Bureau of Motor Vehicles for unanswered summonses

40.____

Question 41-60.

DIRECTIONS: In answering Questions 41 through 60 select the lettered word or phrase which means MOST NEARLY the same as the word in capitals.

41. IMPLY
    A. agree to   B. hint at   C. laugh at
    D. mimic   E. reduce

41.____

42. APPRAISAL
    A. allowance   B. composition   C. prohibition
    D. quantity   E. valuation

42.____

43. DISBURSE
    A. approve   B. expend   C. prevent
    D. relay   E. restrict

43.____

44. POSTERITY
    A. back payment   B. current procedure   C. final effort
    D. future generations   E. rare specimen

44.____

45. PUNCTUAL
    A. clear   B. honest   C. polite
    D. prompt   E. prudent

45.____

46. PRECARIOUS
    A. abundant   B. alarmed   C. cautious
    D. insecure   E. placid

46.____

47. FOSTER
    A. delegate   B. demote   C. encourage
    D. plead   E. surround

47.____

48. PINNACLE
    A. center   B. crisis   C. outcome
    D. peak   E. personificaton

    48.____

49. COMPONENT
    A. flattery   B. opposite   C. part
    D. revision   E. trend

    49.____

50. SOLICIT
    A. ask   B. prohibit   C. promise
    D. revoke   E. surprise

    50.____

51. LIAISON
    A. asset   B. coordination   C. difference
    D. policy   E. procedure

    51.____

52. ALLEGE
    A. assert   B. break   C. irritate
    D. reduce   E. wait

    52.____

53. INFILTRATION
    A. consumption   B. disposal   C. enforcement
    D. penetration   E. seizure

    53.____

54. SALVAGE
    A. announce   B. combine   C. prolong
    D. save   E. try

    54.____

55. MOTIVE
    A. attack   B. favor   C. incentive
    D. patience   E. tribute

    55.____

56. PROVOKE
    A. adjust   B. incite   C. leave
    D. obtain   E. practice

    56.____

57. SURGE
    A. branch   B. contract   C. revenge
    D. rush   E. want

    57.____

58. MAGNIFY
    A. attract   B. demand   C. generate
    D. increase   E. puzzle

    58.____

59. PREPONDERANCE
    A. decision   B. judgment   C. outweighing
    D. submission   E. warning

    59.____

60. ABATE
    A. assist
    B. coerce
    C. diminish
    D. indulge
    E. trade

Question 61-65.

DIRECTIONS: Questions 61 through 65 are to be answered on the basis of the table which appears below.

VALUE OF PROPERTY STOLEN – 2019 AND 2020
LARCENY

Category	2019 Number of Offenses	2019 Value of Stolen Property	2020 Number of Offenses	2020 Value of Stolen Property
Pocket-picking	20	$1,950	10	$950
Purse-snatching	175	5,750	20	12,500
Shoplifting	155	7,950	225	17,350
Automobile thefts	1,040	127,050	860	108,000
Thefts of auto accessories	1,135	34,950	970	24,400
Bicycle thefts	355	8,250	240	6,350
All other thefts	1,375	187,150	1,300	153,150

61. Of the total number of larcenies reported for 2019, automobile thefts accounted for MOST NEARLY
    A. 5%   B. 15%   C. 25%   D. 50%   E. 75%

62. The LARGEST percentage decrease in the value of the stolen property from 2019 to 2020 was in the category of
    A. pocket-picking
    B. automobile thefts
    C. thefts of auto accessories
    D. bicycle thefts
    E. all other thefts

63. In 2020, the average amount of each theft was LOWEST for the category of
    A. pocket-picking
    B. purse-snatching
    C. shoplifting
    D. thefts of auto accessories

64. The category which had the LARGEST numerical reduction in the number of offenses from 2019 to 2020 was
    A. pocket-picking
    B. automobile thefts
    C. thefts of auto accessories
    D. bicycle thefts
    E. all other thefts

65. When the categories are ranked for each year, according to the number of offenses committed in each category (largest number to rank first), the number of categories which will have the same rank in 2019 as in 2020 is
    A. 3   B. 4   C. 5   D. 6   E. 7

13 (#1)

66. A parade is marching up an avenue for 60 city blocks. A sample count of the number of people watching the parade on one side of the street in the block is taken, first, in a block near the end of the parade, and then in a block at the middle; the former count is 4,000 and the latter is 6,000.
If the average for the entire parade is assumed to be the average of the two samples, then the estimated number of persons watching the entire parade is MOST NEARLY
   A. 240,000   B. 300,000   C. 480,000   D. 600,000   E. 720,000

66.____

67. Suppose that the revenue from parking meters in a city was 5% greater in 2019 than in 2018, and 2% less in 2020 than in 2019.
If the revenue in 2018 was $1,500,000, then the revenue in 2020 was
   A. $1,541,500   B. $1,542,000   C. $1,542,500
   D. $1,543,000   E. $1,543,500

67.____

68. A radio motor patrol car completes a ten mile trip in twenty minutes.
If it does one-half the distance at a speed of twenty miles an hour, its speed, in miles per hour, for the remainder of the distance must be
   A. 30   B. 40   C. 50   D. 60   E. 70

68.____

69. A public beach has two parking areas. Their capacities are in the ratio of two to one and, on a certain day, are filled to 60% and 40% of capacity, respectfully.
The entire parking facilities of the beach on that day are MOST NEARLY _____ filled.
   A. 38%   B. 43%   C. 48%   D. 53%   E. 58%

69.____

70. While on foot patrol, an officer walks north for eleven blocks, turns around and walks south for six blocks, turns around and walks north for two blocks, then makes a right turn and walks one block.
In relation to his starting point, he is now _____ blocks away and facing _____.
   A. twenty; east   B. eight; east   C. seven; west
   D. nine; north   E. seven; north

70.____

Question 71-73.

DIRECTIONS: Questions 71 through 73 are to be answered on the basis of the following paragraph.

    When police officers search for a stolen car, they first check for the color of the car, then for make, model, year, body damage, and finally license number. The first five can be detected from almost any angle, while the recognition of the license number is often not immediately apparent. The serial number and motor number, though less likely to be changed than the easily substituted license number, cannot be observed in initial detection of the stolen car.

71. According to the above paragraph, the one of the following features which is LEAST readily observed in checking for a stolen car in moving traffic is
   A. license number   B. serial number   C. model
   D. make   E. color

71.____

72. The feature of a car that cannot be determined from most angles of observation is the
    A. make
    B. model
    C. year
    D. license number
    E. color

73. Of the following, the feature of a stolen car that is MOST likely to be altered by a car thief shortly after the car is stolen is the
    A. license number
    B. motor number
    C. color
    D. model
    E. minor body damage

Question 74-75.

DIRECTIONS: Questions 74 and 75 are to be answered on the basis of the following paragraph.

The racketeer is primarily concerned with business affairs, legitimate or otherwise, and preferably those which are close to the margin of legitimacy. He gets his best opportunities from business organizations which meet the need of large sections of the public for goods or services which are defined as illegitimate by the same public, such as prostitution, gambling, illicit drugs or liquor. In contrast to the thief, the racketeer and the establishments he controls deliver goods and services for money received.

74. From the above paragraph, it can be deduced that suppression of racketeers is difficult because
    A. victims of racketeers are not guilty of violating the law
    B. racketeers are generally engaged in fully legitimate enterprises
    C. many people want services which are not obtainable through legitimate sources
    D. the racketeers are well organized
    E. laws prohibiting gambling and prostitution are unenforceable

75. According to the above paragraph, racketeering, unlike theft, involves
    A. objects of value
    B. payment for goods received
    C. organized gangs
    D. public approval
    E. unlawful activities

Question 76-78.

DIRECTIONS: Questions 76 through 78 are to be answered on the basis of the following paragraph.

A number of crimes, such as robbery, assault, rape, certain forms of theft and burglary, are highly visible crimes in that it is apparent to all concerned that they are criminal acts prior to or at the time they are committed. In contrast to these, check forgeries, especially those committed by first offenders, have low visibility. There is little in the criminal act or in the interaction between the check passer and the person cashing the check to identify it as a crime. Closely related to this special quality of the forgery crime is the fact that, while it is formally defined and treated as a felonious or infamous crime, it is informally held by the legally untrained public to be a relatively harmless form of crime.

76. According to the above paragraph, crimes of high visibility
    A. are immediately recognized as crimes by the victims
    B. take place in public view
    C. always involve violence or the threat of violence
    D. usually are committed after dark
    E. can be observed from a distance

77. According to the above paragraph,
    A. the public regards check forgery as a minor crime
    B. the law regards check forgery as a minor crime
    C. the law distinguishes between check forgery and other forgery
    D. it is easier to spot inexperienced check forgers than other criminals
    E. it is more difficult to identify check forgers than other criminals

78. As used in the above paragraph, an *infamous* crime is
    A. a crime attracting great attention from the public
    B. more serious than a felony
    C. less serious than a felony
    D. more or less serious than a felony, depending upon the surrounding circumstances
    E. the same as a felony

Question 79-81.

DIRECTIONS: Questions 79 through 81 are to be answered on the basis of the following paragraph.

Criminal science is largely the science of identification. Progress in this field has been marked and sometimes very spectacular because new techniques, instruments, and facts flow continuously from the scientist. But the crime laboratories are undermanned, trade secrets still prevail, and inaccurate conclusions are often the result. However, modern gadgets cannot substitute for the skilled intelligent investigator; he must be their master.

79. According to the above paragraph, criminal science
    A. excludes the field of investigation
    B. is primarily interested in establishing identity
    C. is based on the equipment used in crime laboratories
    D. uses techniques different from those used in other sciences
    E. is essentially secret in nature

80. Advances in criminal science have been, according to the above paragraph,
    A. extremely limited
    B. slow but steady
    C. unusually reliable
    D. outstanding
    E. infrequently worthwhile

81. A problem that has not been overcome completely in crime work is, according to the above paragraph,
    A. unskilled investigators
    B. the expense of new equipment and techniques
    C. an insufficient number of personnel in crime laboratories
    D. inaccurate equipment used in laboratories
    E. conclusions of the public about the value of this field

81.____

Question 82-84.

DIRECTIONS: Questions 82 through 84 are to be answered on the basis of the following paragraph.

The New York City Police Department will accept for investigation no report of a person missing from his residence if such residence is located outside of New York City. The person reporting same will be advised to report such fact to the police department of the locality where the missing person lives, which will, if necessary, communicate officially with the New York City Police Department. However, a report will be accepted of a person who is missing from a temporary residence in New York City, but the person making the report will be instructed to make a report also to the police department of the locality where the missing person lives.

82. According to the above paragraph, a report to the New York City Police Department of a missing person whose permanent residence is outside of New York City will
    A. always be investigated provided that a report is also made to his local police authorities
    B. never be investigated unless requested officially by his local police authorities
    C. be investigated in cases of temporary New York City residence, but a report should always be made to his local police authorities
    D. be investigated if the person making the report is a New York City resident
    E. always be investigated and a report will be made to the local police authorities by the New York City Police Department

82.____

83. Of the following, the MOST likely reason for the procedure described in the above paragraph is that
    A. non-residents are not entitled to free police service from New York City
    B. local police authorities would resent interference in their jurisdiction
    C. local police authorities sometimes try to unload their problems on the New York City Police
    D. local police authorities may be better able to conduct an investigation
    E. few persons are erroneously reported as missing

83.____

84. Mr. Smith, who lives in Jersey City, and Mr. Jones, who lives in Newark, arrange to meet in New York City, but Mr. Jones does not keep the appointment. Mr. Smith telephones Mr. Jones several times the next day and gets no answer. Mr. Smith believes that something has happened to Mr. Jones.

84.____

According to the above paragraph, Mr. Smith should apply to the police authorities of
A. Jersey City
B. Newark
C. Newark and New York City
D. Jersey City and New York City
E. Newark, Jersey City, and New York City

Question 85-87.

DIRECTIONS: Questions 85 through 87 are to be answered on the basis of the following paragraph.

Some early psychologists believed that the basic characteristic of the criminal type was inferiority of intelligence, if not outright feeblemindedness. They were misled by the fact that they had measurements for all kinds of criminals but, until World War I gave them a draft army sample, they had no information on a comparable group of non-criminal adults. As soon as acceptable measurements could be taken of criminals and a comparable group of non-criminals, concern with feeblemindedness or with low intelligence as a type took on less and less significance in research in criminology.

85. According to the above paragraph, some early psychologists were in error because they did not
    A. distinguish among the various types of criminals
    B. devise a suitable method of measuring intelligence
    C. measure the intelligence of non-criminals as a basis for comparison
    D. distinguish between feeblemindedness and inferiority of intelligence
    E. clearly define the term *intelligence*

86. The above paragraph implies that studies of the intelligence of criminals and non-criminals
    A. are useless because it is impossible to obtain comparable groups
    B. are not meaningful because only the less intelligent criminals are detected
    C. indicate that criminals are more intelligent than non-criminals
    D. indicate that criminals are less intelligent than non-criminals
    E. do not indicate that there are any differences between the two groups

87. According to the above paragraph, studies of World War I draft gave psychologists vital information concerning
    A. adaptability to army life of criminals and non-criminals
    B. criminal tendencies among draftees
    C. the intelligence scores of large numbers of men
    D. differences between intelligence scores of draftees and volunteers
    E. the behavior of men under abnormal conditions

Question 88-90.

DIRECTIONS: Questions 88 through 90 are to be answered on the basis of the following paragraph.

The use of a roadblock is simply an adaptation to police practices of the military concept of encirclement. Successful operation of a roadblock plan depends almost entirely on the amount of advance study and planning given to such operations. A thorough and detailed examination of the roads and terrain under the jurisdiction of a given police agency should be made with the locations of the roadblocks pinpointed in advance The first principle to be borne in mind in the location of each roadblock is the time element. Its location must be at a point beyond which the fugitive could not have possibly traveled in the time elapsed from the commission of the crime to the arrival of the officers at the roadblock.

88. According to the above paragraph,
    A. military operations have made extensive use of roadblocks
    B. the military concept of encirclement is an adaptation of police use of roadblocks
    C. the technique of encirclement has been widely used by military forces
    D. a roadblock is generally more effective than encirclement
    E. police use of roadblocks is based on the idea of military encirclement

89. According to the above paragraph,
    A. the factor of time is the sole consideration in the location of a roadblock
    B. the maximum speed possible in the method of escape is of major importance in roadblock location
    C. the time of arrival of officers at the site of a proposed roadblock is of little importance
    D. if the method of escape is not known, it should be assumed that the escape is by automobile
    E. a roadblock should be sited as close to the scene of the crime as the terrain will permit

90. According to the above paragraph,
    A. advance study and planning are of minor importance in the success of roadblock operations
    B. a thorough and detailed examination of all roads within a radius of fifty miles should precede the determination of a roadblock location
    C. consideration of terrain features is important in planning the location of roadblocks
    D. the pinpointing of roadblocks should be performed before any advance study is made
    E. a roadblock operation can seldom be successfully undertaken by a single police agency

KEY (CORRECT ANSWERS)

1. E	21. E	41. B	61. C	81. C
2. C	22. A	42. E	62. A	82. C
3. A	23. A	43. B	63. D	83. D
4. A	24. C	44. D	64. B	84. B
5. D	25. D	45. D	65. C	85. C
6. C	26. B	46. D	66. D	86. E
7. B	27. D	47. C	67. E	87. C
8. A	28. A	48. D	68. D	88. E
9. C	29. E	49. C	69. D	89. B
10. A	30. C	50. A	70. B	90. C
11. D	31. E	51. B	71. B	
12. A	32. C	52. A	72. D	
13. E	33. B	53. D	73. A	
14. E	34. C	54. D	74. C	
15. E	35. B	55. C	75. B	
16. A	36. A	56. B	76. A	
17. B	37. E	57. D	77. A	
18. E	38. D	58. D	78. E	
19. B	39. A	59. C	79. B	
20. C	40. B	60. C	80. D	

EXAMINATION SECTION
TEST 1

DIRECTIONS: Each question or incomplete statement is followed by several suggested answers or completions. Select the one that BEST answers the question or completes the statement. *PRINT THE LETTER OF THE CORRECT ANSWER IN THE SPACE AT THE RIGHT.*

1. Upon arriving at the scene of an accident in which a pedestrian was struck and killed by an automobile, an officer's first action was to clear the scene of spectators.
   Of the following, the PRINCIPAL reason for this action is that
   A. important evidence may be inadvertently destroyed by the crowd
   B. this is a fundamental procedure in first aid work
   C. the operator of the vehicle may escape in the crowd
   D. witnesses will speak more freely if other persons are not present

   1.____

2. In questioning witnesses, an officer is instructed to avoid leading questions or questions that will suggest the answer.
   Accordingly, when questioning a witness about the appearance of a suspect, it would be BEST for him to ask:
   A. What kind of hat did he wear?   B. Did he wear a felt hat?
   C. What did he wear?   D. Didn't he wear a hat?

   2.____

3. The only personal description the police have of a particular criminal was made several years ago.
   Of the following, the item in the description that will be MOST useful in identifying him at the present time is the
   A. color of his eyes   B. color of his hair
   C. number of teeth   D. weight

   3.____

4. Crime statistics indicate that property crimes such as larceny, burglary, and robbery are more numerous during winter months than in summer.
   The one of the following explanations that MOST adequately accounts for this situation is that
   A. human needs, such as clothing, food, heat, and shelter, are greater in winter
   B. criminal tendencies are aggravated by climatic changes
   C. there are more hours of darkness in winter and such crimes are usually committed under cover of darkness
   D. urban areas are more densely populated during winter months, affording greater opportunity for such crimes

   4.____

5. When automobile tire tracks are to be used as evidence, a plaster cast is made of them.
   Of the following, the MOST probable reason for taking a photograph is that
   A. photographs can be duplicated more easily than castings
   B. less skill is required for photographing than casting
   C. the tracks may be damaged in the casting process
   D. photographs are more easily transported than castings

5.____

6. It is generally recommended that an officer, in lifting a revolver that is to be sent to the police laboratory for ballistics tests and fingerprint examination, do so by insetting a pencil through the trigger guard rather than into the barrel of the weapon.
   The reason for preferring this procedure is that
   A. every precaution must be taken not to eliminate fingerprints on the weapon
   B. there is a danger of accidentally discharging the weapon by placing the pencil in the barrel
   C. the pencil may make scratches inside the barrel that will interfere with the ballistics tests
   D. a weapon can more easily be lifted by the trigger guard

6.____

7. PHYSICIAN is to PATIENT as ATTORNEY is to
   A. court B. client C. counsel D. judge

7.____

8. JUDGE is to SENTENCE as JURY is to
   A. court B. foreman C. defendant D. verdict

8.____

9. REVERSAL is to AFFIRMANCE as CONVICTION is to
   A. appeal B. acquittal C. error D. mistrial

9.____

10. GENUINE is to TRUE as SPURIOUS is to
    A. correct B. conceived C. false D. speculative

10.____

11. ALLEGIANCE is to LOYALTY as TREASON is to
    A. felony B. faithful C. obedience D. rebellion

11.____

12. CONCUR is to AGREE as DIFFER is to
    A. coincide B. dispute C. join D. repeal

12.____

13. A person who has an uncontrollable desire to steal without need is called a
    A. dipsomaniac   B. kleptomaniac
    C. monomaniac   D. pyromaniac

13.____

14. In the sentence, "The placing of any inflammable substance in any building or the placing of any device or contrivence capable of producing fire, for the purpose of causing a fire is an attempt to burn," the MISSPELLED word is
    A. inflammable B. substance C. device D. contrivence

14.____

15. In the sentence, "The word 'break' also means obtaining an entrance into a building by any artifice used for that purpose, or by colussion with any person therein," the MISSPELLED word is

    A. obtaining   B. entrance   C. artifice   D. colussion

    15.____

16. In the sentence, "Any person who with intent to provoke a breech of the peace causes a disturbance or is offensive to others may be deemed to have committed disorderly conduct," the MISSPELLED word is

    A. breech   B. disturbance   C. offensive   D. committed

    16.____

17. In the sentence, "When the offender inflicts a grevious harm upon the person from whose possession, or in his presence, property is taken, he is guilty of robbery, the MISSPELLED word is

    A. offender   B. grevious   C. possession   D. presence

    17.____

18. In the sentence, "A person who wilfully encourages or advises another person in attempting to take the latter's life is guilty of a felony," the MISSPELLED word is

    A. wilfully   B. encourages   C. advises   D. attempting

    18.____

19. The treatment to be given the offender cannot alter the fact of his offense; but we can take measures to reduce the chances of similar acts in the future. We should banish the criminal, not in order to exact revenge nor directly to encourage reform, but to deter him and others from further illegal attacks on society.
    According to this paragraph, the PRINCIPAL reason for punishing criminals is to
    A. prevent the commission of future crimes
    B. remove them safely from society
    C. avenge society
    D. teach them that crime does not pay

    19.____

20. Even the most comprehensive and best substantiated summaries of the total volume of criminal acts would not contribute greatly to an understanding of the varied social and biological factors which are sometimes assumed to enter into crime causation, nor would they indicate with any degree of precision the needs of police forces in combating crime.
    According to this statement,
    A. crime statistics alone do not determine the needs of police forces in combating crime
    B. crime statistics are essential to a proper understanding of the social factors of crime
    C. social and biological factor which enter the crime causation have little bearing on police needs
    D. a knowledge of the social and biological factors of crime is essential to a proper understanding of crime statistics

    20.____

21. The police officer's art consists in applying and enforcing a multitude of laws and ordinances in such degree or proportion and in such manner that the greatest degree of social protection will be secured. The degree of enforcement and the method of application will vary with each neighborhood and community.
According to the foregoing paragraph,
   A. each neighborhood or community must judge for itself to what extent the law is to be enforced
   B. a police officer should only enforce those laws which are designed to give the greatest degree of social protection
   C. the manner and intensity of law enforcement is not necessarily the same in all communities
   D. all laws and ordinances must be enforced in a community with the same degree of intensity

22. Police control in the sense of regulating the details of police operations involves such matters as the technical means for so organizing the available personnel that competent police leadership, when secured, can operate effectively. It is concerned not so much with the extent to which popular controls can be trusted to guide and direct the course of police protection a with the administrative relationships which should exist between the component parts of the police organism.
According to the foregoing statement, police control is
   A. solely a matter of proper personnel assignment
   B. the means employed to guide and direct the course of police protection
   C. principally concerned with the administrative relationships between units of a police organization
   D. the sum total of means employed in rendering police protection

23. Two patrol cars hurry to the scene of an accident from different directions. The first proceeds at the rate of 45 miles per hour and arrives in four minutes. Although the second car travels over a route which is three-fourths of a mile longer, it arrives at the scene only a half-minute later.
The speed of the second car, expressed in miles per hour, is
   A. 50   B. 55   C. 60   D. 65

24. A motorcycle officer issued 72 traffic summonses in January, 60 in February and 83 in March.
In order to average 75 summonses per month for the four months of January, February, March, and April, during April he will have to issue _____ summonses.
   A. 80   B. 85   C. 90   D. 95

25. In a unit of the Police Department to which 40 officers are assigned, the sick report record during 2022 was as follows: 1 was absent 8 days, 5 were absent 3 days each, 4 were absent 5 days each, 10 were absent 2 days each, 8 were absent 4 days each, 5 were absent 1 day each.
The average number of days on sick report for all the members of this unit is MOST NEARLY
   A. ½   B. 1   C. 2 ½   D. 3

Questions 26-30.

DIRECTIONS: Column I lists various statements of fact. Column II is a list of crimes. Next to the numbers corresponding to the number preceding the statements of fact in Column I, place the letter preceding the crime listed in Column II with which Jones should be charged. In answering these questions, the following definitions of crimes should be applied, bearing in mind that ALL elements contained in the definitions must be present in order to charge a person with that crime.

BURGLARY is breaking and entering a building with intent to commit some crime therein. EMBEZZLEMENT is the appropriation to one's use of another's property which has been entrusted to one's care or which has come lawfully into one's possession. EXTORTION is taking or obtaining property from another with his consent, induced by a wrongful use of force or fear. LARCENY is taking and carrying away the personal property of another with intent to deprive or defraud the true owner of the use and benefit of such property. ROBBERY is the unlawful taking of the personal property of another from his person or in his presence by force or violence, or fear of injury.

COLUMN I

26. Jones, believing Smith had induced his wife to leave him, went to Smith's home armed with a knife with which he intended to assault Smith. When his knock was unanswered, he forced open the door of Smith's home and entered but, finding the house empty, he threw away the knife and left.

27. Jones was employed as a collection agent by Smith. When Smith refused to reimburse him for certain expenses he claimed to have incurred in connection with his work, Jones deducted this amount from sums he had collected for Smith.

28. Jones spent the night in a hotel. During the night he left his room, went downstairs to the desk, stole money and returned to his room.

29. Jones, a building inspector, found that the elevators in Smith's building were being operated without a permit. He threatened to report the matter and have the elevators shut down unless Smith paid him a sum of money. Smith paid the amount demanded

30. Jones held-up Smith on the street and, pointing a revolve at him, demanded his money. Smith, without resisting, handed Jones his money. When Jones was apprehended, it was discovered that the revolver was a toy.

COLUMN II

A. burglary
B. embezzlement
C. extortion
D. larceny
E. robbery
F. no crime

26._____

27._____

28._____

29._____

30._____

Questions 31-40.

DIRECTIONS: Questions 31 through 40 consist of statements from which a term is missing. Each of these statements can be completed correctly with one of the terms in the following list. In the space opposite the number corresponding to the number of the question, place the LETTER preceding the term in the following list which MOST accurately completes the statement.

- A. affidavit
- B. appeal
- C. arraignment
- D. arrest
- E. bench warrant
- F. habeas corpus
- G. indictment
- H. injunction
- I. sentence
- J. subpoena

31. A _____ is a writ calling witnesses to court.   31.____

32. _____ is a method used to obtain a review of a case in court of superior jurisdiction.   32.____

33. A judgment passed by a court on a person on trial as a criminal offender is called a _____.   33.____

34. _____ is a writ or order requiring a person to refrain from a particular act.   34.____

35. _____ is the name given to a writ commanding the bringing of the body of a certain person before a certain court.   35.____

36. A _____ is a court order directing that an offender be brought into court.   36.____

37. The calling of a defendant before the court to answer an accusation is called _____.   37.____

38. The accusation in writing, presented by the grand jury to a competent court charging a person with a public offense is an _____.   38.____

39. A sworn declaration in writing is an _____.   39.____

40. _____ is the taking of a person into custody for the purpose of holding him to answer a criminal charge.   40.____

Questions 41-55.

DIRECTIONS: Questions 41 through 55 consist of statements from which a term is missing. Each of these statements can be completed correctly with one of the terms in the following list. In the space opposite the number corresponding to the number of the question, place the LETTER preceding the term in the following list which MOST accurately completes the statement.

A. accessory   B. accomplice   C. alibi
D. autopsy   E. ballistics   F. capital
G. confidence man   H. commission   I. conspiracy
J. corroborated   K. grand jury   L. homicide
M. misdemeanors   N. penology   O. perjury

41. _____ is the dissection of a dead human body to determine the cause of death. 41._____

42. The general term which mean the killing of one person by another is _____. 42._____

43. _____ is the science of the punishment of crime. 43._____

44. False swearing constitutes the crime of _____. 44._____

45. A combination of two or more persons to accomplish a criminal or unlawful act is called _____. 45._____

46. By _____ is meant evidence showing that a defendant was in another place when the crime was committed. 46._____

47. _____ is a term frequently used to describe a person engaged in a kind of swindling operation. 47._____

48. A _____ offense is one for which a life sentence or death penalty is prescribed by law. 48._____

49. A violation of a law may be either an act of omission or an act of _____. 49._____

50. An _____ is a person who is liable to prosecution for the identical offense charged against a defendant on trial. 50._____

51. A person would be an _____ who after the commission of a crime aided in the escape of one he knew to be an offender. 51._____

52. An official body called to hear complaints and to determine whether there is ground for criminal prosecution is known as the _____. 52._____

53. Crimes are generally divided into two classes, namely felonies and _____. 53._____

54. _____ is the science of the motion of projectiles. 54._____

55. Testimony of a witness which is confirmed by another witness is _____. 55._____

Questions 56-60.

DIRECTIONS: Next to the question number which corresponds with the number of each item in Column I, place the letter preceding the adjective in Column II which BEST describes the persons in Column I.

COLUMN I	COLUMN II	
56. A talkative woman	A. abstemious	56.____
57. A person on a reducing diet	B. pompous C. erudite	57.____
58. A scholarly professor	D. benevolent E. docile	58.____
59. A man who seldom speaks	F. loquacious G. indefatigable	59.____
60. A charitable person	H. taciturn	60.____

Questions 61-65.

DIRECTIONS: Next to the question number which corresponds with the number preceding each profession in Column I, place the letter preceding the word in Column II which BEST explains the subject of that profession.

COLUMN I	COLUMN II	
61. Geologist	A. animals	61.____
62. Oculist	B. eyes C. feet	62.____
63. Podiatrist	D. fortune-telling E. language	63.____
64. Palmist	F. rocks G. stamps	64.____
65. Zoologist	H. woman	65.____

Questions 66-70.

DIRECTIONS: Next to the question number corresponding to the number of each of the words in Column I, place the letter preceding the word in Column II that is MOST NEARLY OPPOSITE to it in meaning.

COLUMN I	COLUMN II	
66. comely	A. beautiful	66.____
67. eminent	B. cowardly C. kind	67.____
68. frugal	D. sedate E. shrewd	68.____
69. gullible	F. ugly G. unknown	69.____
70. valiant	H. wasteful	70.____

KEY (CORRECT ANSWERS)

1.	A	16.	A	31.	J	46.	C	61.	F
2.	C	17.	B	32.	B	47.	G	62.	B
3.	A	18.	A	33.	I	48.	F	63.	C
4.	C	19.	A	34.	H	49.	H	64.	D
5.	C	20.	A	35.	F	50.	B	65.	A
6.	C	21.	C	36.	E	51.	A	66.	F
7.	B	22.	C	37.	C	52.	L	67.	G
8.	D	23.	A	38.	G	53.	N	68.	H
9.	B	24.	B	39.	A	54.	E	69.	E
10.	C	25.	C	40.	D	55.	K	70.	B
11.	D	26.	A	41.	D	56.	F		
12.	B	27.	B	42.	M	57.	A		
13.	B	28.	D	43.	O	58.	C		
14.	D	29.	C	44.	P	59.	H		
15.	D	30.	E	45.	J	60.	D		

EXAMINATION SECTION
TEST 1

DIRECTIONS: Each question or incomplete statement is followed by several suggested answers or completions. Select the one that BEST answers the question or completes the statement. *PRINT THE LETTER OF THE CORRECT ANSWER IN THE SPACE AT THE RIGHT.*

1. An indictment is a

    A. formal charge
    B. overdue payment
    C. bill of particulars relating to a dispute
    D. felony

2. In a trial, a hostile witness is a(n) _____ witness.

    A. controversial B. unfriendly
    C. combative D. evasive

3. Which of the following was an event from 1999 that may reduce the number of guns in this country?

    A. The passage of a strict gun law in Congress
    B. Gun shows were restricted by Congress
    C. The Colt Corporation restricted the sale of its guns
    D. An embargo was placed on guns coming into this country

4. In the state, headlights should be used when visibility is equal to a minimum or less than _____ feet.

    A. 500 B. 750 C. 1,000 D. 1,250

5. You are required to dim your headlights when an approaching vehicle is within _____ feet of your vehicle.

    A. 500 B. 400 C. 300 D. 200

6. *Some features of the arrangement of contents in the following pages may perplex some readers.*
   The word *perplex*, as used in the above sentence, means MOST NEARLY

    A. interest B. enlighten
    C. turnoff D. confuse

7. Hearsay evidence means

    A. false evidence
    B. evidence that needs to be verified
    C. it is generally not admissible in court
    D. the person testifying is unsure of its truth

Questions 8-9.

DIRECTIONS: Questions 8 and 9 refer to the following paragraph.

The variations in report writing range from such picayune details as using A.M. or a.m. to more substantive issues as the inclusion or omission of a report summary in the first paragraph.

8. In the above paragraph, the word *picayune* means MOST NEARLY 8.____

   A. grammatic
   B. debatable
   C. trivial
   D. tendentious

9. In the above paragraph, the word *substantive* means MOST NEARLY 9.____

   A. cursory
   B. meaningless
   C. critical
   D. substantial

10. In accordance with the driver's manual issued by the state, you must report an accident when damage is _____ or more. 10.____

    A. $500 B. $1,000 C. $1,500 D. $2,000

11. It is easier to pass a heavy truck on a highway 11.____

    A. when the roadway is level
    B. when going uphill
    C. when going downhill
    D. on a concrete pavement

12. In most states, motorcyclists are required to use 12.____

    A. headlights and taillights only after sundown
    B. headlights and taillights at all times
    C. taillights only during daylight hours
    D. headlights only during daylight hours

13. DNA refers to 13.____

    A. a person who dies upon arriving at a hospital
    B. genetic material
    C. a chemical reaction
    D. a powerful drug

14. An odometer measures the _____ an automobile. 14.____

    A. speed of
    B. velocity of
    C. distance traveled by
    D. revolutions per second of the engine of

15. *Profiling has recently become a controversial issue in police work.* 15.____
    Profiling, as used in the above sentence, relates to paying special attention to

    A. a recognizable class of people
    B. people of low income

C. people who exceed the speed limits
D. the class of people who drive expensive cars

16. Most highways have a minimum speed of _____ MPH. 16._____

    A. 40 B. 35 C. 30 D. 25

17. The lowest automobile accident rate occurs in the _____ year age group. 17._____

    A. 20 to 35 B. 35 to 50 C. 50 to 65 D. 65 to 80

18. *Writing is characterized as narrative description, exposition, and argument.* 18._____
    Exposition, as used in the above sentence, means MOST NEARLY

    A. describing the circumstances of the situation
    B. the explanation of a piece of information
    C. explaining your conclusions
    D. giving the pros and cons of a conclusion

19. A report states that the latent prints have been sent to the laboratory. The word *latent,* as 19._____
    used in the above statement, means MOST NEARLY

    A. missing B. visible C. hidden D. damaged

20. After being *acquitted* in the first trial, O.J. Simpson faced a second trial. The second trial 20._____
    was not double jeopardy because

    A. evidence was withheld from the jury
    B. he was tried on different criminal charges
    C. the second trial was a civil trial
    D. the first trial was against the weight of the evidence

21. To *loiter* means MOST NEARLY to 21._____

    A. gather in a group of five or more
    B. create suspicion of wrongdoing while hanging around
    C. obstruct pedestrian movement
    D. linger in an aimless way

22. The minimum automobile insurance required for property damage in New York State is 22._____

    A. $3,000 B. $5,000 C. $10,000 D. $20,000

23. The maximum speed limit in a village or town is usually _____ MPH. 23._____

    A. 20 B. 25 C. 30 D. 40

24. The purpose of the *two second rule* in driving is to 24._____

    A. give you enough time to stop if there is a traffic signal ahead
    B. give you enough clearance to cut into another lane when passing a car
    C. keep enough room between your vehicle and the one ahead
    D. provide enough room when entering a highway

25. In most states, you may be arrested for driving with a blood alcohol content of _____ percent or more.   25.____

  A. .05   B. .10   C. .15   D. .20

KEY (CORRECT ANSWERS)

1. A
2. B
3. C
4. C
5. A

6. D
7. C
8. C
9. D
10. B

11. B
12. B
13. B
14. C
15. A

16. A
17. B
18. B
19. C
20. C

21. D
22. B
23. C
24. C
25. B

TEST 2

DIRECTIONS: Each question or incomplete statement is followed by several suggested answers or completions. Select the one that BEST answers the question or completes the statement. *PRINT THE LETTER OF THE CORRECT ANSWER IN THE SPACE AT THE RIGHT.*

1. A yellow sign showing two children in black indicates a school crossing. The shape of the sign is a   1.____

     A. square   B. rectangle   C. hexagon   D. pentagon

2. Personal vehicles driven by volunteer firefighters responding to alarms are allowed to display _____ lights.   2.____

     A. blue   B. green   C. red   D. amber

3. The color amber is closest to   3.____

     A. green   B. yellow   C. purple   D. blue

4. Larceny in the legal sense means   4.____

    A. the unlawful taking away of another person's property without his consent
    B. overcharging another person who is making a purchase
    C. deceiving another person as to the value of an item he wishes to purchase
    D. adding a service charge to an agreed price to an item that is purchased

5. A misdemeanor in law refers to   5.____

    A. a financial dispute between two litigants
    B. a minor offense
    C. a burglary where a small amount of goods was stolen
    D. unruly behavior in public

6. An overt act means MOST NEARLY a(n)   6.____

    A. foolish act   B. act done publicly
    C. illegal act   D. outrageous act

7. A defense lawyer works for a client *pro bono*. This means he   7.____

    A. gets paid only if he wins the case
    B. gets paid a fixed fee
    C. works for free
    D. represents his client at half his usual fee

8. Corpus delicti refers to the   8.____

    A. missing person   B. murderer
    C. scene of the crime   D. dead victim

9. The shape of a stop sign is   9.____

    A. triangular   B. square
    C. six-sided   D. eight-sided

63

10. Service signs are _____ with white letters and symbols.
    A. blue   B. green   C. yellow   D. red

11. Destination signs are _____ with white letters and symbols.
    A. blue   B. green   C. yellow   D. red

12. According to the driver's manual, you are prohibited from passing if you cannot safely return to the right lane before any approaching vehicle comes within _____ feet of your car.
    A. 100   B. 150   C. 200   D. 250

13. When parking near a hydrant, you must be clear of the hydrant a minimum distance of _____ feet.
    A. 5   B. 10   C. 15   D. 20

14. When parking your vehicle between two parked vehicles, you must park a maximum of _____ inches from the curb.
    A. 12   B. 15   C. 18   D. 21

15. In order to insure approval, the framers of the Constitution agreed to add a series of amendments after approval to protect people's rights.
    The number of amendments that were added is
    A. six   B. eight   C. ten   D. twelve

16. The amendment number that insures a person's right to bear arms is
    A. one   B. two   C. three   D. five

17. The amendment number that prevents a person from incriminating himself is
    A. one   B. three   C. five   D. seven

18. The right of a person to be secure in his house, and against unreasonable search is amendment number
    A. two   B. four   C. six   D. eight

19. The right of people to assemble peaceably is amendment number
    A. one   B. two   C. three   D. four

20. 90 kilometers per hour is equivalent to _____ MPH.
    A. 40   B. 45   C. 50   D. 55

21. A commercial driver's license is required if the vehicle being driven has a gross weight rating of equal to or more than _____ pounds.
    A. 24,000   B. 26,000   C. 28,000   D. 30,000

22. One kilogram is equivalent to _____ pounds.
    A. 2.2   B. 2.4   C. 2.6   D. 2.8

23. Failing to stop for a school bus in New York State is worth _____ points on your license. 23.____
    A. 3　　　　　B. 4　　　　　C. 5　　　　　D. 6

24. In the state, the minimum liability insurance required against the death of one person is 24.____
    A. $30,000　　B. $50,000　　C. $100,000　　D. $150,000

25. Before a person is arrested, he is read a statement by the arresting officer. The name associated with this procedure is 25.____
    A. Megan　　B. Zenger　　C. Scott　　D. Miranda

KEY (CORRECT ANSWERS)

1. D
2. A
3. B
4. A
5. B

6. B
7. C
8. D
9. D
10. A

11. B
12. C
13. C
14. A
15. C

16. B
17. C
18. B
19. A
20. D

21. B
22. A
23. C
24. B
25. D

TEST 3

DIRECTIONS: Each question or incomplete statement is followed by several suggested answers or completions. Select the one that BEST answers the question or completes the statement. *PRINT THE LETTER OF THE CORRECT ANSWER IN THE SPACE AT THE RIGHT.*

1. In legal terms, a deposition is
   A. a statement made by a person in open court
   B. a statement under oath, but not in open court
   C. the testimony made by a defendant under oath in open court
   D. a statement under oath that is mainly hearsay

2. In an automobile accident, first check to see if the injured person is breathing. If not, apply
   A. MPR   B. IBR   C. FHR   D. CPR

3. Hazard vehicles, such as snow plows and tow trucks, display _____ -colored lights.
   A. blue   B. green   C. amber   D. red

4. The hand signal shown at the right indicates
   A. caution because there is an obstruction ahead
   B. a right turn
   C. a left turn
   D. a stop

5. A felony is a
   A. crime only where someone is murdered
   B. major crime
   C. crime only where someone is injured
   D. crime only where major physical damage occurs

6. *Embezzlement* means MOST NEARLY
   A. deceiving   B. the hiding of funds
   C. stealing   D. investing illegally

7. The writer should be wary of using an entire paragraph for information, while necessary is not really of great importance.
   The word *wary* in the above sentence means MOST NEARLY
   A. uncertain   B. cautious
   C. certain   D. serious

8. Hearsay evidence is evidence that
   A. is usually admissible in court
   B. can be inferred from preceding evidence
   C. is based on what another person said out of court
   D. is implied in the testimony of a witness

9. *Excessive bail shall not be required* is amendment number

   A. two B. four C. six D. eight

10. The writ of habeas corpus is used to

    A. insure a defendant receives a fair trial
    B. insure a defendant's Fifth Amendment rights
    C. reduce or eliminate bail
    D. prevent a person from being detained illegally

11. The number of justices in the United States Supreme Court is

    A. 6 B. 7 C. 8 D. 9

12. The *blue wall* refers to law enforcement officers who

    A. do not publicly condemn fellow officers regardless of facts
    B. set up roadblocks
    C. support their superiors
    D. do their utmost to improve their image

13. The difference between burglary and robbery is

    A. burglary is breaking into a building to commit theft, while robbery is the use of violence in taking property from a person
    B. the money value taken in a burglary is less than $10,000, whereas in a robbery the money value taken is more than $10,000
    C. burglary takes place at night, whereas robbery takes place in the daytime
    D. burglary takes place indoors, whereas robbery takes place outdoors

14. The Federal government announced new guidelines relating to automobiles. These standards relate to

    A. automobile weight   B. gas mileage requirements
    C. car infant seats   D. bumper heights

15. General Motors was involved in a famous lawsuit relating to the Chevy Corvair based on

    A. its crashworthiness
    B. faulty design of the brake system
    C. failure of the transmissions
    D. location of the gas tanks

16. State legislatures are considering restrictions on the use of cellular phones while driving an automobile. The main argument for the restrictions is that

    A. driving with one hand is hazardous
    B. conversations on the phone are a distraction
    C. cellular phones interfere with the ignition system
    D. the driver is unlikely to hear sirens or hornblowing

17. *Much of their business involves the unpredictable and the bizarre.*
    The word *bizarre*, as used in the above statement, means MOST NEARLY

    A. weird   B. routine
    C. complicated   D. life-threatening

18. The federal government seized 145 metric tons of cocaine coming into the United States from South America.
A metric ton is equal to _____ pounds.

    A. 1,800	B. 2,000	C. 2,200	D. 2,400

19. A kilogram is most nearly _____ pounds.

    A. 2.0	B. 2.2	C. 2.4	D. 2.6

20. A narcotic drug used in medicine, but less habit-forming than morphine, is

    A. cocaine	B. methadone	C. LSD	D. heroin

21. Of the following, the one that is a hazard for the large recreational vehicles is

    A. their inability to meet the emission requirements
    B. their bumper height above the ground does not match the height of the bumpers on the smaller-sized vehicles
    C. because the driver is high above the ground, his ability to see his surroundings is impaired
    D. because of the high center of gravity of the recreational vehicles, they become unstable at high speeds

22. State inspection procedures on emissions focus on

    A. hydrocarbons and CO_2
    B. CO and CO_2
    C. SO_2 and CO
    D. hydrocarbons and CO

23. In order to bring a case before a Grand Jury, the prosecutor must present a prima facie case of guilt before the Grand Jury.
Prima facie in the above statement means MOST NEARLY

    A. overwhelming evidence to convict
    B. sufficient to convict unless rebutted by the defense
    C. possibly sufficient to convict by an objective jury
    D. with additional evidence would be sufficient to convict

24. The KKK was denied a permit to hold a parade in New York City. The Klan sued in court claiming a violation of their rights under the _____ Amendment.

    A. First	B. Third	C. Fifth	D. Eighth

25. In a jury trial for a felony, a jury of twelve must have

    A. a majority decision
    B. 9 members finding the defendant guilty
    C. 11 members finding the defendant guilty
    D. a unanimous finding of guilt

KEY (CORRECT ANSWERS)

1.	B	11.	D
2.	D	12.	A
3.	C	13.	A
4.	D	14.	C
5.	B	15.	D
6.	C	16.	B
7.	B	17.	A
8.	C	18.	C
9.	D	19.	B
10.	D	20.	B

21. B
22. D
23. B
24. A
25. D

TEST 4

DIRECTIONS: Each question or incomplete statement is followed by several suggested answers or completions. Select the one that BEST answers the question or completes the statement. *PRINT THE LETTER OF THE CORRECT ANSWER IN THE SPACE AT THE RIGHT.*

1. State law defines a juvenile as _____ years of age or less.   1.___
   A. 15   B. 16   C. 17   D. 18

2. A writ of habeas corpus is an order to   2.___
   A. dismiss charges against a detained person
   B. reduce the charges against a detained person
   C. have a detained person confront his accusers
   D. have a detained person brought before a court

3. A person is brought into a police station to face charges. The person brought in when interrogated refuses to tell more than his name and address.   3.___
   In the face of his silence, the proper course to be followed by the interviewer is to
   A. remind the detainee that he is guilty of obstruction of justice
   B. stop the interrogation
   C. remind the detainee that his unwillingness to cooperate will result in high bail
   D. tell the interviewee he is required to cooperate with the police

4. *The implication in most discussions on police discretion is that it is the police administrator who should undertake to spell out policies and rules.*   4.___
   In the above statement, the word *discretion* means MOST NEARLY
   A. the power to judge or act
   B. behavior
   C. competence
   D. ability to reach a conclusion

5. A nickname for amphetamine is   5.___
   A. ice   B. pot   C. downer   D. grass

6. A nickname for cocaine is   6.___
   A. speed   B. red devils
   C. snow   D. Mary Jane

7. A nickname for marijuana is   7.___
   A. ice   B. downer   C. snow   D. grass

8. A nickname for barbiturates is   8.___
   A. angel dust   B. quaaludes
   C. meth   D. downers

70

9. Of the following, the most widely used drug is

   A. LSD B. crack C. marijuana D. cocaine

10. Crack is related to

    A. angel dust
    B. quaaludes
    C. LSD
    D. cocaine

11. The police department is changing the type of ammunition they use. The new bullets will have a softer head. The main reason for this change is that

    A. it will not ricochet if it hits a wall
    B. it will cause less injury to a person struck by the bullet
    C. the bullet is less expensive
    D. it will be easier to recover

12. Of the following weapons, the one that is of the semiautomatic type is the

    A. Colt revolver
    B. 45
    C. AK-47
    D. Springfield rifle

13. A *Saturday Night Special* is a

    A. semi-automatic gun
    B. small, cheaply made weapon
    C. gun used for hunting
    D. difficult gun to conceal

14. One inch is equal to _____ centimeters.

    A. 2.54 B. 2.64 C. 2.74 D. 2.84

15. A gun control bill was passed in Congress that was named after President Reagan's press secretary who was shot in an attack on the President. The name of the bill was the _____ bill.

    A. McClure
    B. Brady
    C. Volkmer
    D. Everett Koop

16. In New York City, if you are caught carrying a concealed gun for which you do not have a permit, you can be jailed for a maximum of _____ months.

    A. 3 B. 6 C. 9 D. 12

17. The Federal Firearm License Law is designed to ensure that individuals who obtain licenses have a legitimate reason for doing so and to deny guns to

    A. people who carry large amounts of money on their person
    B. people who have a criminal record
    C. senior citizens
    D. people under 22 years old

18. According to government studies, the number of guns in the United States is over _____ million.

    A. one hundred
    B. one hundred and twenty
    C. one hundred and fifty
    D. two hundred

19. According to statistics, when a woman is killed with a gun, it is LEAST likely to be by

A. her husband B. a relative
C. a stranger D. a friend

20. Federal law states that a person is prohibited from buying a gun who is under the age of

   A. sixteen B. eighteen
   C. twenty D. twenty-two

21. Of the following countries in South America, the one that is the largest exporter of drugs into the United States is

   A. Columbia B. Venezuela
   C. Chile D. Argentina

22. Of the following, the state in the United States that allows citizens to carry concealed guns is

   A. Arizona B. New Mexico
   C. Texas D. Oklahoma

23. A bullet has a diameter of 9 mm. Its diameter, in inches, is MOST NEARLY _____ inch.

   A. 1/4 B. 3/8 C. 1/2 D. 5/8

24. The repeal of the amendment to the Constitution barring the manufacture and selling of whiskey occurred under the administration of President

   A. Roosevelt B. Hoover C. Truman D. Coolidge

25. The shrub from which cocaine is derived is

   A. cacao B. hemp C. liana D. coca

KEY (CORRECT ANSWERS)

1. D		11. A	
2. D		12. C	
3. B		13. B	
4. A		14. A	
5. A		15. B	
6. C		16. D	
7. D		17. B	
8. D		18. D	
9. C		19. C	
10. D		20. B	

21. A
22. C
23. B
24. A
25. D

EXAMINATION SECTION
TEST 1

DIRECTIONS: Each question or incomplete statement is followed by several suggested answers or completions. Select the one that BEST answers the question or completes the statement. *PRINT THE LETTER OF THE CORRECT ANSWER IN THE SPACE AT THE RIGHT.*

1. Which of the following events would typically cause the GREATEST amount of stress in a person's life?
    A. A major change in financial status
    B. Vacation
    C. Pregnancy
    D Marital separation

    1.____

2. A local shopping center has experienced a recent rash of shoplifting. Officer Jones is patrolling the mall parking lot frequently.
Which situation below should Officer Jones regard as MOST suspicious?
    A. A man running out a store entrance with a shopping bag from the store under his arm
    B. A car parked for a long time near the front entrance of the store
    C. A woman loading a pile of clothes, some with plastic security tags still attached, into the trunk of her car
    D. A young man walking around looking in through the windows of various parked cars

    2.____

3. An officer is faced with the responsibility of telling a woman her husband has been murdered. While the officers should phrase the news as gently as possible, he or she should also demonstrate empathy nonverbally.
The BEST way to do this is to
    A. stand with arms crossed
    B. hold the woman closely
    C. maintain eye contact
    D. tell the woman you understand her pain

    3.____

4. Cognitive symptoms of anxiety include
    A. rapid heart rate   B. feelings of fear of helplessness
    C. poor social functioning   D. euphoria

    4.____

5. Which of the following is MOST likely to help a person to improve her attitude?
    A. Avoiding people who make her feel bad about herself
    B. Learning to become more goal-oriented
    C. Learning to look more clearly at her own faults
    D. Taking charge of an unruly situation

    5.____

6. A suspect has been handcuffed, but refuses to take a seat in the patrol car after several requests.
   The arresting officer should
   A. tap the suspect behind the knees with the baton, just hard enough so that the suspect's legs will fold and he can be inserted into the car
   B. tighten the handcuffs until the pain compel compliance
   C. try to frighten the suspect with threats
   D. inform the suspect of the consequences for resisting arrest

7. Each of the following is likely to be a cause of stress on the job, EXCEPT
   A. work overload
   B. differences in organizational and personal values
   C. a narrowly-defined role
   D. time pressures

8. In communicating with people, especially in stressful or high-conflict situations, nonverbal communication is
   A. more important than the verbal message
   B. less important than the verbal message
   C. universal across all cultures
   D. typically contradictory to the verbal message

9. Problem-oriented police work does NOT
   A. help officers get to the roots of a crime problem
   B. offer a proactive model for policing
   C. focus on responding to calls for service
   D. have any impact on preventing or reducing crime

10. The difference between assertiveness and aggressiveness is that
    A. assertiveness is not potentially harmful to others
    B. aggressiveness involves strangers
    C. aggressiveness has to do with achieving goals
    D. assertiveness is always negative

11. As an officer and his partner arrive to investigate a reported domestic disturbance, the husband and wife are still arguing. In the presence of the officers, each spouse makes a verbal threat of physical harm against the other. In resolving this conflict, the FINAL step that should be taken by the officers is to
    A. indicate the consequences if this behavior continues
    B. empathize with each of the spouses
    C. present the spouses with problem-solving strategies
    D. describe the behaviors that appeared to cause the disturbance

12. Elements of community policing include
    I. the police   II. the business community
    III. the media   IV. religious institutions
    The CORRECT ANSWER IS:
    A. I, II   B. I, II, III   C. I, III   D. I, II, III, IV

13. In a grocery store parking lot, a pair of officers arrest both the buyer and seller in an alleged drug transaction in a grocery store parking lot. After the suspects have been handcuffed and placed in a patrol car, one of the officers notices a wad of bills on the ground where the transaction took place. The officer pockets the money and decides to keep it, telling herself that the money is "dirty" and that she has more of a right to it than either of the criminal suspects. Legally, the officer has committed a crime; ethically, she has committed a(n)
    A. rationalization   B. kickback   C. stereotyping   D. deviance

14. Probably the MOST effective way to deal with on-the-job stress is to
    A. find alternative employment
    B. take early retirement
    C. participate in a personal wellness program
    D. acquire assertiveness skills that will help confront the people responsible for the stress

Questions 15-16.

DIRECTIONS: Questions 15 and 16 deal with the following situation.

A pharmacist has complained to the police department that several drug addicts in his neighborhood have been attempting to obtain drugs legally, usually by passing fake prescriptions.

15. Which of the following people should arouse the MOST suspicion when approaching the prescription counter?
    A. A middle-aged woman who appears homeless and is poorly groomed
    B. A young African-American male in a hooded sweatshirt on a hot day
    C. A man in his thirties who glances around furtively and brings a large amount of nonprescription items to the counter for purchase
    D. None of the above should be regarded as suspicious on the basis of their appearance alone

16. After refusing to fill several prescriptions, the pharmacist describes or gives each of the prescriptions to an investigating officer.
    Which of the following MOST warrants investigation?
    A. A written investigation that is covered with several coffee rings
    B. A prescription written on a Post-It note
    C. A written prescription for pain killers with a date indicating it was written more than a week ago
    D. A prescription that is phoned in by a doctor

17. An individual's personality, whether normal or deviant, will ALWAYS
    A. refer to the person's deep inner self, rather than just superficial aspects
    B. involve unique characteristics that are all different from another person's
    C. be a product of social and cultural environments, with no biological foundation
    D. be organized into patterns that are observable and measurable to some degree

18. Change in a person's life that is due to personal growth is almost always
    A. negative   B. dramatic   C. positive   D. minor

19. Residents in an urban neighborhood have complained of a recent increase in gang-related graffiti in their community.
    Which of the following should be regarded as MOST suspicious by an officer on patrol?
    A. One young man walking down the street and flashing gang signs at passing cars
    B. A pair of teenagers riding their bicycles in a tenement parking lot late at night
    C. A group of teenagers hanging out in a convenience store parking lot, leaning against a wall that is covered with graffiti
    D. A group of teenagers hanging out in a convenience store parking lot. One of the teenagers has a spray paint can.

20. Common symptoms of stress include each of the following EXCEPT
    A. digestive problem   B. sluggishness
    C. sleep problems   D. emotional instability

21. The general goal of community policing is
    A. a lower overall crime rate
    B. conviction of criminals who are caught in the community
    C. fewer violent crimes
    D. a higher quality of life in the community

22. In most settings, the simplest and most effective method of stopping sexual harassment is to
    A. threaten the person with legal or administrative consequences
    B. ignore it
    C. avoid the person as much as possible
    D. ask or tell the person to stop

23. Of the following types of crime, the one MOST likely to have a widespread impact on a victims community is
    A. hate or bias crime   B. workplace violence
    C. theft   D. sexual assault

24. Functional roles of the police include:
    I. Crime prevention   II. Order maintenance
    III. Public service   IV. Criminal prosecution
    The CORRECT answer is:
    A. I only   B. I, II   C. I, II, III   D. I, II, III, IV

25. A pre-existing thought or belief that people have about members of a given group—whether the belief is positive, negative, or neutral—is
    A. ethnocentrism   B. a stereotype
    C. self-centeredness   D. discrimination

KEY (CORRECT ANSWERS)

1. D
2. C
3. C
4. B
5. B

6. D
7. C
8. A
9. C
10. A

11. A
12. D
13. A
14. C
15. D

16. B
17. D
18. B
19. D
20. B

21. D
22. D
23. A
24. C
25. B

TEST 2

DIRECTIONS: Each question or incomplete statement is followed by several suggested answers or completions. Select the one that BEST answers the question or completes the statement. *PRINT THE LETTER OF THE CORRECT ANSWER IN THE SPACE AT THE RIGHT.*

1. Role expectations for police officers generally
    A. are consistent across the country, with a strong focus on peacekeeping
    B. change from community to community, depending on the local culture
    C. direct them to be more lenient with juvenile offenders
    D. direct them to be self-reliant in both preventing and investigating crime

    1._____

2. Officer Shinjo takes a complaint from a woman who says she is being stalked by a man who is a classmate in one of her night business courses. The man has sent her unwanted gifts and left numerous unanswered telephone messages, but she did not become concerned until last night, when she noticed the man following her home from class. She asks Officer Shinjo what to do about the situation.
    At least part of Officer Shinjo's advice to the woman should include the suggestion that she
    A. immediately apply for a restraining order
    B. create a logbook to document each of the stalking incidents in as much detail as possible
    C. answer one of the man's telephone calls and try to explain that the unwanted attention is making her uncomfortable
    D. call the man herself and threaten legal action if he doesn't stop bothering her

    2._____

3. Which of the following is an element of self-direction?
    A. Knowing when to seek help from others
    B. Being able to get from one geographic location to another without a map
    C. Establishing and reaching both short- and long-term goals
    D. Adopting healthier lifestyle habits

    3._____

4. Each of the following factors is typically associated with ethnicity, EXCEPT
    A. culture   B. language
    C. economic status   D. physical characteristics

    4._____

5. Among the communication skills necessary for effective communication with people, the foundation upon which all others are based is considered to be
    A. confrontation   B. authoritativeness
    C. attending behavior   D. observation

    5._____

6. Which of the following offers the BEST definition of the word "ethics"?
    A. An individual's means of obtaining what he wants from and for other people in a society
    B. Standards of conduct that express a society's concept of right and wrong

    6._____

C. A formal code of conduct that delineates a strict set of rules and framework for punishment
D. Morality and the consequences of behaviors

7. Which of the following is a measurement of a rate? 7.____
   A. The ratio of the number of new African-American arrestees for drug-related crimes in the 35-49 age bracket during a specific year, compared to the number of African-Americans in the same age group in the entire community
   B. The number of white females, aged 18-25, who are arrested each year on child endangerment charges
   C. The percentage change in the number of property crimes in a given year, compared to the previous year
   D. The ratio of the number of persons currently under prosecution for violent crimes to the number of people, aged 14-55, in the entire community

8. In recent weeks, several patrons at a local restaurant have had their cars broken into by having a window smashed in, and then having valuable items taken from the car. Officer Jackson is patrolling the restaurant parking lot. 8.____
   Which situation below should she regard as MOST suspicious?
   A. A young man in a hooded sweatshirt walking around the parking lot at lunchtime, carrying a long, heavy flashlight
   B. A car parked so as to partially block other cars from exiting the parking lot
   C. A man's voice raised in anger coming from the parking lot
   D. Several young men leaning against the outside of the parking lot fence in the early evening, bouncing a basketball and apparently waiting for the arrival of another person

9. Among the skills important to effective communication with people, the MOST complex and difficult to master are those that help to 9.____
   A. encourage   B. confront   C. influence   D. summarize

10. The FIRST step in dealing with an alcohol or drug addiction is to 10.____
    A. admit there is a problem
    B. talk to a counselor or close friend
    C. stop taking the drug or drinking alcohol
    D. join a support group or enter a rehabilitation center

11. Key elements of police professionalism include: 11.____
    I. an advanced education
    II. a clearly stated code of ethics
    III. accountability through peer review
    IV. demonstrated understanding of the field's core body of knowledge
    The CORRECT answer is:
    A. I, II   B. I, III, IV   C. II, III, IV   D. I, II, III, IV

12. A factor that makes a police officer susceptible to corruption is that the officer
    A. is typically different from most members of society
    B. can be sure that if a suspect is arrested, the suspect will be prosecuted and punished
    C. is usually better off financially than most of the people she interacts with in carrying out her duties
    D. has the professional discretion not to enforce the law

13. In resolving an ethical dilemma, a police officer's FIRST step should generally be to
    A. identify the ethical issues that are in conflict
    B. identify the people and organizations likely to be affected by the decision
    C. consult with colleagues and appropriate experts
    D. examine the reasons in favor of and opposed to each possible course of action

14. During a lengthy interview with a witness, an officer decides to use "reflection of meaning" strategies in order to clarify the information he's being given.
    This strategy would involve each of the following EXCEPT
    A. trying to paraphrase longer statements offered by the witness
    B. closing with a check on the witness's words, such as "So do I understand this correctly?"
    C. beginning sentences with phrases such as "You mean….." or "Sounds as if you saw….."
    D. offering an interpretation of the witness's words

15. Officer McGee is meeting with several community members to determine a course of action for reducing gang-related activities in the area.
    Each of the following is a guideline to be used by an officer in building a constructive relationship with community members, EXCEPT
    A. viewing community members as equals
    B. adopting a completely neutral tone of voice when speaking with people
    C. using a shared vocabulary of easily understood, nonoffensive words
    D. asking for the input of community members before making any suggestions

16. In solving a complex problem, the FIRST step is always to
    A. develop a plan   B. gather information
    C. define the problem   D. envision contingencies

17. Role conflict can occur when an officer encounters two sets of expectations that are inconsistent with each other. Role strain can occur when an officer's role is limited by what he or she is authorized to do.
    The MAIN difference between these two is that role
    A. conflict is relatively rare among police officers
    B. conflict can be resolved; role strain cannot
    C. strain creates stressful situations for officers
    D. strain has a greater influence on the officer's exercise of discretion

4 (#2)

18. Generally, police community relations differs from public relations in that they
    A. consider the needs of the community first
    B. are much more successful in reducing social problems
    C. are without inherent spheres of interest
    D. encourage two-way communications

    18.____

19. Factors that place a man at risk as a potential batterer include each of the following, EXCEPT
    A. poverty
    B. drug or alcohol use
    C. 30-45 years of age
    D. witnessing spousal abuse between parents

    19.____

20. The four major categories of commonly abused substances include
    A. stimulants   B. alcohol   C. nicotine   D. caffeine

    20.____

21. After receiving their monthly assistance payments from the local social services agency, some members of the homeless community immediately use the money to carry out drug transactions.
    In his patrol of the area around the agency, which situation below should Officer Garcia regard as MOST suspicious?
    A. A group of several homeless people who meet every day in a local park, where they sit together for about three hours and then move on
    B. A homeless woman who walks up and down the entire length of a busy city street all day long, endlessly smoking cigarettes
    C. An abandoned car that sits on a privately-owned lot and is used as a sleeping place by several homeless people throughout the day
    D. A single man remaining in the same area for several hours at a time, during which many homeless people approach him and greet him with handshakes

    21.____

22. The MOST significant factor that requires police to perform functions other than law enforcement is
    A. greater public trust relative to other agencies or institutions
    B. a broader resource base
    C. round-the-clock availability
    D. the level of police interaction with community members

    22.____

23. A "minority" group is a group that is discriminated against on the basis of
    A. physical or cultural characteristics
    B. the size of the group relative to the majority
    C. race
    D. the group's degree of conformity to the norms of the majority

    23.____

24. An officer is talking with a resident of a high-crime urban neighborhood about a recent increase in drug-related activities. Because of the active police presence in the area, some residents are suspicious of the police.
    Each of the following nonverbal cues is a likely indicator of distrust on the part of a listener, EXCEPT

    24.____

A. holding arms crossed over one's chest
B. steady eye contact
C. clenched jaw
D. shoulders angled away from speaker

25. Personality characteristics necessary for the successful performance of police duties include
    I. dependent style in problem-solving
    II. emotional expressiveness in interpersonal communication
    III. cohesiveness in group performance
    IV. emotional restraint
    The CORRECT answer is:
    A. I, III   B. I, II, IV   C. II, III, IV   D. I, II, III, IV

25.____

KEY (CORRECT ANSWERS)

1.	B		11.	D
2.	B		12.	D
3.	C		13.	A
4.	C		14.	D
5.	C		15.	B
6.	B		16.	C
7.	B		17.	B
8.	A		18.	D
9.	C		19.	C
10.	A		20.	A

21.	D
22.	C
23.	A
24.	B
25.	C

READING COMPREHENSION
UNDERSTANDING AND INTERPRETING WRITTEN MATERIAL
EXAMINATION SECTION
TEST 1

DIRECTIONS: The following questions are intended to test your ability to read with comprehension and to understand and interpret written materials, particularly legal passages. It will be necessary for you to read each paragraph carefully because the questions are based only on the material contained therein.
Each question has several suggested answers. *PRINT THE LETTER OF THE CORRECT ANSWER IN THE SPACE AT THE RIGHT.*

Questions 1-3.

DIRECTIONS: Answer Questions 1 to 3 *SOLELY* on the basis of the following statement:
    Foot patrol has some advantages over all other methods of patrol. Maximum opportunity is provided for observation within range of the senses and for close contact with people and things that enable the patrolman to provide a maximum service as an information source and counselor to the public and as the eyes and ears of the police department. A foot patrolman loses no time in alighting from a vehicle, and the performance of police tasks is not hampered by responsibility for his vehicle while afoot. Foot patrol, however, does not have many of the advantages of a patrol car. Lack of both mobility and immediate communication with headquarters lessens the officer's value in an emergency. The area that he can cover effectively is limited and, therefore, this method of patrol is costly.

1. According to this paragraph, the foot patrolman is the eyes and ears of the police department because he is

    A. in direct contact with the station house
    B. not responsible for a patrol vehicle
    C. able to observe closely conditions on his patrol post
    D. a readily available information source to the public

1.____

2. The *MOST* accurate of the following statements concerning the various methods of patrol, according to this paragraph, is that

    A. foot patrol should sometimes be combined with motor patrol
    B. foot patrol is better than motor patrol
    C. helicopter patrol has the same advantages as motor patrol
    D. motor patrol is more readily able to communicate with superior officers in an emergency

2.____

3. According to this paragraph, it is *CORRECT* to state that foot patrol is

    A. *economical* since increased mobility makes more rapid action possible
    B. *expensive* since the area that can be patrolled is relatively small
    C. *economical* since vehicle costs need not be considered
    D. *expensive* since giving information to the public is time-consuming

3.____

Questions 4-6.

DIRECTIONS: Answer Questions 4 to 6 SOLELY on the basis of the following statement:
All applicants for an original license to operate a catering establishment shall be fingerprinted. This shall include the officers, employees, and stockholders of the company and the members of a partnership. In case of a change, by addition or substitution, occurring during the existence of a license, the person added or substituted shall be fingerprinted. However, in the case of a hotel containing more than 200 rooms, only the officer or manager filing the application is required to be fingerprinted. The police commissioner may also at his discretion exempt the employees and stockholders of any company. The fingerprints shall be taken on one copy of form C.E. 20 and on two copies of C.E. 21. One copy of form C.E. 21 shall accompany the application. Fingerprints are not required with a renewal application.

4. According to this paragraph, an employee added to the payroll of a licensed catering establishment which is not in a hotel, must

    A. always be fingerprinted
    B. be fingerprinted unless he has been previously fingerprinted for another license
    C. be fingerprinted unless exempted by the police commissioner
    D. be fingerprinted only if he is the manager or an officer of the company

5. According to this paragraph, it would be MOST accurate to state that

    A. form C.E. 20 must accompany a renewal application
    B. form C.E. 21 must accompany all applications
    C. form C.E. 21 must accompany an original application
    D. both forms C.E. 20 and C.E. 21 must accompany all applications

6. A hotel of 270 rooms has applied for a license to operate a catering establishment on the premises. According to the instructions for fingerprinting given in this paragraph, the

    A. officers, employees, and stockholders shall be fingerprinted
    B. officers and manager shall be fingerprinted
    C. employees shall be fingerprinted
    D. officer filing the application shall be fingerprinted

Questions 7-9.

DIRECTIONS: Answer Questions 7 to 9 SOLELY on the basis of the following statement:
It is difficult to instill in young people inner controls on aggressive behavior in a world marked by aggression. The slum child's environment, full of hostility, stimulates him to delinquency; he does that which he sees about him. The time to act against delinquency is before it is committed. It is clear that juvenile delinquency, especially when it is committed in groups or gangs, leads almost inevitably to an adult criminal life unless it is checked at once. The first signs of vandalism and disregard for the comfort, health, and property of the community should be considered as storm warnings which cannot be ignored. The delinquent's first crime has the underlying element of testing the law and its ability to hit back.

7. A *suitable* title for this entire paragraph based on the material it contains is: 7._____

   A. The Need for Early Prevention of Juvenile Delinquency
   B. Juvenile Delinquency as a Cause of Slums
   C. How Aggressive Behavior Prevents Juvenile Delinquency
   D. The Role of Gangs in Crime

8. According to this paragraph, an *INITIAL* act of juvenile crime *usually* involves a(n) 8._____

   A. group or gang activity
   B. theft of valuable property
   C. test of the strength of legal authority
   D. act of physical violence

9. According to this paragraph, acts of juvenile delinquency are *most likely* to lead to a criminal career when they are 9._____

   A. acts of vandalism
   B. carried out by groups or gangs
   C. committed in a slum environment
   D. such as to impair the health of the neighborhood

Questions 10-12.

DIRECTIONS: Answer Questions 10 to 12 *SOLELY* on the basis of the following statement:
The police laboratory performs a valuable service in crime investigation by assisting in the reconstruction of criminal action and by aiding in the identification of persons and things. When studied by a technician, physical things found at crime scenes often reveal facts useful in identifying the criminal and in determining what has occurred. The nature of substances to be examined and the character of the examinations to be made vary so widely that the services of a large variety of skilled scientific persons are needed in crime investigations. To employ such a complete staff and to provide them with equipment and standards needed for all possible analyses and comparisons is beyond the means and the needs of any but the largest police departments. The search of crime scenes for physical evidence also calls for the services of specialists supplied with essential equipment and assigned to each tour of duty so as to provide service at any hour.

10. If a police department employs a large staff of technicians of various types in its laboratory, it will affect crime investigation to the extent that 10._____

    A. most crimes will be speedily solved
    B. identification of criminals will be aided
    C. search of crime scenes for physical evidence will become of less importance
    D. investigation by police officers will not usually be required

11. According to this paragraph, the *MOST* complete study of objects found at the scenes of crimes is 11._____

    A. always done in all large police departments
    B. based on assigning one technician to each tour of duty
    C. probably done only in large police departments
    D. probably done in police departments of communities with low crime rates

12. According to this paragraph, a large variety of skilled technicians is useful in criminal investigations because

    A. crimes cannot be solved without their assistance as a part of the police team
    B. large police departments need large staffs
    C. many different kinds of tests on various substances can be made
    D. the police cannot predict what methods may be tried by wily criminals

Questions 13-14.

DIRECTIONS: Answer Questions 13 and 14 SOLELY on the basis of the following statement:
The emotionally unstable person is always potentially a dangerous criminal, who causes untold misery to other persons and is a source of considerable trouble and annoyance to law enforcement officials. Like his fellow criminals he will be a menace to society as long as he is permitted to be at large. Police activities against him serve to sharpen his wits, and imprisonment gives him the opportunity to learn from others how to commit more serious crimes when he is released. This criminal's mental structure makes it impossible for him to profit by his experience with the police officials, by punishment of any kind or by sympathetic understanding and treatment by well-intentioned persons, professional and otherwise.

13. According to the above paragraph, the MOST accurate of the following statements concerning the relationship between emotional instability and crime is that

    A. emotional instability is proof of criminal activities
    B. the emotionally unstable person can become a criminal
    C. all dangerous criminals are emotionally unstable
    D. sympathetic understanding will prevent the emotionally unstable person from becoming a criminal

14. According to the above paragraph, the effect of police activities on the emotionally unstable criminal is that

    A. police activities aid this type of criminal to reform
    B. imprisonment tends to deter this type of criminal from committing future crimes
    C. contact with the police serves to assist sympathetic understanding and medical treatment
    D. police methods against this type of criminal develop him for further unlawful acts

Questions 15-17.

DIRECTIONS: Answer Questions 15 to 17 SOLELY on the basis of the following statement:
Proposals to license gambling operations are based on the belief that the human desire to gamble cannot be suppressed and, therefore, it should be licensed and legalized with the people sharing in the profits, instead of allowing the underworld to benefit. If these proposals are sincere, then it is clear that only one is worthwhile at all. Legalized gambling should be completely controlled and operated by the state with all the profits used for its citizens. A state agency should be set up to operate and control the gambling business. It should be as completely removed from politics as possible. In view of the inherent nature of the gambling business, with its close relationship to lawlessness and crime, only a man of the highest integrity should be eligible to become head of this agency. However, state gambling would encourage mass gambling with its attending social and economic evils in the same manner as other forms of legal gambling; but there is no justification whatever for the business of gambling to be legalized and then permitted to operate for private profit or for the benefit of any political organization.

15. The CENTRAL thought of this paragraph may be correctly expressed as the   15._____
    A. need to legalize gambling in the state
    B. state operation of gambling for the benefit of the people
    C. need to license private gambling establishments
    D. evils of gambling

16. According to this paragraph, a problem of legalized gambling which will *still* occur if the   16._____
    state operates the gambling business is
    A. the diversion of profits from gambling to private use
    B. that the amount of gambling will tend to diminish
    C. the evil effects of any form of mass gambling
    D. the use of gambling revenues for illegal purposes

17. According to this paragraph, to legalize the business of gambling would be   17._____
    A. *justified* because gambling would be operated only by a man of the highest integrity
    B. *justified* because this would eliminate politics
    C. *unjustified* under any conditions because the human desire to gamble cannot be suppressed
    D. *unjustified* if operated for private or political profit

Questions 18-20.

DIRECTIONS: Answer Questions 18 to 20 *SOLELY* on the basis of the following statement:
Whenever, in the course of the performance of their duties in an emergency, members of the force operate the emergency power switch at any location on the transit system and thereby remove power from portions of the track, or they are on the scene where this has been done, they will bear in mind that, although power is removed, further dangers exist; namely, that a train may coast into the area even though the power is off, or that the rails may be energized by a train which may be in a position to transfer electricity from a live portion of the third rail through its shoe beams. Employees must look in each direction before stepping upon, crossing, or standing close to tracks, being particularly careful not to come into contact with the third rail.

18. According to this paragraph, whenever an emergency occurs which has resulted in operating the emergency power switch, it is *MOST* accurate to state that   18._____
    A. power is shut off and employees may perform their duties in complete safety
    B. there may still be power in a portion of the third rail
    C. the switch will not operate if a portion of the track has been broken
    D. trains are not permitted to stop in the area of the emergency

19. An *important* precaution which this paragraph urges employees to follow after operating   19._____
    the emergency power switch, is to
    A. look carefully in both directions before stepping near the rails
    B. inspect the nearest train which has stopped to see if the power is on
    C. examine the third rail to see if the power is on
    D. check the emergency power switch to make sure it has operated properly

20. A trackman reports to you, a patrolman, that a dead body is lying on the road bed. You operate the emergency power switch. A train which has been approaching comes to a stop near the scene.
In order to act in accordance with the instructions in the above paragraph, you *should*

   A. climb down to the road bed and remove the body
   B. direct the train motorman to back up to the point where his train will not be in position to transfer electricity through its shoe beams
   C. carefully cross over the road bed to the body, avoiding the third rail and watching for train movements
   D. have the train motorman check to see if power is on before crossing to the tracks

21. The treatment to be given the offender cannot alter the fact of his offense; but we can take measures to reduce the chances of similar acts in the future. We should banish the criminal, not in order to exact revenge nor directly to encourage reform, but to deter him and others from further illegal attacks on society.
According to this paragraph, the *PRINCIPAL* reason for punishing criminals is to

   A. prevent the commission of future crimes
   B. remove them from society
   C. avenge society
   D. teach them that crime does not pay

22. Even the most comprehensive and best substantiated summaries of the total volume of criminal acts would not contribute greatly to an understanding of the varied social and biological factors which are sometimes assumed to enter into crime causation, nor would they indicate with any degree of precision the needs of police forces in combating crime.
According to this statement,

   A. crime statistics alone do not determine the needs of police forces in combating crime
   B. crime statistics are essential to a proper understanding of the social factors of crime
   C. social and biological factors which enter into crime causation have little bearing on police needs
   D. a knowledge of the social and biological factors of crime is essential to a proper understanding of crime statistics

23. The policeman's art consists of applying and enforcing a multitude of laws and ordinances in such degree or proportion and in such manner that the greatest degree of social protection will be secured. The degree of enforcement and the method of application will vary with each neighborhood and community.
According to the foregoing paragraph,

   A. each neighborhood or community must judge for itself to what extent the law is to be enforced
   B. a policeman should only enforce those laws which are designed to give the greatest degree of social protection
   C. the manner and intensity of law enforcement is not necessarily the same in all communities
   D. all laws and ordinances must be enforced in a community with the same degree of intensity

24. Police control in the sense of regulating the details of police operations, involves such matters as the technical means for so organizing the available personnel that competent police leadership, when secured, can operate effectively. It is concerned not so much with the extent to which popular controls can be trusted to guide and direct the course of police protection as with the administrative relationships which should exist between the component parts of the polie organism. According to the foregoing statement, police control is

    A. solely a matter of proper personnel assignment
    B. the means employed to guide and direct the course of police protection
    C. principally concerned with the administrative relationships between units of a police organization
    D. the sum total of means employed in rendering police protection

25. Police Department Rule 5 states that a Deputy Commissioner acting as Police Commissioner shall carry out the orders of the Police Commissioner, previously given, and such orders shall not, except in cases of extreme emergency, be countermanded. This means, most nearly, that, except in cases of extreme emergency,

    A. the orders given by a Deputy Commissioner acting as Police Commissioner may not be revoked
    B. a Deputy Commissioner acting as Police Commissioner should not revoke orders previously given by the Police Commissioner
    C. a Deputy Commissioner acting as Police Commissioner is vested with the same authority to issue orders as the Police Commissioner himself
    D. only a Deputy Commissioner acting as Police Commissioner may issue orders in the absence of the Police Commissioner himself

KEY (CORRECT ANSWERS)

1.	C		11.	C
2.	D		12.	C
3.	B		13.	B
4.	C		14.	D
5.	C		15.	B
6.	D		16.	C
7.	A		17.	D
8.	C		18.	B
9.	B		19.	A
10.	B		20.	C

21. A
22. A
23. C
24. C
25. B

TEST 2

Questions 1-2.

DIRECTIONS: Answer Questions 1 and 2 SOLELY on the basis of the following statement:
The medical examiner may contribute valuable data to the investigator of fires which cause fatalities. By careful examination of the bodies of any victims, he not only establishes cause of death, but may also furnish, in many instances, answers to questions relating to the identity of the victim and the source and origin of the fire. The medical examiner is of greatest value to law enforcement agencies because he is able to determine the exact cause of death through an examination of tissue of apparent arson victims. Thorough study of a burned body or even of parts of a burned body will frequently yield information which illuminates the problems confronting the arson investigator and the police.

1. According to the above paragraph, the MOST important task of the medical examiner in the investigation of arson is to obtain information concerning the

    A. identity of arsonists
    B. cause of death
    C. identity of victims
    D. source and origin of fires

2. The CENTRAL thought of the above paragraph is that the medical examiner aids in the solution of crimes of arson when

    A. a person is burnt to death
    B. identity of the arsonist is unknown
    C. the cause of the fire is known
    D. trained investigators are not available

Questions 3-6.

DIRECTIONS: Answer Questions 3 to 6 SOLELY on the basis of the following statement:
A foundling is an abandoned child whose identity is unknown. Desk officers shall direct the delivery, by a policewoman, if available, of foundlings actually or apparently under two years of age, to the Foundling Hospital, or if actually or apparently two years of age or over, to the Children's Center. In all other cases of dependent or neglected children, other than foundlings, requiring shelter, desk officers shall provide for obtaining such shelter as follows: between 9 a.m. and 5 p.m., Monday through Friday, by telephone direct to the Bureau of Child Welfare, in order to ascertain the shelter to which the child shall be sent; at all other times, direct the delivery of a child actually or apparently under two years of age to the Foundling Hospital, or, if the child is actually or apparently two years of age or over, to the Children's Center.

3. According to this paragraph, it would be MOST correct to state that

    A. a foundling as well as a neglected child may be delivered to the Foundling Hospital
    B. a foundling but not a neglected child may be delivered to the Children's Center
    C. a neglected child requiring shelter, regardless of age, may be delivered to the Bureau of Child Welfare
    D. the Bureau of Child Welfare may determine the shelter to which a foundling may be delivered

4. According to this paragraph, the desk officer shall provide for obtaining shelter for a neglected child, apparently under two years of age, by

   A. directing its delivery to the Children's Center if occurrence is on a Monday between 9 a.m. and 5 p.m.
   B. telephoning the Bureau of Child Welfare if occurrence is on a Sunday
   C. directing its delivery to the Foundling Hospital if occurrence is on a Wednesday at 4 p.m.
   D. telephoning the Bureau of Child Welfare if occurrence is at 10 a.m. on a Friday

4.____

5. According to this paragraph, the desk officer should direct delivery to the Foundling Hospital of any child who is

   A. actually under 2 years of age and requires shelter
   B. apparently under two years of age and is neglected or dependent
   C. actually 2 years of age and is a foundling
   D. apparently under 2 years of age and has been abandoned

5.____

6. A 12-year-old neglected child requiring shelter is brought to a police station on Thursday at 2 p.m. Such a child should be sent to

   A. a shelter selected by the Bureau of Child Welfare
   B. a shelter selected by the desk officer
   C. the Children's Center
   D. the Foundling Hospital when a brother or sister, under 2 years of age, also requires shelter

6.____

Questions 7-9.

DIRECTIONS: Answer Questions 7 to 9 *SOLELY* on the basis of the following statement:
In addition to making the preliminary investigation of crimes, patrolmen should serve as eyes, ears, and legs for the detective division. The patrol division may be used for surveillance, to serve warrants and bring in suspects and witnesses, and to perform a number of routine tasks for the detectives which will increase the time available for tasks that require their special skills and facilities. It is to the advantage of individual detectives, as well as of the detective division, to have patrolmen working in this manner; more cases are cleared by arrest and a greater proportion of stolen property is recovered when, in addition to the detective regularly assigned, a number of patrolmen also work on the case. Detectives may stimulate the interest and participation of patrolmen by keeping them currently informed of the presence, identity, or description, hangouts, associates, vehicles and method of operation of each criminal known to be in the community.

7. According to this paragraph, a patrolman should

   A. assist the detective in certain of his routine functions
   B. be considered for assignment as a detective on the basis of his patrol performance
   C. leave the scene once a detective arrives
   D. perform as much of the detective's duties as time permits

7.____

8. According to this paragraph, patrolmen should aid detectives by

   A. accepting assignments from detectives which give promise of recovering stolen property
   B. making arrests of witnesses for the detective's interrogation
   C. performing all special investigative work for detectives
   D. producing for questioning individuals who may aid the detective in his investigation

9. According to this paragraph, detectives can keep patrolmen interested by

   A. ascertaining that patrolmen are doing investigative work properly
   B. having patrolmen directly under his supervision during an investigation
   C. informing patrolmen of the value of their efforts in crime prevention
   D. supplying the patrolmen with information regarding known criminals in the community

Questions 10-11.

DIRECTIONS: Answer Questions 10 and 11 *SOLELY* on the basis of the following statement:
State motor vehicle registration departments should and do play a vital role in the prevention and detection of automobile thefts. The combatting of theft is, in fact, one of the primary purposes of the registration of motor vehicles. As of recent date, there were approximately 61,309,000 motor vehicles registered in the United States. That same year some 200,000 of them were stolen. All but 6 percent have been or will be recovered. This is a very high recovery ratio compared to the percentage of recovery of other stolen personal property. The reason for this is that automobiles are carefully identified by the manufacturers and carefully registered by many of the states.

10. The *CENTRAL* thought of this paragraph is that there is a close relationship between the

    A. number of automobiles registered in the United States *and* the number stolen
    B. prevention of automobile thefts *and* the effectiveness of police departments in the United States
    C. recovery of stolen automobiles *and* automobile registration
    D. recovery of stolen automobiles *and* of other stolen property

11. According to this paragraph, the high recovery ratio for stolen automobiles is due to

    A. state registration and manufacturer identification of motor vehicles
    B. successful prevention of automobile thefts by state motor vehicle departments
    C. the fact that only 6% of stolen vehicles are not properly registered
    D. the high number of motor vehicles registered in the United States

Questions 12-15.

DIRECTIONS: Answer Questions 12 to 15 *SOLELY* on the basis of the following statement:
It is not always understood that the term "physical evidence" embraces any and all objects, living or inanimate. A knife, gun, signature, or burglar tool is immediately recognized as physical evidence. Less often is it considered that dust, microscopic fragments of all types, even an odor, may equally be physical evidence and often the most important of all. It is well established that the most useful types of physical evidence are generally microscopic in dimensions, that is, not noticeable by the eye and, therefore, most likely to be overlooked by

the criminal and by the investigator. For this reason, microscopic evidence persists for months or years after all other evidence has been removed and found inconclusive. Naturally, there are limitations to the time of collecting microscopic evidence as it may be lost or decayed. The exercise of judgment as to the possibility or profit of delayed action in collecting the evidence is a field in which the expert investigator should judge.

12. The *one* of the following which the above paragraph does *NOT* consider to be physical evidence is a

    A. criminal thought
    B. minute speck of dust
    C. raw onion smell
    D. typewritten note

13. According to the above paragraph, the re-checking of the scene of a crime

    A. is *useless* when performed years after the occurrence of the crime
    B. is *advisable* chiefly in crimes involving physical violence
    C. *may turn up* microscopic evidence of value
    D. *should be delayed* if the microscopic evidence is not subject to decay or loss

14. According to the above paragraph, the criminal investigator *should*

    A. give most of his attention to weapons used in the commission of the crime
    B. ignore microscopic evidence until a requiest is received from the laboratory
    C. immediately search for microscopic evidence and ignore the more visible objects
    D. realize that microscopic evidence can be easily overlooked

15. According to the above paragraph,

    A. a delay in collecting evidence must definitely diminish its value to the investigator
    B. microscopic evidence exists for longer periods of time than other physical evidence
    C. microscopic evidence is generally the most useful type of physical evidence
    D. physical evidence is likely to be overlooked by the criminal and by the investigator

Questions 16-18.

DIRECTIONS: Answer Questions 16 to 18 *SOLELY* on the basis of the following statement:
Sometimes, but not always, firing a gun leaves a residue of nitrate particles on the hands. This fact is utilized in the paraffin test which consists of applying melted paraffin and gauze to the fingers, hands, and wrists of a suspect until a cast of approximately 1/8 of an inch is built up. The heat of the paraffin causes the pores of the skin to open and release any particles embedded in them. The paraffin cast is then removed and tested chemically for nitrate particles. In addition to gunpowder, fertilizers, tobacco ashes, matches, and soot are also common sources of nitrates on the hands.

16. Assume that the paraffin test has been given to a person suspected of firing a gun and that nitrate particles have been found. It would be *CORRECT* to conclude that the suspect

    A. is guilty
    B. is innocent
    C. may be guilty or innocent
    D. is probably guilty

17. In testing for the presence of gunpowder particles on human hands, the characteristic of paraffin which makes it MOST serviceable is that it

    A. causes the nitrate residue left by a fired gun to adhere to the gauze
    B. is waterproof
    C. melts at a low temperature
    D. helps to distinguish between gunpowder nitrates and other types

18. According to the above paragraph, in the paraffin test, the nitrate particles are removed from the pores because the paraffin

    A. enlarges the pores
    B. contracts the pores
    C. reacts chemically with nitrates
    D. dissolves the particles

Questions 19-21.

DIRECTIONS: Answer Questions 19 to 21 SOLELY on the basis of the following statement:
   Pickpockets operate most effectively when there are prospective victims in either heavily congested areas or in lonely places. In heavily populated areas, the large number of people about them covers the activities of these thieves. In lonely spots, they have the advantage of working unobserved. The main factor in the pickpocket's success is the selection of the "right" victim, A pickpocket's victim must, at the time of the crime, be inattentive, distracted, or unconscious. If any of these conditions exist, and if the pickpocket is skilled in his operations, the stage is set for a successful larceny. With the coming of winter, the crowds move southward—and so do most of the pickpockets. However, some pickpockets will remain in certain areas all year around. They will concentrate on theater districts, bus and railroad terminals, hotels or large shopping centers. A complete knowledge of the methods of this type of criminal and the ability to recognize them come only from long years of experience in performing patient surveillance and trailing of them. This knowledge is essential for the effective control and apprehension of this type of thief.

19. According to this paragraph, the pickpocket is LEAST likely to operate in a

    A. baseball park with a full capacity attendance
    B. station in an outlying area late at night
    C. moderately crowded dance hall
    D. over-crowded department store

20. According to this paragraph, the one of the following factors which is NOT necessary for the successful operation of the pickpocket is that

    A. he be proficient in the operations required to pick pockets
    B. the "right" potential victims be those who have been the subject of such a theft previously
    C. his operations be hidden from the view of others
    D. the potential victim be unaware of the actions of the pickpocket

21. According to this paragraph, it would be MOST correct to conclude that police officers who are successful in apprehending pickpockets

    A. are generally those who have had lengthy experience in recognizing all types of criminals
    B. must, by intuition, be able to recognize potential "right" victims

C. must follow the pickpockets in their southward movement
D. must have acquired specific knowledge and skills in this field

Questions 22-23.

DIRECTIONS: Answer Questions 22 and 23 SOLELY on the basis of the following statement:
For many years, slums had been recognized as breeding disease, juvenile delinquency, and crime which not only threatened the health and welfare of the people who lived there, but also weakened the structure of society as a whole. As far back as 1834, a sanitary inspection report in the city pointed out the connection between insanitary, overcrowded housing and the spread of epidemics. Down through the years, evidence of slum-produced evils accumulated as the slums themselves continued to spread. This spread of slums was nationwide. Its symptoms and its ill effects were peculiar to no locality, but were characteristic of the country as a whole and imperiled the national welfare.

22. According to this paragraph, people who live in slum dwellings

   A. cause slums to become worse
   B. are threatened by disease and crime
   C. create bad housing
   D. are the chief source of crime in the country

23. According to this paragraph, the effects of juvenile delinquency and crime in slum areas were

   A. to destroy the structure of society
   B. noticeable in all parts of the country
   C. a chief cause of the spread of slums
   D. to spread insanitary conditions in the city

Questions 24-25.

DIRECTIONS: Questions 24 and 25 pertain to the following section of the Penal Law:
Section 1942. A person who, after having been three times convicted within this state, of felonies or attempts to commit felonies, or under the law of any other state, government or country, of crimes which if committed within this state would be felonious, commits a felony, other than murder, first or second degree, or treason, within this state, shall be sentenced upon conviction of such fourth, or subsequent, offense to imprisonment in a state prison for an indeterminate term the minimum of which shall be not less than the maximum term provided for first offenders for the crime for which the individual has been convicted, but, in any event, the minimum term upon conviction for a felony as the fourth, or subsequent, offense, shall be not less than fifteen years, and the maximum thereof shall be his natural life.

24. Under the terms of the above stated portion of Section 1942 of the Penal Law, a person must receive the increased punishment therein provided *if*

   A. he is convicted of a felony and has been three times previously convicted of felonies
   B. he has been three times previously convicted of felonies, regardless of the nature of his present conviction

C. his fourth conviction is for murder, first or second degree, or treason
D. he has previously been convicted three times of murder, first or second degree, or treason

25. Under the terms of the above stated portion of Section 1942 of the Penal Law, a person convicted of a felony for which the penalty is imprisonment for a term not to exceed ten years, and who has been three times previously convicted of felonies in this state, shall be sentenced to a term the *minimum* of which shall be

    A. ten years
    B. fifteen years
    C. indeterminate
    D. his natural life

25.____

KEY (CORRECT ANSWERS)

1.	B	11.	A
2.	A	12.	A
3.	A	13.	C
4.	D	14.	D
5.	D	15.	C
6.	A	16.	C
7.	A	17.	A
8.	D	18.	A
9.	D	19.	C
10.	C	20.	B

21. D
22. B
23. B
24. A
25. B

READING COMPREHENSION
UNDERSTANDING AND INTERPRETING WRITTEN MATERIAL
EXAMINATION SECTION
TEST 1

DIRECTIONS: Each question or incomplete statement is followed by several suggested answers or completions. Select the one that BEST answers the question or completes the statement. *PRINT THE LETTER OF THE CORRECT ANSWER IN THE SPACE AT THE RIGHT.*

Questions 1-6.

DIRECTIONS: Questions 1 through 6 are to be answered SOLELY on the basis of the following passage.

Delinquency and crime and reactions to them are social products and are socially defined. Society, as a whole, not individuals, creates and defines rules, pejoratively labels those who break rules, and prescribes ways for reacting to the labeled person. Moreover, at times the societal process of defining, labeling, and reacting may not affect behavior but at other times it is influential in determining both who shall enter the correctional process and what its outcome will be.

What's more, the labeling process is often a means of isolating offenders from, rather than integrating them in, effective participation in such major societal institutions as schools, businesses, unions, and political, community, and fraternal organizations. These institutions are the major access routes to a successful, non-delinquent career. Those who are in power in them are the gatekeepers of society and, if offenders and correctional programs are isolated from them, then the personal wishes and characteristics of offenders will have little bearing on whether correctional programs succeed or fail.

1. According to the above passage, the MAJOR determinant of whether an offender will succeed in society is his
    A. self-confidence and general intelligence
    B. degree of participation in the major societal institutions
    C. attitude toward the entire criminal justice system
    D. overall criminal record

2. The above passage suggests that the isolation of offenders from certain groups within society through the labeling process is
    A. intentional   B. unlawful   C. beneficial   D. irreversible

3. Of the following, the MOST appropriate title for the passage is
    A. Methods of Reforming the Attitudes of Society
    B. Unjust Justice
    C. Delinquency and Crime
    D. Society's Rejection of Offenders

4. According to the passage, delinquency and crime are created by the
   A. characteristics of offenders
   B. correctional process itself
   C. operations of society
   D. gatekeepers of major institutions

4.____

5. Of the following suggested methods of helping offenders adjust to society, the one which the passage would be LEAST likely to favor would be to
   A. establish cooperative relations between correctional programs in cooperation with influential members of society
   B. keep the public informed of current developments in the corrections field by contributing information to local newspapers
   C. create an organizational structure within correctional institutions which, wherever practicable, resembles life in society
   D. encourage offenders to maintain close ties with other offenders with whom they become friendly while incarcerated

5.____

6. According to the passage, the rehabilitation of the offender is MOST likely to be determined by
   A. the individual inmate himself
   B. dynamic reformation programs
   C. society as a whole
   D. the specific correctional institution

6.____

Questions 7-10.

DIRECTIONS: Questions 7 through 10 are to be answered SOLELY on the basis of the following passage.

Urban crime rates are generally higher than those prevailing in rural areas. This apparent preponderance of urban crime has been observed by many criminologists both here and abroad and, although the factual basis for their conclusion that more crime occurs in urban areas does not lend itself to close measurement, there seems to be sufficient reason to accept it at face value. But there is an increasing body of evidence accumulating in the United States indicative that a profound change in these relationships may be in progress. For murder and rape, the rural crime rate of this country now equals the urban rate. As to all homicides, it exceeds the urban crime rate of the New England, Middle Atlantic, and North Central states, and shows such impressive advances for aggravated assault and robbery as to greatly reduce the former disparity. Such changes raise the question whether rural crimes, reacting to new means of transport and consequent interchange of population, which are urban influences, may not now be in the process of attaining urban crime levels. Certain it is that crimes against the person have for centuries been relatively more numerous in rural areas than crimes against property. Hence, the new trend is in a sense an extension of a condition of long standing.

7. According to the above passage, the statement that crime rates are generally higher in urban areas than in rural areas
   A. has not been definitely established although there is strong evidence to support such a view
   B. is justified but does not necessarily indicate that more crime is actually committed in urban areas

7.____

C. has been definitely established despite some contrary evidence submitted by criminologists
D. is not justified since the facts gathered by many criminologists do not lend themselves to close measurement

8. Concerning the present relationship between rural and urban crime rates, it would be MOST correct to state, according to the above passage, that for
   A. aggravated assault and robbery, the urban rate remained stationary while the rural rate increased
   B. murder and rape, the rural rate equals the urban rate in the Middle Atlantic states
   C. aggravated assault and robbery, the rural rate was formerly lower than the urban rate
   D. murder and rape, the urban rate is less than the rural rate in the North Central states

9. The development of new means of transport, according to the above passage,
   A. may or may not be an urban influence but it definitely contributed to a rise in rural crime levels
   B. is an urban influence and may or may not contribute to a rise in rural crime levels
   C. may or may not be an urban influence and may or may not contribute to a rise in rural crime levels
   D. is an urban influence and has definitely contributed to a rise in rural crime levels

10. The new trend is BEST defined, according to the above passage, as a tendency for crime against
    A. the person to be more numerous in rural areas than they have been in the past in urban areas
    B. property to be less numerous in urban areas than they are in rural areas
    C. the person to be more numerous in rural areas than they have been in the past
    D. property to be more numerous in urban areas than they have been in urban areas

Questions 11-15.

DIRECTIONS: Questions 11 through 15 are to be answered SOLELY on the basis of the following passage.

If we are to study crime in its widest social setting, we will find a variety of conduct which, although criminal in the legal sense, is not offensive to the moral conscience of a considerable number of persons. Traffic violations for example, do not brand the offender as guilty of moral offense. In fact, the recipient of a traffic ticket is usually simply the subject of some good-natured joking by his friends. Although there may be indignation among certain groups of citizens against gambling and liquor law violations, these activities are often tolerated, if not openly supported, by the more numerous residents of the community. Indeed, certain social and service clubs regularly conduct gambling games and lotteries for the purpose of raising funds. Some communities regard violations involving the sale of liquor with little concern in order to profit from increased license fees and taxes paid by dealers. The thousand and one forms of political graft and corruption which infest our urban centers only occasionally arouse public condemnation and official action.

11. According to the above passage, all types of illegal conduct are
    A. condemned by all elements of the community
    B. considered a moral offense, although some are tolerated by a few citizens
    C. violations of the law, but some are acceptable to certain elements of the community
    D. found in a social setting which is not punishable by law

12. According to the above paragraph, traffic violations are GENERALLY considered by society as
    A. crimes requiring the maximum penalty set by the law
    B. more serious than violations of the liquor laws
    C. offenses against the morals of the community
    D. relatively minor offenses requiring minimum punishment

13. According to the above passage, a lottery conducted for the purpose of raising funds for a church
    A. is considered a serious violation of law
    B. may be tolerated by a community which has laws against gambling
    C. may be conducted under special laws demanded by the more numerous residents
    D. arouses indignation in most communities

14. On the basis of the passage, the MOST likely reaction in the community to a police raid on a gambling casino would be
    A. more an attitude of indifference than interest in the raid
    B. general approval of the raid
    C. condemnation of the raid by most people
    D. demand for further action, since this raid is not sufficient to end gambling activities

15. The one of the following which BEST describes the central thought of this passage and would be MOST suitable as a title for it is
    A. Crime and the Police
    B. Public condemnation of Graft and Corruption
    C. Gambling is Not Always a Vicious Business
    D. Public Attitude Toward Law Violations

Questions 16-18.

DIRECTIONS: Questions 16 through 18 are to be answered SOLELY on the basis of the following passage.

The rise of urban-industrial society has complicated the social arrangements needed to regulate contacts between people. As a consequence, there has been an unprecedented increase in the volume of laws and regulations designed to control individual conduct and to govern the relationship of the individual to others. In a century there has been an eight-fold increase in the crimes for which one may be prosecuted.

For these offenses, the courts have the ultimate responsibility for redressing wrongs and convicting the guilty. The body of legal precepts gives the impression of an abstract and even-handed dispensation of justice. Actually, the personnel of the agencies applying these precept are faced with the difficulties of fitting abstract principles to highly variable situations emerging from the dynamics of everyday life. It is inevitable that discrepancies should exist between precept and practice.

The legal institutions serve as a framework for the social order by their slowness to respond to the caprices of transitory fad. This valuable contribution exacts a price in terms of the inflexibility of legal institutions in responding to new circumstances. This possibility is promoted by the changes in values and norms of the dynamic larger culture of which the legal precepts are a part.

16. According to the above passage, the increase in the number of laws and regulations during the twentieth century can be attributed to the
    A. complexity of modern industrial society
    B. increased seriousness of offenses committed
    C. growth of individualism
    D. anonymity of urban living

17. According to the above passage, which of the following presents a problem to the staff of legal agencies?
    A. The need to eliminate the discrepancy between precept and practice
    B. The necessity to apply abstract legal precepts to rapidly changing conditions
    C. The responsibility for reducing the number of abstract legal principles
    D. The responsibility for understanding offenses in terms of the real life situations from which they emerge

18. According to the above passage, it can be concluded that legal institutions affect social institutions by
    A. preventing change
    B. keeping pace with its norms and values
    C changing its norms and values
    D. providing stability

Questions 19-21.

DIRECTIONS: Questions 19 through 21 are to be answered SOLELY on the basis of the following passage.

This research lends additional emphasis to the contention that crime, as reported and recorded in the United States, is largely a function of social and cultural factors rather than biological, psychological, or entirely chance of factors. In the absence of significant biological variations or significant differences in basic mental processes on a regional or sectional basis, all other things being equal, one would expect a rather even crime rate from state to state. Since vast differences in crime rates on a sectional basis are found to persist over a period of time, one may hypothesize that subcultural variations of a regional or sectional nature are responsible for these regional or sectional patterns of crime. Even if this hypothesis cannot be accepted due to underreporting of crime, the least that the data may be said to demonstrate is a distinctly sectional variation in reporting and recording practices, indicating great disparities in sectional reactions to various types of human, or more specifically, criminal behavior.

19. According to the above passage, sectional crime rates
    A. are not affected significantly by entirely chance factors in the absence of psychological factors
    B. can be affected by biological variations or differences in basic mental processes
    C. vary little with significant biological factors in the population
    D. vary significantly in the absence of variable social and cultural factors

20. According to the above passage, great differences in the crime pattern and incidence in different sections of the United States may be said to be, assuming adequate reporting,
    A. a function of sectional variations in reporting and recording practices
    B. based on the specificity of some types of criminal behavior and the lack of a pattern in others
    C. based primarily on differences in the extent of urbanization of the population
    D. the result of regional cultural variations that are persistent over a period of time

21. According to the above passage, the statement that is MOST acceptable concerning the interpretation of crime data distribution by states or regions is that
    A. a more or less even crime rate from state to state indicates absence of significant biological variations
    B. consistent patterns of crime incidence are solely attributable to similar cultural and social factors
    C. failure to report crime that has occurred is indicative of differences in reaction to different types of crimes committed
    D. uniform reporting practices tend to eliminate sectional disparities in causality of crime

Questions 22-26.

DIRECTIONS: Questions 22 through 26 are to be answered SOLELY on the basis of the following passage.

Criminals were once considered sinners who chose to offend against the laws of God and man. They were severely punished for their crimes. Modern criminologists regard society itself as in large part responsible for the crimes committed against it. Poverty, poor living conditions, and inadequate education are all causes of crime. Crime is fundamentally the result of society's failure to provide a decent life for all the people. It is especially common in times when values are changing, as after a war, or in countries where people of different backgrounds and values are thrown together, as in the United States. Crimes, generally speaking, are fewer in countries where there is a settled way of life and a traditional respect for law.

22. This passage deals with
 A. criminals
 B. society
 C. the reasons for crime
 D. crime in the United States

23. The MAIN idea of this passage is that
 A. crime is common when values are changing
 B. crime is the result of poverty
 C. traditional respect for law prevents a crime
 D. society is largely responsible for crime

24. According to the passage, which is NOT a cause of crime?
 A. Poverty
 B. Wickedness
 C. Ethnic mixing
 D. Unsettled way of life

25. Crime is MOST common in
 A. periods of instability
 B. the United States
 C. wartime
 D. suburbs

26. To prevent crime, the author implies that society should
 A. provide stiffer penalties for criminals
 B. provide a decent way of life are everyone
 C. segregate the poor
 D. give broader powers to the police

Questions 27-30.

DIRECTIONS: Questions 27 through 30 are to be answered SOLELY on the basis of the following passage.

Perpetrators of crimes are often described by witnesses or victims in terms of salient facial features. The Bertillon System of identification which preceded the widespread use of fingerprints was based on body measurements. Recently, there have been developments in the quantification of procedures used in the classification and comparison of facial characteristics. Devices are now available which enable a trained operator, with the aid of a witness, to form a composite picture of a suspect's face and to translate that composite into a numerical code. Further developments in this area are possible, using computers to develop efficient sequences of questions so that witnesses may quickly arrive at the proper description.

Recent studies of voice analysis and synthesis, originally motivated by problems of efficient telephone transmission, have led to the development of the audio-frequency profile or *voice print*. Each voice print may be sufficiently unique to permit development of a classification system that will make possible identification of the source of a voice print. This method of identification, using an expert to identify the voice patterns, has been introduced in more than 40 cases by 15 different police departments. As with all identification systems that rely on experts to perform the identification, controlled laboratory tests are needed to establish with care the relative frequency of errors of omission and commission made by experts.

27. The MOST appropriate title for the above passage is
   A. Technology in Modern Investigative Detection
   B. Identification By Physical Features
   C. Verification of Identifications By Experts
   D. The Use of Electronic Identification Techniques

27.____

28. According to the above passage, computers may be used in conjunction with which of the following identification techniques?
   A. Fingerprints
   B. Bertillon System
   C. Voice prints
   D. Composite Facial Pictures

28.____

29. According to the above passage, the ability to identify individuals based on facial characteristics has improved as a result of
   A. an increase in the number of facial types which can be shown to witnesses
   B. information which is derived from other body measurements
   C. coded classification and comparison techniques
   D. greater reliance upon experts to make the identifications

29.____

30. According to the above passage, it is CORRECT to state that audio-frequency profiles or voice prints
   A. have been decisive in many prosecutions
   B. reduce the number of errors made by experts
   C. developed as a result of problems in telephonic communications
   D. are unlikely to result in positive identifications

30.____

KEY (CORRECT ANSWERS)

1.	B	11.	C	21.	C
2.	A	12.	D	22.	C
3.	D	13.	B	23.	A
4.	C	14.	A	24.	B
5.	D	15.	D	25.	A
6.	C	16.	A	26.	B
7.	B	17.	B	27.	B
8.	C	18.	D	28.	D
9.	D	19.	D	29.	C
10.	C	20.	D	30.	C

TEST 2

DIRECTIONS: Each question or incomplete statement is followed by several suggested answers or completions. Select the one that BEST answers the question or completes the statement. *PRINT THE LETTER OF THE CORRECT ANSWER IN THE SPACE AT THE RIGHT.*

Questions 1-7.

DIRECTIONS: Questions 1 through 7 are to be answered SOLELY on the basis of the following rules. These rules are not intended to be an exact copy of the rules of any institution.

SECTION OF RULES

All members of the department shall treat as confidential the official business of the department. An employee shall under no circumstances impart information to anyone relating to the official business of the department, except when she is a witness under oath in a court of law. When answering a department telephone, an employee shall give the name of the institution to which she is attached, her rank, and full name. Officers shall not give the name of any bondsman or attorney to inmates. The head of the institution shall be notified immediately when an inmate requests an officer for the name of a bondsman or attorney. All inmates awaiting trial shall be advised that they are entitled to one free telephone call within the city. All other telephone calls must be paid for by the inmate. Officers assigned to the examination of parcels or letters for inmates shall do so with utmost care. Failure to discover contraband shall be presumptive evidence of negligence. When an officer is assigned to accompany an inmate to court, to the District Attorney's office, or elsewhere, she must handcuff the inmate and must, under no circumstances, visit any places except such as are designated in the document calling for the inmate's presence.

1. Assume that Mary Jones is assigned to the House of Detention as a Correction Officer with shield number 781.
   When she answers the institution's phone, she should say
   A. House of Detention, Officer Mary Jones
   B. House of Detention, Officer Mary Jones, shield number 781
   C. Officer Mary Jones, shield number 781
   D. This is the House of Detention, Officer Jones speaking

2. An inmate awaiting trial asks for permission to make a telephone call to New Jersey.
   She should be
   A. allowed to make the call if she has not made any other free calls
   B. permitted to make the call at her own expense
   C. told that only local telephone calls are permitted
   D. told that she will have to pay all charges

3. An inmate awaiting trial asks you for the name of a lawyer who will not charge a large fee, as she does not have much money.
   You should
   A. bring her request to the attention of the head of the institution
   B. remind her that under the rules inmates are forbidden to ask an officer for the name of an attorney
   C. tell her that you don't know any lawyers who charge low fees
   D. tell her the state will furnish a lawyer without charge

3.____

4. A supervisor has an inmate whose case received a great deal of publicity in the newspapers. One day a reporter comes to the supervisor's home to interview him about this prisoner.
   The supervisor should
   A. give him only such information as has already appeared in the daily press
   B. give him only such information which is not considered confidential
   C. tell him that he is prohibited by the rules from discussing the case with him
   D. tell him that an interview will be granted if he can produce a letter from the Commissioner giving him permission for the interview

4.____

5. An officer is assigned to deliver a prisoner to the hospital prison ward in accordance with a court order. He is given a department car and chauffeur for this purpose. Before he leaves, the Superintendent of the prison also gives him some important official papers requiring the Commissioner's immediate attention for delivery to Central Office. On the way to the hospital, he will pass Central Office.
   He should stop at Central Office
   A. and send the chauffeur in with the papers while he waits in the car with the prisoner
   B. on his way back from the hospital, after he has delivered his prisoner
   C. to deliver the papers, leaving the handcuffed prisoner in the car in charge of the chauffeur
   D. to deliver the papers, taking the handcuffed prisoner with him

5.____

6. According to the rules, if an article of contraband is successfully smuggled into the prison in a package for an inmate, it is
   A. possible that the contraband may have been extremely well concealed
   B. possible that the employee who inspected the package did not realize that the article in question constituted contraband
   C. probable that the employee who inspected the package was careless
   D. sufficient cause to make the employee who inspected the package subject to dismissal

6.____

7. According to the rules,
   A. an employee may testify about official business in court
   B. only a competent court or the District Attorney can order a prisoner to be produced

7.____

C. sentenced inmates are not allowed to make telephone calls out of the institution
D. while packages for inmates are censored, their personnel mail is not

Questions 8-11.

DIRECTIONS: Questions 8 through 11 are to be answered SOLELY on the basis of the following passage.

Female criminality is very much under-reported, especially if one considers offenses such as shoplifting, thefts by prostitutes, offenses against children, and homicide. There are even certain offenses such as homosexuality and exhibitionism that go practically unprosecuted if committed by women. Female offenders are really protected by men, even by victims, who are usually disinclined to complain to authorities. Since women play much less active role in society than men do, one must be prepared for the fact that women are often the instigators of crimes committed by men and, as instigators, they are hard to detect. There are several crimes that are ordinarily highly detectable in men but have very low detectability in women. Her roles as homemaker, mother, nurse, wife, and so forth, permit the female to commit a crime and yet screen that crime from public view—for example, slowly poisoning her husband or treating her children abusively. In addition, law enforcement officers, judges, and juries are much more lenient toward women than toward men. Such considerations lead to the conclusion that criminality of women is *largely masked criminality*. Consequently, official statistics and records of criminality should be expected to under-report female offenses. The true measure of female crime must be sought from unofficial sources. The masked character of female crime and its gross under-reporting are consistent with the official view that the female is a very low risk for crime.

8. What has the writer inferred about the incidence of female offenses?
    A. It gives an adequate representation of the number of crimes committed by men but instigated by women.
    B. It is not to be considered an important area of criminality.
    C. It is understated because the classic female role makes her less visible to social scrutiny.
    D. In every crime the incidence of male offenses is more difficult than that of women.

8.____

9. Judges are inclined to be lenient toward female offenders because
    A. the role of the woman in society has stereotyped her as maternal and non-hostile
    B. the majority of their crimes does not physically harm others
    C. they commit crimes which are difficult to detect
    D. official statistics report them as less likely to commit crimes

9.____

10. Of the following, the title MOST suitable for this passage is
    A. Male Criminality
    B. The Petty Offender
    C. The Female Murderer
    D. Exposing Female Criminality

10.____

11. According to the passage, which of the following crimes is LEAST likely to be prosecuted against a woman? 11.____
    A. Child abuse
    B. Exhibitionism
    C. Homicide
    D. Prostitution

Questions 12-16.

DIRECTIONS: Questions 12 through 16 are to be answered SOLELY on the basis of the following passage. Each of the questions consist of two statements. Read the passage carefully, and then mark your answer
  A. if both statements are correct according to the information given in the passage
  B. if both statements are incorrect according to the information given in the passage
  C. if one statement is correct and one is incorrect according to the information given in the passage
  D. if the correctness or incorrectness of one or both of the statements cannot be determined from the information given in the passage.

The twentieth century has opened to women many pursuits from which they were formerly excluded and thus has given them new opportunities for crime. Can we assume that as a result of this development female crime will change its nature and become like masculine crime through losing its masked character? In periods of pronounced social stress, such as war, in which women assume many roles otherwise open only to men, experience indicates that crimes of women against property increase. Can we assume, further, that simultaneously the amount of undiscovered female crime decreases? Further study contradicts the validity of this assumption. Their new roles have become wage earners and household heads, but they have not stopped being the homemakers, the rearers of children, the nurses, or the shoppers. With the burden of their social functions increased, their opportunities for crime have not undergone a process of substitution so much as a process of increase.

12. I. As women assumed increased social burdens, there was a marked change in the character of their opportunities for crime. 12.____
    II. Although the crimes committed by women have increased, they are still fewer in number than those committed by men.

13. I. Male crime is less masked in character than female crime. 13.____
    II. The opportunities of women to commit crimes have increased in the last fifty years.

14. I. In wartime, when they have increased employment opportunities, women commit fewer crimes against property. 14.____
    II. When the social equality of women increases, the number of undetected crimes which they commit decreases.

15. I. In the period between 1900 and 1968, women did not gain many new opportunities for employment. 15.____
    II. In a family unit, the role of the shopper is traditionally that of the wife rather than that of the husband.

16. I. The crime rate increases in periods of social stress, such as war.
    II. Because women have not wanted to be limited to their traditional roles of homemaker and rearer of children, they have sought social equality with men.

Questions 17-18.

DIRECTIONS: Questions 1 through 6 are to be answered SOLELY on the basis of the following passage.

The public has become increasingly aware that rehabilitation that great battle cry of prison reform is one of the great myths of twentieth century penology. The hard truth is that punishment and retribution are the primary, if not the only, functions served by most correctional institutions. Courts can provide enlightened rule-making to assist prison reform and ombudsmen can give prisoners a forum to consider their complaints but the results would be limited. The corrections system will never run with any real efficiency until: (a) prisoners want to be reformed; (b) prison administrators want to help them reform; (c) courts want to help both toward a system of reform; and (d) they all define reform in the same way. If this is not done, the criminal justice system will continue to operate on the model of concentric layers of coercion, a grossly inefficient model.

17. According to the above passage, all of the following will be required in order to improve the correction system EXCEPT
    A. commitment to reform by prison administrators
    B. development by penal experts of criteria for meaningful rehabilitation
    C. acceptance by prisoners of the need for their cooperation
    D. assistance by the courts in providing a system where reform is possible

18. According to the above passage, meaningful prison reform is MOST likely to result from
    A. the appointment of ombudsmen to replace the courts in ruling on prisoners' complaints
    B. coordination by sociologists of efforts to improve prison conditions
    C. a realization by society that rehabilitation of prisoners is no longer a realistic objective
    D. the joint efforts of those directly concerned and a common understanding of the goals to be achieved

Questions 19-25.

DIRECTIONS: Each of Questions 19 through 25 begins with a statement. Your answer to each of these questions MUST be based only upon this statement and not on any other information you may have.

19. At any given moment, the number of people coming out of prisons in the United States is substantially as great as the number entering them.
Of the following, the MOST reasonable assumption on the basis of the preceding statement is that

- A. most prisoners in the United States are recidivists
- B. the crime rate in this country is decreasing
- C. the crime rate in this country is increasing
- D. the prison population of this country is constant

20. The indeterminate sentence usually sets a lower limit for the time to be served, and an upper limit. In some cases, there is a maximum limit, but no minimum; in some, a minimum but no maximum; and in others, neither a maximum nor a minimum, the time to be served being determined by the prisoner's conduct and other considerations.
In the preceding statement, the one of the following which is NOT given as a characteristic of the indeterminate sentence is that
    - A. sometimes the maximum time which must be served is not set at the time of sentence
    - B. sometimes the minimum time which must be served is not set at the time of sentence
    - C. the exact length of time to be served is fixed at the time of sentence
    - D. the length of time to be served may vary with the prisoner's behavior

21. Overcrowding in a prison makes segregation of prisoners more difficult, complicates the maintenance of order and discipline, and endangers health and morals.
Of the following, the MOST reasonable assumption based on the preceding statement is that
    - A. if prisoners are allowed to associate too freely their health and morals will be endangered
    - B. in a prison that is not overcrowded there will not be any problems of order and discipline
    - C. it is undesirable for the inmate population to exceed unduly the intended capacity of a prison
    - D. segregation of prisoners is carried on mainly for the purpose of better prison administration

22. Most non-professional shoplifters are women of comfortable means who could buy the things they steal.
Of the following, the MOST valid conclusion which can be drawn from the preceding statement is that
    - A. some well-to-do women are shoplifters
    - B. most professional shoplifters are men
    - C. few women practice shoplifting as a profession
    - D. most shoplifters suffer from a mental ailment rather than from a moral deficiency

23. Since accomplices and instigators are harder to detect and successfully prosecute than overt perpetrators, most women offenders therefore escape punishment.
Of the following, the MOST valid conclusion which can be drawn from the preceding statement is that

A. judges deal more leniently with females than with male offenders
B. men who are accomplices or instigators of crimes are easier to detect and prosecute than woman
C. successful prosecution of women offenders depends to a large extent on their successful detection
D. women are more often accomplices in, rather than actual perpetrators of, criminal acts

24. Through the juvenile court, the recognition of social responsibility in the delinquent acts of an individual has been established.
The MOST accurate of the following statements on the basis of the preceding statement is that
    A. delinquent behavior is an evidence of an individual's social irresponsibility
    B. some individuals are responsible for their delinquent acts
    C. the juvenile court is evidence of society's willingness to assume some blame for the anti-social behavior of its younger members
    D. the juvenile court takes into consideration the age, social background, and offense of the individual before deciding upon his punishment

24._____

25. The way to win more offenders to lasting good behavior is to provide treatment to each offender based on an understanding of the causes of his actions and of his emotional needs in the light of modern insight into human nature.
Of the following, the MOST valid inference which can be drawn from the preceding statement is that
    A. few offenders are reformed today because they are not led to an understanding of the causes of their criminal actions
    B. individualized attention is required to achieve reform in criminals
    C. penologists have a better understanding of the causes of criminal behavior because of recent developments in the study of human nature
    D. unsolved emotional conflicts frequently result in criminal acts

25._____

KEY (CORRECT ANSWERS)

1.	A	11.	B
2.	B	12.	D
3.	A	13.	A
4.	C	14.	B
5.	B	15.	C
6.	C	16.	D
7.	A	17.	B
8.	C	18.	D
9.	A	19.	D
10.	D	20.	C

21. C
22. A
23. D
24. C
25. B

REPORT WRITING

EXAMINATION SECTION
TEST 1

DIRECTIONS: Each question or incomplete statement is followed by several suggested answers or completions. Select the one that BEST answers the question or completes the statement. *PRINT THE LETTER OF THE CORRECT ANSWER IN THE SPACE AT THE RIGHT.*

1. Police Officer Johnson responds to the scene of an assault and obtains the following information:
   Time of Occurrence: 8:30 P.M.
   Place of Occurrence: 120-18 119th Avenue, Apt. 2A
   Suspects: John Andrews, victim's ex-husband and unknown white male
   Victim: Susan Andrews
   Injury: Broken right arm
   Officer Johnson is preparing a complaint report on the incident.
   Which one of the following expresses the above information MOST clearly and accurately?

   A. Susan Andrews was assaulted at 120-18 119th Avenue, Apt. 2A. At 8:30 P.M., her ex-husband, John Andrews, and an unknown white male broke her arm.
   B. At 8:30 P.M., Susan Andrews was assaulted at 120-18 119th Avenue, Apt. 2A, by her ex-husband, John Andrews, and an unknown white male. Her right arm was broken.
   C. John Andrews, an unknown white male, and Susan Andrews' ex-husband, assaulted and broke her right arm at 8:30 P.M., at 120-18 119th Avenue, Apt. 2A.
   D. John Andrews, ex-husband of Susan Andrews, broke her right arm with an unknown white male at 120-18 119th Avenue, at 8:30 P.M. in Apt. 2A.

2. While on patrol, Officers Banks and Thompson see a man lying on the ground bleeding. Officer Banks records the following details about the incident:
   Time of Incident: 3:15 P.M.
   Place of Incident: Sidewalk in front of 517 Rock Avenue
   Incident: Tripped and fell
   Name of Injured: John Blake
   Injury: Head wound
   Action Taken: Transported to Merry Hospital
   Officer Banks is completing a report on the incident.
   Which one of the following expresses the above information MOST clearly and accurately?

   A. At 3:15 P.M., Mr. John Blake was transported to Merry Hospital. He tripped and fell, injuring his head on sidewalk in front of 517 Rock Avenue.
   B. Mr. John Blake tripped and fell on the sidewalk at 3:15 P.M. in front of 517 Rock Avenue. He was transported to Merry Hospital while he sustained a head wound.
   C. Mr. John Blake injured his head when he tripped and fell on the sidewalk in front of 517 Rock Avenue at 3:15 P.M. He was transported to Merry Hospital.
   D. A head was wounded on the sidewalk in front of 517 Rock Avenue at 3:15 P.M. Mr. John Blake tripped and fell and was transported to Merry Hospital.

3. When assigned to investigate a complaint, a police officer should

    I. Interview witnesses and obtain facts
    II. Conduct a thorough investigation of circumstances concerning the complaint
    III. Prepare a complaint report
    IV. Determine if the complaint report should be closed or referred for further investigation
    V. Enter complaint report on the Complaint Report Index and obtain a complaint report number at the station house

While on patrol, Police Officer John is instructed by his supervisor to investigate a complaint by Mr. Stanley Burns, who was assaulted by his brother-in-law, Henry Traub. After interviewing Mr. Burns, Officer John learns that Mr. Traub has been living with Mr. Burns for the past two years. Officer John accompanies Mr. Burns to his apartment but Mr. Traub is not there. Officer John fills out the complaint report and takes the report back to the station house where it is entered on the Complaint Report Index and assigned a complaint report number. Officer John's actions were

  A. *improper,* primarily because he should have stayed at Mr. Burns' apartment and waited for Mr. Traub to return in order to arrest him
  B. *proper,* primarily because after obtaining all the facts, he took the report back to the station house and was assigned a complaint report number
  C. *improper,* primarily because he should have decided whether to close the report or refer it for further investigation
  D. *proper,* primarily because he was instructed by his supervisor to take the report from Mr. Burns even though it involved his brother-in-law

4. Police Officer Waters was the first person at the scene of a fire which may have been the result of arson. He obtained the following information:

Place of Occurrence: 35 John Street, Apt. 27
Time of Occurrence: 4:00 P.M.
Witness: Daisy Logan
Incident: Fire (possible arson)
Suspect: Male, white, approximately 18 years old, wearing blue jeans and a plaid shirt, running away from the incident Officer Waters is completing a report on the incident.

Which one of the following expresses the above information MOST clearly and accurately?

  A. At 4:00 P.M., Daisy Logan saw a white male, approximately 18 years old who was wearing blue jeans and a plaid shirt, running from the scene of a fire at 35 John Street, Apt. 27.
  B. Seeing a fire at 35 John Street, a white male approximately 18 years old, wearing blue jeans and a plaid shirt, was seen running from Apt. 27 at 4:00 P.M. reported Daisy Logan.
  C. Approximately 18 years old and wearing blue jeans and a plaid shirt, Daisy Logan saw a fire and a white male running from 35 John Street, Apt. 27 at 4:00 P.M.
  D. Running from 35 John Street, Apt. 27, the scene of the fire, reported Daisy Logan at 4:00 P.M., was a white male approximately 18 years old and wearing blue jeans and a plaid shirt.

5. Police Officer Sullivan obtained the following information at the scene of a two-car accident:

   Place of Occurrence: 2971 William Street
   Drivers and Vehicles Involved: Mrs. Wilson, driver of blue 2004 Toyota Camry; Mr. Bailey, driver of white 2001 Dodge
   Injuries Sustained: Mr. Bailey had a swollen right eye; Mrs. Wilson had a broken left hand

   Which one of the following expresses the above information MOST clearly and accurately?

   A. Mr. Bailey, owner of a white 2001 Dodge, at 2971 William Street, had a swollen right eye. Mrs. Wilson, with a broken left hand, is the owner of the blue 2004 Toyota Camry. They were in a car accident.
   B. Mrs. Wilson got a broken left hand and Mr. Bailey a swollen right eye at 2971 William Street. The vehicles involved in the car accident were a 2001 Dodge, white, owned by Mr. Bailey, and Mrs. Wilson's blue 2004 Toyota Camry.
   C. Mrs. Wilson, the driver of the blue 2004 Toyota Camry, and Mr. Bailey, the driver of the white 2001 Dodge, were involved in a car accident at 2971 William Street. Mr. Bailey sustained a swollen right eye, and Mrs. Wilson broke her left hand.
   D. Mr. Bailey sustained a swollen right eye and Mrs. Wilson broke her left hand in a car accident at 2971 William Street. They owned a 2001 white Dodge and a 2004 blue Toyota Camry.

6. Officer Johnson has issued a summons to a driver and has obtained the following information:

   Place of Occurrence: Corner of Foster Road and Woodrow Avenue
   Time of Occurrence: 7:10 P.M.
   Driver: William Grant
   Offense: Driving through a red light
   Age of Driver: 42
   Address of Driver: 23 Richmond Avenue

   Officer Johnson is making an entry in his Memo Book regarding the incident.
   Which one of the following expresses the above information MOST clearly and accurately?

   A. William Grant, lives at 23 Richmond Avenue at 7:10 P.M., went through a red light. He was issued a summons at the corner of Foster Road and Woodrow Avenue. The driver is 42 years old.
   B. William Grant, age 42, who lives at 23 Richmond Avenue, was issued a summons for going through a red light at 7:10 P.M. at the corner of Foster Road and Woodrow Avenue.
   C. William Grant, age 42, was issued a summons on the corner of Foster Road and Woodrow Avenue for going through a red light. He lives at 23 Richmond Avenue at 7:10 P.M.
   D. A 42-year-old man who lives at 23 Richmond Avenue was issued a summons at 7:10 P.M. William Grant went through a red light at the corner of Foster Road and Woodrow Avenue.

7. Police Officer Frome has completed investigating a report of a stolen auto and obtained   7._____
the following information:
Date of Occurrence: October 26, 2004
Place of Occurrence: 51st Street and 8th Avenue
Time of Occurrence: 3:30 P.M.
Crime: Auto theft
Suspect: Michael Wadsworth
Action Taken: Suspect arrested
Which one of the following expresses the above information
MOST clearly and accurately?

   A. Arrested on October 26, 2004 was a stolen auto at 51st Street and 8th Avenue at 3:30 P.M. driven by Michael Wadsworth.
   B. For driving a stolen auto at 3:30 P.M., Michael Wadsworth was arrested at 51st Street and 8th Avenue on October 26, 2004.
   C. On October 26, 2004 at 3:30 P.M., Michael Wadsworth was arrested at 51st Street and 8th Avenue for driving a stolen auto.
   D. Michael Wadsworth was arrested on October 26, 2004 at 3:30 P.M. for driving at 51st Street and 8th Avenue. The auto was stolen.

8. Police Officer Wright has finished investigating a report of Grand Larceny and has   8._____
obtained the following information:
Time of Occurrence: Between 1:00 P.M. and 2:00 P.M.
Place of Occurrence: In front of victim's home, 85 Montgomery Avenue
Victim: Mr. Williams, owner of the vehicle
Crime: Automobile broken into
Property Taken: Stereo valued at $1,200
Officer Wright is preparing a report on the incident. Which one of the following
expresses the above information MOST clearly and accurately?

   A. While parked in front of his home Mr. Williams states that between 1:00 P.M. and 2:00 P.M. an unknown person broke into his vehicle. Mr. Williams, who lives at 85 Montgomery Avenue, lost his $1,200 stereo.
   B. Mr. Williams, who lives at 85 Montgomery Avenue, states that between 1:00 P.M. and 2:00 P.M. his vehicle was parked in front of his home when an unknown person broke into his car and took his stereo worth $1,200.
   C. Mr. Williams was parked in front of 85 Montgomery Avenue, which is his home, when it was robbed of a $1,200 stereo. When he came out, he observed between 1:00 P.M. and 2:00 P.M. that his car had been broken into by an unknown person.
   D. Mr. Williams states between 1:00 P.M. and 2:00 P.M. that an unknown person broke into his car in front of his home. Mr. Williams further states that he was robbed of a $1,200 stereo at 85 Montgomery Avenue.

9. Police Officer Fontaine obtained the following details relating to a suspicious package:

   Place of Occurrence: Case Bank, 2 Wall Street
   Time of Occurrence: 10:30 A.M.
   Date of Occurrence: October 10, 2004
   Complaint: Suspicious package in doorway
   Found By: Emergency Service Unit

   Officer Fontaine is preparing a report for department records.
   Which one of the following expresses the above information MOST clearly and accurately?

   A. At 10:30 A.M., the Emergency Service Unit reported they found a package on October 10, 2004 which appeared suspicious. This occurred in a doorway at 2 Wall Street, Case Bank.
   B. A package which appeared suspicious was in the doorway of Case Bank. The Emergency Service Unit reported this at 2 Wall Street at 10:30 A.M. on October 10, 2004 when found.
   C. On October 10, 2004 at 10:30 A.M., a suspicious package was found by the Emergency Service Unit in the doorway of Case Bank at 2 Wall Street.
   D. The Emergency Service Unit found a package at the Case Bank. It appeared suspicious at 10:30 A.M. in the doorway of 2 Wall Street on October 10, 2004.

10. Police Officer Reardon receives the following information regarding a case of child abuse:

    Victim: Joseph Mays
    Victim's Age: 10 years old
    Victim's Address: Resides with his family at 42 Columbia Street, Apt. 1B
    Complainant: Victim's uncle, Kevin Mays
    Suspects: Victim's parents

    Police Officer Reardon is preparing a report to send to the Department of Social Services.
    Which one of the following expresses the above information MOST clearly and accurately?

    A. Kevin Mays reported a case of child abuse to his ten-year-old nephew, Joseph Mays, by his parents. He resides with his family at 42 Columbia Street, Apt. 1B.
    B. Kevin Mays reported that his ten-year-old nephew, Joseph Mays, has been abused by the child's parents. Joseph Mays resides with his family at 42 Columbia Street, Apt. 1B.
    C. Joseph Mays has been abused by his parents. Kevin Mays reported that his nephew resides with his family at 42 Columbia Street, Apt. 1B. He is ten years old.
    D. Kevin Mays reported that his nephew is ten years old. Joseph Mays has been abused by his parents. He resides with his family at 42 Columbia Street, Apt. 1B.

11. While on patrol, Police Officer Hawkins was approached by Harry Roland, a store owner, who found a leather bag valued at $200.00 outside his store. Officer Hawkins took the property into custody and removed the following items:

2 Solex watches, each valued at	$500.00
4 14-kt. gold necklaces, each valued at	$315.00
Cash	$519.00
1 diamond ring, valued at	$400.00

    Officer Hawkins is preparing a report on the found property.
    Which one of the following is the TOTAL value of the property and cash found?

    A. $1,734   B. $3,171   C. $3,179   D. $3,379

12. While on patrol, Police Officer Blake observes a man running from a burning abandoned building. Officer Blake radios the following information:

Place of Occurrence:	310 Hall Avenue
Time of Occurrence:	8:30 P.M.
Type of Building:	Abandoned
Suspect:	Male, white, about 35 years old
Crime:	Arson

    Officer Blake is completing a report on the incident.
    Which one of the following expresses the above information MOST clearly and accurately?

    A. An abandoned building located at 310 Hall Avenue was on fire at 8:30 P.M. A white male, approximately 35 years old, was observed fleeing the scene.
    B. A white male, approximately 35 years old, at 8:30 P.M. was observed fleeing 310 Hall Avenue. The fire was set at an abandoned building.
    C. An abandoned building was set on fire. A white male, approximately 35 years old, was observed fleeing the scene at 8:30 P.M. at 310 Hall Avenue.
    D. Observed fleeing a building at 8:30 P.M. was a white male, approximately 35 years old. An abandoned building, located at 310 Hall Avenue, was set on fire.

13. Police Officer Winters responds to a call regarding a report of a missing person. The following information was obtained by the Officer:

Time of Occurrence:	3:30 P.M.
Place of Occurrence:	Harrison Park
Reported By:	Louise Dee - daughter
Description of Missing Person:	Sharon Dee, 70 years old, 5'5", brown eyes, black hair - mother

    Officer Winters is completing a report on the incident. Which one of the following expresses the above information MOST clearly and accurately?

    A. Mrs. Sharon Dee, reported missing by her daughter, Louise, was seen in Harrison Park. The last time she saw her was at 3:30 P.M. She is 70 years old with black hair, brown eyes, and 5'5".
    B. Louise Dee reported that her mother, Sharon Dee, is missing. Sharon Dee is 70 years old, has black hair, brown eyes, and is 5'5". She was last seen at 3:30 P.M. in Harrison Park.
    C. Louise Dee reported Sharon, her 70-year-old mother at 3:30 P.M., to be missing after being seen last at Harrison Park. Described as being 5'5", she has black hair and brown eyes.

D. At 3:30 P.M. Louise Dee's mother was last seen by her daughter in Harrison Park. She has black hair and brown eyes. Louise reported Sharon is 5'5" and 70 years old.

14. While on patrol, Police Officers Mertz and Gallo receive a call from the dispatcher regarding a crime in progress.
    When the Officers arrive, they obtain the following information:
    Time of Occurrence: 2:00 P.M.
    Place of Occurrence: In front of 2124 Bristol Avenue
    Crime: Purse snatch
    Victim: Maria Nieves
    Suspect: Carlos Ortiz
    Witness: Jose Perez, who apprehended the subject
    The Officers are completing a report on the incident.
    Which one of the following expresses the above information MOST clearly and accurately?

    A. At 2:00 P.M., Jose Perez witnessed Maria Nieves. Her purse was snatched. The suspect, Carlos Ortiz, was apprehended in front of 2124 Bristol Avenue.
    B. In front of 2124 Bristol Avenue, Carlos Ortiz snatched the purse belonging to Maria Nieves. Carlos Ortiz was apprehended by a witness to the crime after Jose Perez saw the purse snatch at 2:00 P.M.
    C. At 2:00 P.M., Carlos Ortiz snatched a purse from Maria Nieves in front of 2124 Bristol Avenue. Carlos Ortiz was apprehended by Jose Perez, a witness to the crime.
    D. At 2:00 P.M., Carlos Ortiz was seen snatching the purse of Maria Nieves as seen and apprehended by Jose Perez in front of 2124 Bristol Avenue.

15. Police Officers Willis and James respond to a crime in progress and obtain the following information:
    Time of Occurrence: 8:30 A.M.
    Place of Occurrence: Corner of Hopkin Avenue and Amboy Place
    Crime: Chain snatch
    Victim: Mrs. Paula Evans
    Witness: Mr. Robert Peters
    Suspect: White male
    Officers Willis and James are completing a report on the incident.
    Which one of the following expresses the above information MOST clearly and accurately?

    A. Mrs. Paula Evans was standing on the corner of Hopkin Avenue and Amboy Place at 8:30 A.M. when a white male snatched her chain. Mr. Robert Peters witnessed the crime.
    B. At 8:30 A.M., Mr, Robert Peters witnessed Mrs. Paula Evans and a white male standing on the corner of Hopkin Avenue and Amboy Place. Her chain was snatched.
    C. At 8:30 A.M., a white male was standing on the corner of Hopkin Avenue and Amboy Place. Mrs. Paula Evans' chain was snatched, and Mr. Robert Peters witnessed the crime.

D. At 8:30 A.M., Mr. Robert Peters reported he witnessed a white male snatching Mrs. Paula Evans' chain while standing on the corner of Hopkin Avenue and Amboy Place.

16. Police Officers Cleveland and Logan responded to an assault that had recently occurred. The following information was obtained at the scene:

    Place of Occurrence: Broadway and Roosevelt Avenue
    Time of Occurrence: 1:00 A.M.
    Crime: Attempted robbery, assault
    Victim: Chuck Brown, suffered a broken tooth
    Suspect: Lewis Brown, victim's brother

    Officer Logan is completing a report on the incident.
    Which one of the following expresses the above information MOST clearly and accurately?

    A. Lewis Brown assaulted his brother Chuck on the corner of Broadway and Roosevelt Avenue. Chuck Brown reported his broken tooth during the attempted robbery at 1:00 A.M.
    B. Chuck Brown had his tooth broken when he was assaulted at 1:00 A.M. on the corner of Broadway and Roosevelt Avenue by his brother, Lewis Brown, while Lewis was attempting to rob him.
    C. An attempt at 1:00 A.M. to rob Chuck Brown turned into an assault at the corner of Broadway and Roosevelt Avenue when his brother Lewis broke his tooth.
    D. At 1:00 A.M., Chuck Brown reported that he was assaulted during his brother's attempt to rob him. Lewis Brown broke his tooth. The incident occurred on the corner of Broadway and Roosevelt Avenue.

16._____

17. Police Officer Mannix has just completed an investigation regarding a hit-and-run accident which resulted in a pedestrian being injured. Officer Mannix has obtained the following information:

    Make and Model of Car: Pontiac, Trans Am
    Year and Color of Car: 2006, white
    Driver of Car: Male, black
    Place of Occurrence: Corner of E. 15th Street and 8th Avenue
    Time of Occurrence: 1:00 P.M.

    Officer Mannix is completing a report on the accident.
    Which one of the following expresses the above information MOST clearly and accurately?

    A. At 1:00 P.M., at the corner of E. 15th Street and 8th Avenue, a black male driving a white 2006 Pontiac Trans Am was observed leaving the scene of an accident after injuring a pedestrian with the vehicle.
    B. On the corner of E. 15th Street and 8th Avenue, a white Pontiac, driven by a black male, a 2006 Trans Am injured a pedestrian and left the scene of the accident at 1:00 P.M.
    C. A black male driving a white 2006 Pontiac Trans Am injured a pedestrian and left with the car while driving on the corner of E. 15th Street and 8th Avenue at 1:00 P.M.
    D. At the corner of E. 15th Street and 8th Avenue, a pedestrian was injured by a black male. He fled in his white 2006 Pontiac Trans Am at 1:00 P.M.

17._____

18. The following details were obtained by Police Officer Dwight at the scene of a family dispute:

    Place of Occurrence: 77 Baruch Drive
    Victim: Andrea Valdez, wife of Walker
    Violator: Edward Walker
    Witness: George Valdez, victim's brother
    Crime: Violation of Order of Protection
    Action Taken: Violator arrested

    Police Officer Dwight is preparing a report on the incident.
    Which one of the following expresses the above information MOST clearly and accurately?

    A. George Valdez saw Edward Walker violate his sister's Order of Protection at 77 Baruch Drive. Andrea Valdez's husband was arrested for this violation.
    B. Andrea Valdez's Order of Protection was violated at 77 Baruch Drive. George Valdez saw his brother-in-law violate his sister's Order. Edward Walker was arrested.
    C. Edward Walker was arrested for violating an Order of Protection held by his wife, Andrea Valdez. Andrea's brother, George Valdez, witnessed the violation at 77 Baruch Drive.
    D. An arrest was made at 77 Baruch Drive when an Order of Protection held by Andrea Valdez was violated by her husband. George Valdez, her brother, witnessed Edward Walker.

19. The following details were obtained by Police Officer Jackson at the scene of a robbery:

    Place of Occurrence: Chambers Street, northbound A platform
    Victim: Mr. John Wells
    Suspect: Joseph Miller
    Crime: Robbery, armed with knife, wallet taken
    Action Taken: Suspect arrested

    Officer Jackson is completing a report on the incident.
    Which one of the following expresses the above information MOST clearly and accurately?

    A. At Chambers Street northbound A platform, Joseph Miller used a knife to remove the wallet of John Wells while waiting for the train. Police arrested him.
    B. Mr. John Wells, while waiting for the northbound A train at Chambers Street, had his wallet forcibly removed at knifepoint by Joseph Miller. Joseph Miller was later arrested.
    C. Joseph Miller was arrested for robbery. At Chambers Street, John Wells stated that his wallet was taken. The incident occurred at knifepoint while waiting on a northbound A platform.
    D. At the northbound Chambers Street platform, John Wells was waiting for the A train. Joseph Miller produced a knife and removed his wallet. He was arrested.

20. Police Officer Bellows responds to a report of drugs being sold in the lobby of an apartment building. He obtains the following information at the scene:

Time of Occurrence: 11:30 P.M.
Place of Occurrence: 1010 Bath Avenue
Witnesses: Mary Markham, John Silver
Suspect: Harry Stoner
Crime: Drug sales
Action Taken: Suspect was gone when police arrived

Officer Bellows is completing a report of the incident. Which one of the following expresses the above information MOST clearly and accurately?

- A. Mary Markham and John Silver witnessed drugs being sold and the suspect flee at 1010 Bath Avenue. Harry Stoner was conducting his business at 11:30 P.M. before police arrival in the lobby.
- B. In the lobby, Mary Markham reported at 11:30 P.M. she saw Harry Stoner, along with John Silver, selling drugs. He ran from the lobby at 1010 Bath Avenue before police arrived.
- C. John Silver and Mary Markham reported that they observed Harry Stoner selling drugs in the lobby of 1010 Bath Avenue at 11:30 P.M. The witnesses stated that Stoner fled before police arrived.
- D. Before police arrived, witnesses stated that Harry Stoner was selling drugs. At 1010 Bath Avenue, in the lobby, John Silver and Mary Markham said they observed his actions at 11:30 P.M.

21. While on patrol, Police Officer Fox receives a call to respond to a robbery. Upon arriving at the scene, he obtains the following information:

Time of Occurrence: 6:00 P.M.
Place of Occurrence: Sal's Liquor Store at 30 Fordham Road
Victim: Sal Jones
Suspect: White male wearing a beige parka
Description of Crime: Victim was robbed in his store at gunpoint

Officer Fox is completing a report on the incident. Which one of the following expresses the above information MOST clearly and accurately?

- A. I was informed at 6:00 P.M. by Sal Jones that an unidentified white male robbed him at gunpoint at 30 Fordham Road while wearing a beige parka at Sal's Liquor Store.
- B. At 6:00 P.M., Sal Jones was robbed at gunpoint in his store. An unidentified white male wearing a beige parka came into Sal's Liquor Store at 30 Fordham Road, he told me.
- C. I was informed at 6:00 P.M. while wearing a beige parka an unidentified white male robbed Sal Jones at gunpoint at Sal's Liquor Store at 30 Fordham Road.
- D. Sal Jones informed me that at 6:00 P.M. he was robbed at gunpoint in his store, Sal's Liquor Store, located at 30 Fordham Road, by an unidentified white male wearing a beige parka.

22. The following details were obtained by Police Officer Connors at the scene of a bank robbery:

Time of Occurrence:	10:21 A.M.
Place of Occurrence:	Westbury Savings and Loan
Crime:	Bank Robbery
Suspect:	Male, dressed in black, wearing a black woolen face mask
Witness:	Mary Henderson of 217 Westbury Ave.
Amount Stolen:	$6141 U.S. currency

Officer Connors is completing a report on the incident. Which one of the following expresses the above information MOST clearly and accurately?

- A. At 10:21 A.M., the Westbury Savings and Loan was witnessed being robbed by Mary Henderson of 217 Westbury Avenue. The suspect fled dressed in black with a black woolen face mask. He left the bank with $6141 in U.S. currency.
- B. Dressed in black wearing a black woolen face mask, Mary Henderson of 217 Westbury Avenue saw a suspect flee with $6141 in U.S. currency after robbing the Westbury Savings and Loan. The robber was seen at 10:21 A.M.
- C. At 10:21 A.M., Mary Henderson of 217 Westbury Avenue, witness to the robbery of the Westbury Savings and Loan, reports that a male, dressed in black, wearing a black face mask, did rob said bank and fled with $6141 in U.S. currency.
- D. Mary Henderson, of 217 Westbury Avenue, witnessed the robbery of the Westbury Savings and Loan at 10:21 A.M. The suspect, a male, was dressed in black and was wearing a black woolen face mask. He fled with $6141 in U.S. currency.

23. At the scene of a dispute, Police Officer Johnson made an arrest after obtaining the following information:

Place of Occurrence:	940 Baxter Avenue
Time of Occurrence:	3:40 P.M.
Victim:	John Mitchell
Suspect:	Robert Holden, arrested at scene
Crime:	Menacing
Weapon:	Knife
Time of Arrest:	4:00 P.M.

Officer Johnson is completing a report of the incident.
Which one of the following expresses the above information MOST clearly and accurately?

- A. John Mitchell was menaced by a knife at 940 Baxter Avenue. Robert Holden, owner of the weapon, was arrested at 4:00 P.M., twenty minutes later, at the scene.
- B. John Mitchell reports at 3:40 P.M. he was menaced at 940 Baxter Avenue by Robert Holden. He threatened him with his knife and was arrested at 4:00 P.M. at the scene.
- C. John Mitchell stated that at 3:40 P.M. at 940 Baxter Avenue he was menaced by Robert Holden, who was carrying a knife. Mr. Holden was arrested at the scene at 4:00 P.M.
- D. With a knife, Robert Holden menaced John Mitchell at 3:40 P.M. The knife belonged to him, and he was arrested at the scene of 940 Baxter Avenue at 4:00 P.M.

24. Officer Nieves obtained the following information after he was called to the scene of a large gathering:

Time of Occurrence:	2:45 A.M.
Place of Occurrence:	Mulberry Park
Complaint:	Loud music
Complainant:	Mrs. Simpkins, 42 Mulberry Street, Apt. 25
Action Taken:	Police officer dispersed the crowd

Officer Nieves is completing a report on the incident. Which one of the following expresses the above information MOST clearly and accurately?

A. Mrs. Simpkins, who lives at 42 Mulberry Street, Apt. 25, called the police to make a complaint. A large crowd of people were playing loud music in Mulberry Park at 2:45 A.M. Officer Nieves responded and dispersed the crowd.
B. Officer Nieves responded to Mulberry Park because Mrs. Simpkins, the complainant, lives at 42 Mulberry Street, Apt. 25. Due to a large crowd of people who were playing loud music at 2:45 A.M., he immediately dispersed the crowd.
C. Due to a large crowd of people who were playing loud music in Mulberry Park at 2:45 A.M., Officer Nieves responded and dispersed the crowd. Mrs. Simpkins called the police and complained. She lives at 42 Mulberry Street, Apt. 25.
D. Responding to a complaint by Mrs. Simpkins, who resides at 42 Mulberry Street, Apt. 25, Officer Nieves dispersed a large crowd in Mulberry Park. They were playing loud music. It was 2:45 A.M.

25. While patroling the subway, Police Officer Clark responds to the scene of a past robbery where he obtains the following information:

Place of Occurrence:	Northbound E train
Time of Occurrence:	6:30 P.M.
Victim:	Robert Brey
Crime:	Wallet and jewelry taken
Suspects:	2 male whites armed with knives

Officer Clark is completing a report on the incident.
Which one of the following expresses the above information MOST clearly and accurately?

A. At 6:30 P.M., Robert Brey reported he was robbed of his wallet and jewelry. On the northbound E train, two white males approached Mr. Brey. They threatened him before taking his property with knives.
B. While riding the E train northbound, two white men approached Robert Brey at 6:30 P.M. They threatened him with knives and took his wallet and jewelry.
C. Robert Brey was riding the E train at 6:30 P.M. when he was threatened by two whites. The men took his wallet and jewelry as he was traveling northbound.
D. Robert Brey reports at 6:30 P.M. he lost his wallet to two white men as well as his jewelry. They were carrying knives and threatened him aboard the northbound E train.

KEY (CORRECT ANSWERS)

1. B
2. C
3. C
4. A
5. C

6. B
7. C
8. B
9. C
10. B

11. D
12. A
13. B
14. C
15. A

16. B
17. A
18. C
19. B
20. C

21. D
22. D
23. C
24. A
25. B

TEST 2

DIRECTIONS: Each question or incomplete statement is followed by several suggested answers or completions. Select the one that BEST answers the question or completes the statement. *PRINT THE LETTER OF THE CORRECT ANSWER IN THE SPACE AT THE RIGHT.*

1. Police Officer Johnson has just finished investigating a report of a burglary and has obtained the following information:
   Place of Occurrence: Victim's residence
   Time of Occurrence: Between 8:13 P.M. and 4:15 A.M.
   Victim: Paul Mason of 1264 Twentieth Street, Apt. 3D
   Crime: Burglary
   Damage: Filed front door lock
   Officer Johnson is preparing a report of the incident. Which one of the following expresses the above information MOST clearly and accurately?

   A. Paul Mason's residence was burglarized at 1264 Twentieth Street, Apt. 3D, between 8:13 P.M. and 4:15 A.M. by filing the front door lock.
   B. Paul Mason was burglarized by filing the front door lock and he lives at 1264 Twentieth Street, Apt. 3D, between 8:13 P.M. and 4:15 A.M.
   C. Between 8:13 P.M. and 4:15 A.M., the residence of Paul Mason, located at 1264 Twentieth Street, Apt. 3D, was burglarized after the front door lock was filed.
   D. Between 8:13 P.M. and 4:15 A.M., at 1264 Twentieth Street, Apt. 3D, after the front door lock was filed, the residence of Paul Mason was burglarized.

1.____

2. Police Officer Lowell has just finished investigating a burglary and has received the following information:
   Place of Occurrence: 117-12 Sutphin Boulevard
   Time of Occurrence: Between 9:00 A.M. and 5:00 P.M.
   Victim: Mandee Cotton
   Suspects: Unknown
   Officer Lowell is completing a report on this incident.
   Which one of the following expresses the above information MOST clearly and accurately?

   A. Mandee Cotton reported that her home was burglarized between 9:00 A.M. and 5:00 P.M. Ms. Cotton resides at 117-12 Sutphin Boulevard. Suspects are unknown.
   B. A burglary was committed at 117-12 Sutphin Boulevard reported Mandee Cotton between 9:00 A.M. and 5:00 P.M. Ms. Cotton said unknown suspects burglarized her home.
   C. Unknown suspects burglarized a home at 117-12 Sutphin Boulevard between 9:00 A.M. and 5:00 P.M. Mandee Cotton, homeowner, reported.
   D. Between the hours of 9:00 A.M. and 5:00 P.M., it was reported that 117-12 Sutphin Boulevard was burglarized. Mandee Cotton reported that unknown suspects are responsible.

2.____

3. Police Officer Dale has just finished investigating a report of attempted theft and has obtained the following information:

Place of Occurrence: In front of 103 W. 105th Street
Time of Occurrence: 11:30 A.M.
Victim: Mary Davis
Crime: Attempted theft
Suspect: Male, black, scar on right side of face
Action Taken: Drove victim around area to locate suspect

Officer Dale is preparing a report on the incident. Which one of the following expresses the above information MOST clearly and accurately?

A. Mary Davis was standing in front of 103 W. 105th Street when Officer Dale arrived after an attempt to steal her pocketbook failed at 11:30 A.M. Officer Dale canvassed the area looking for a black male with a scar on the right side of his face with Ms. Davis in the patrol car.
B. Mary Davis stated that, at 11:30 A.M., she was standing in front of 103 W. 105th Street when a black male with a scar on the right side of his face attempted to steal her pocketbook. Officer Dale canvassed the area with Ms. Davis in the patrol car.
C. Officer Dale canvassed the area by putting Mary Davis in a patrol car looking for a black male with a scar on the right side of his face. At 11:30 A.M. in front of 103 W. 105th Street, she said he attempted to steal her pocketbook.
D. At 11:30 A.M., in front of 103 W. 105th Street, Officer Dale canvassed the area with Mary Davis in a patrol car who said that a black male with a scar on the right side of his face attempted to steal her pocketbook.

4. While on patrol, Police Officer Santoro received a call to respond to the scene of a shooting. The following details were obtained at the scene:

Time of Occurrence: 4:00 A.M.
Place of Occurrence: 232 Senator Street
Victim: Mike Nisman
Suspect: Howard Conran
Crime: Shooting
Witness: Sheila Norris

Officer Santoro is completing a report on the incident.
Which one of the following expresses the above information MOST clearly and accurately?

A. Sheila Norris stated at 4:00 A.M. she witnessed a shooting of her neighbor in front of her building. Howard Conran shot Mike Nisman and ran from 232 Senator Street.
B. Mike Nisman was the victim of a shooting incident seen by his neighbor. At 4:00 A.M., Sheila Norris saw Howard Conran shoot him and run in front of their building. Norris and Nisman reside at 232 Senator Street.
C. Sheila Norris states that at 4:00 A.M. she witnessed Howard Conran shoot Mike Nisman, her neighbor, in front of their building at 232 Senator Street. She further states she saw the suspect running from the scene.
D. Mike Nisman was shot by Howard Conran at 4:00 A.M. His neighbor, Sheila Norris, witnessed him run from the scene in front of their building at 232 Senator Street.

5. Police Officer Taylor responds to the scene of a serious traffic accident in which a car struck a telephone pole, and obtains the following information:

Place of Occurrence: Intersection of Rock Street and Amboy Place
Time of Occurrence: 3:27 A.M.
Name of Injured: Carlos Black
Driver of Car: Carlos Black
Action Taken: Injured taken to Beth-El Hospital

Officer Taylor is preparing a report on the accident. Which one of the following expresses the above information MOST clearly and accurately?

   A. At approximately 3:27 A.M., Carlos Black drove his car into a telephone pole located at the intersection of Rock Street and Amboy Place. Mr. Black, who was the only person injured, was taken to Beth-El Hospital.
   B. Carlos Black, injured at the intersection of Rock Street and Amboy Place, hit a telephone pole. He was taken to Beth-El Hospital after the car accident which occurred at 3:27 A.M.
   C. At the intersection of Rock Street and Amboy Place, Carlos Black injured himself and was taken to Beth-El Hospital. His car hit a telephone pole at 3:27 A.M.
   D. At the intersection of Rock Street and Amboy Place at 3:27 A.M., Carlos Black was taken to Beth-El Hospital after injuring himself by driving into a telephone pole.

6. While on patrol in the Jefferson Housing Projects, Police Officer Johnson responds to the scene of a Grand Larceny.
The following information was obtained by Officer Johnson:

Time of Occurrence: 6:00 P.M.
Place of Occurrence: Rear of Building 12A
Victim: Maria Lopez
Crime: Purse snatched
Suspect: Unknown

Officer Johnson is preparing a report on the incident.
Which one of the following expresses the above information MOST clearly and accurately?

   A. At the rear of Building 12A, at 6:00 P.M., by an unknown suspect, Maria Lopez reported her purse snatched in the Jefferson Housing Projects.
   B. Maria Lopez reported that at 6:00 P.M. her purse was snatched by an unknown suspect at the rear of Building 12A in the Jefferson Housing Projects.
   C. At the rear of Building 12A, Maria Lopez reported at 6:00 P.M. that her purse had been snatched by an unknown suspect in the Jefferson Housing Projects.
   D. In the Jefferson Housing Projects, Maria Lopez reported at the rear of Building 12A that her purse had been snatched by an unknown suspect at 6:00 P.M.

7. Criminal Possession of Stolen Property 2nd Degree occurs when a person knowingly possesses stolen property with intent to benefit himself or a person other than the owner, or to prevent its recovery by the owner, and when the
    I. value of the property exceeds two hundred fifty dollars; or
    II. property consists of a credit card; or
    III. person is a pawnbroker or is in the business of buying, selling, or otherwise dealing in property; or
    IV. property consists of one or more firearms, rifles, or shotguns.

   Which one of the following is the BEST example of Criminal Possession of Stolen Property in the Second Degree?

   A. Mary knowingly buys a stolen camera valued at $225 for her mother's birthday.
   B. John finds a wallet containing $100 and various credit cards. John keeps the money and turns the credit cards in at his local precinct.
   C. Mr. Varrone, a pawnbroker, refuses to buy Mr. Cutter's stolen VCR valued at $230.
   D. Mr. Aquista, the owner of a toy store, knowingly buys a crate of stolen water pistols valued at $260.

8. Police Officer Dale has just finished investigating a report of menacing and obtained the following information:
   Time of Occurrence: 10:30 P.M.
   Place of Occurrence: (Hallway) 77 Hill Street
   Victim: Grace Jackson
   Suspect: Susan, white female, 30 years of age
   Crime: Menacing with a knife

   Officer Dale is preparing a report on the incident.
   Which one of the following expresses the above information MOST clearly and accurately?

   A. At 10:30 P.M., Grace Jackson was stopped in the hallway of 77 Hill Street by a 30-year-old white female known to Grace as Susan. Susan put a knife to Grace's throat and demanded that Grace stay out of the building or Susan would hurt her.
   B. Grace Jackson was stopped in the hallway at knifepoint and threatened to stay away from the building located at 77 Hill Street. The female who is 30 years of age known as Susan by Jackson stopped her at 10:30 P.M.
   C. At 10:30 P.M. in the hallway of 77 Hill Street, Grace Jackson reported a white female 30 years of age put a knife to her throat. She knew her as Susan and demanded she stay away from the building or she would get hurt.
   D. A white female 30 years of age known to Grace Jackson as Susan stopped her in the hallway of 77 Hill Street. She put a knife to her throat and at 10:30 P.M. demanded she stay away from the building or she would get hurt.

9. Police Officer Bennett responds to the scene of a car accident and obtains the following information from the witness:
   Time of Occurrence: 3:00 A.M.
   Victim: Joe Morris, removed to Methodist Hospital
   Crime: Struck pedestrian and left the scene of accident
   Description of Auto: Blue 2008 Pontiac, license plate BOT-3745

   Officer Bennett is preparing an accident report. Which one of the following expresses the above information MOST clearly and accurately?

A. Joe Morris, a pedestrian, was hit at 3:00 A.M. and removed to Methodist Hospital. Also a blue Pontiac, 2008 model left the scene, license plate BOT-3745.
B. A pedestrian was taken to Methodist Hospital after being struck at 3:00 A.M. A blue automobile was seen leaving the scene with license plate BOT-3745. Joe Morris was knocked down by a 2008 Pontiac.
C. At 3:00 A.M., Joe Morris, a pedestrian, was struck by a blue 2008 Pontiac. The automobile, license plate BOT-3745, left the scene. Mr. Morris was taken to Methodist Hospital.
D. Joe Morris, a pedestrian at 3:00 A.M. was struck by a Pontiac. A 2008 model, license plate BOT-3745, blue in color, left the scene and the victim was taken to Methodist Hospital.

10. At 11:30 A.M., Police Officers Newman and Johnson receive a radio call to respond to a reported robbery. The Officers obtained the following information:

Time of Occurrence: 11:20 A.M.
Place of Occurrence: Twenty-four hour newsstand at 2024 86th Street
Victim: Sam Norris, owner
Amount Stolen: $450.00
Suspects: Two male whites

Officer Newman is completing a complaint report on the incident.
Which one of the following expresses the above information MOST clearly and accurately?

A. At 11:20 A.M., it was reported by the newsstand owner that two male whites robbed $450.00 from Sam Norris. The Twenty-four hour newsstand is located at 2024 86th Street.
B. At 11:20 A.M., Sam Norris, the newsstand owner, reported that the Twenty-four hour newsstand located at 2024 86th Street was robbed by two male whites who took $450.00.
C. Sam Norris, the owner of the Twenty-four hour newsstand located at 2024 86th Street, reported that at 11:20 A.M. two white males robbed his newsstand of $450.00.
D. Sam Norris reported at 11:20 A.M. that $450.00 had been taken from the owner of the Twenty-four hour newsstand located at 2024 86th Street by two male whites.

11. While on patrol, Police Officers Carter and Popps receive a call to respond to an assault in progress. Upon arrival, they receive the following information:

Place of Occurrence: 27 Park Avenue
Victim: John Dee
Suspect: Michael Jones
Crime: Stabbing during a fight
Action Taken: Suspect arrested

The Officers are completing a report on the incident.
Which one of the following expresses the above information MOST clearly and accurately?

A. In front of 27 Park Avenue, Michael Jones was arrested for stabbing John Dee during a fight.
B. Michael Jones was arrested for stabbing John Dee during a fight in front of 27 Park Avenue.

C. During a fight, Michael Jones was arrested for stabbing John Dee in front of 27 Park Avenue.
D. John Dee was stabbed by Michael Jones, who was arrested for fighting in front of 27 Park Avenue.

12. Police Officer Gattuso responded to a report of a robbery and obtained the following information regarding the incident:

Place of Occurrence:	Princess Grocery, 6 Button Place
Time of Occurrence:	6:00 P.M.
Crime:	Robbery of $200
Victim:	Sara Davidson, owner of Princess Grocery
Description of Suspect:	White, female, red hair, blue jeans, and white T-shirt
Weapon:	Knife

Officer Gattuso is preparing a report on the incident.
Which one of the following expresses the above information MOST clearly and accurately?

A. Sara Davidson reported at 6:00 P.M. her store Princess Grocery was robbed at knifepoint at 6 Button Place. A white woman with red hair took $200 from her wearing blue jeans and a white T-shirt.
B. At 6:00 P.M., a red-haired woman took $200 from 6 Button Place at Princess Grocery owned by Sara Davidson, who was robbed by the white woman. She was wearing blue jeans and a white T-shirt and used a knife.
C. In a robbery that occurred at knifepoint, a red-haired white woman robbed the owner of Princess Grocery. Sara Davidson, the owner of the 6 Button Place store which was robbed of $200, said she was wearing blue jeans and a white T-shirt at 6:00 P.M.
D. At 6:00 P.M., Sara Davidson, owner of Princess Grocery, located at 6 Button Place, was robbed of $200 at knifepoint. The suspect is a white female with red hair wearing blue jeans and a white T-shirt.

13. Police Officer Martinez responds to a report of an assault and obtains the following information regarding the incident:

Place of Occurrence:	Corner of Frank and Lincoln Avenues
Time of Occurrence:	9:40 A.M.
Crime:	Assault
Victim:	Mr. John Adams of 31 20th Street
Suspect:	Male, white, 5'11", 170 lbs., dressed in gray
Injury:	Victim suffered a split lip
Action Taken:	Victim transported to St. Mary's Hospital

Officer Martinez is completing a report on the incident. Which one of the following expresses the above information MOST clearly and accurately?

A. At 9:40 A.M., John Adams was assaulted on the corner of Frank and Lincoln Avenues by a white male, 5'11", 170 lbs., dressed in gray, suffering a split lip. Mr. Adams lives at 31 20th Street and was transported to St. Mary's Hospital.
B. At 9:40 A.M., John Adams was assaulted on the corner of Frank and Lincoln Avenues by a white male, 5'11", 170 lbs., dressed in gray, and lives at 31 20th Street. Mr. Adams suffered a split lip and was transported to St. Mary's Hospital.

C. John Adams, who lives at 31 20th Street, was assaulted at 9:40 A.M. on the corner of Frank and Lincoln Avenues by a white male, 5'11", 170 lbs., dressed in gray. Mr. Adams suffered a split lip and was transported to St. Mary's Hospital.

D. Living at 31 20th Street, Mr. Adams suffered a split lip and was transported to St. Mary's Hospital. At 9:40 A.M., Mr. Adams was assaulted by a white male, 5'11", 170 lbs., dressed in gray.

14. The following information was obtained by Police Officer Adams at the scene of an auto accident:

Date of Occurrence:	August 7, 2004
Place of Occurrence:	541 W. Broadway
Time of Occurrence:	12:45 P.M.
Drivers:	Mrs. Liz Smith and Mr. John Sharp
Action Taken:	Summons served to Mrs. Liz Smith

Officer Adams is completing a report on the accident. Which one of the following expresses the above information MOST clearly and accurately?

A. At 541 W. Broadway, Mr. John Sharp and Mrs. Liz Smith had an auto accident at 12:45 P.M. Mrs. Smith received a summons on August 7, 2004.

B. Mrs. Liz Smith received a summons at 12:45 P.M. on August 7, 2004 for an auto accident with Mr. John Sharp at 541 W. Broadway.

C. Mr. John Sharp and Mrs. Liz Smith were in an auto accident. At 541 W. Broadway on August 7, 2004 at 12:45 P.M., Mrs. Smith received a summons.

D. On August 7, 2004 at 12:45 P.M. at 541 W. Broadway, Mrs. Liz Smith and Mr. John Sharp were involved in an auto accident. Mrs. Smith received a summons.

15. Police Officer Gold and his partner were directed by the radio dispatcher to investigate a report of a past burglary. They obtained the following information at the scene:

Date of Occurrence:	April 2, 2004
Time of Occurrence:	Between 7:30 A.M. and 6:15 P.M.
Place of Occurrence:	124 Haring Street, residence of victim
Victim:	Mr. Gerald Palmer
Suspect:	Unknown
Crime:	Burglary
Items Stolen:	Assorted jewelry, $150 cash, TV, VCR

Officer Gold must complete a report on the incident. Which one of the following expresses the above information MOST clearly and accurately?

A. Mr. Gerald Palmer stated that on April 2, 2004, between 7:30 A.M. and 6:15 P.M., while he was at work, someone broke into his house at 124 Haring Street and removed assorted jewelry, a VCR, $150 cash, and a TV.

B. Mr. Gerald Palmer stated while he was at work that somebody broke into his house on April 2, 2004 and between 7:30 A.M. and 6:15 P.M. took his VCR, TV, assorted jewelry, and $150 cash. His address is 124 Haring Street.

C. Between 7:30 A.M. and 6:15 P.M. on April 2, 2004, Mr. Gerald Palmer reported an unknown person at 124 Haring Street took his TV, VCR, $150 cash, and assorted jewelry from his house. Mr. Palmer said he was at work at the time.

D. An unknown person broke into the house at 124 Haring Street and stole a TV, VCR, assorted jewelry, and $150 cash from Mr. Gerald Palmer. The suspect broke in on April 2, 2004 while he was at work, reported Mr. Palmer between 7:30 A.M. and 6:15 P.M.

16. While on patrol, Police Officers Morris and Devine receive a call to respond to a reported burglary. The following information relating to the crime was obtained by the Officers:

Time of Occurrence: 2:00 A.M.
Place of Occurrence: 2100 First Avenue
Witness: David Santiago
Victim: John Rivera
Suspect: Joe Ryan
Crime: Burglary, DVD player stolen

The Officers are completing a report on the incident.
Which one of the following expresses the above information MOST clearly and accurately?

 A. David Santiago, the witness reported at 2:00 A.M. he saw Joe Ryan leave 2100 First Avenue, home of John Rivera, with a DVD player.
 B. At 2:00 A.M. David Santiago reported that he had seen Joe Ryan go into 2100 First Avenue and steal a DVD player. John Rivera lives at 2100 First Avenue.
 C. David Santiago stated that Joe Ryan burglarized John Rivera's house at 2100 First Avenue. He saw Joe Ryan leaving his house at 2:00 A.M. with a DVD player.
 D. David Santiago reported that at 2:00 A.M. he saw Joe Ryan leave John Rivera's house, located at 2100 First Avenue, with Mr. Rivera's DVD player.

17. When a police officer responds to an incident involving the victim of an animal bite, the officer should do the following in the order given:
 I. Determine the owner of the animal
 II. Obtain a description of the animal and attempt to locate it for an examination if the owner is unknown
 III. If the animal is located and the owner is unknown, comply with the Care and Disposition of Animal procedure
 IV. Prepare a Department of Health Form 480BAA and deliver it to the Desk Officer with a written report
 V. Notify the Department of Health by telephone if the person has been bitten by an animal other than a dog or cat.

Police Officer Rosario responds to 1225 South Boulevard where someone has been bitten by a dog. He is met by John Miller who informs Officer Rosario that he was bitten by a large German Shepard. Mr. Miller also states that he believes the dog belongs to someone in the neighborhood but does not know who owns it. Officer Rosario searches the area for the dog but is unable to find it.
What should Officer Rosario do NEXT?

 A. Locate the owner of the animal.
 B. Notify the Department of Health by telephone.
 C. Prepare a Department of Health Form 480BAA.
 D. Comply with the Care and Disposition of Animal procedure.

18. The following details were obtained by Police Officer Howard at the scene of a hit-and-run accident:

Place of Occurrence:	Intersection of Brown Street and Front Street
Time of Occurrence:	11:15 A.M.
Victim:	John Lawrence
Vehicle:	Red Chevrolet, license plate 727PQA
Crime:	Leaving the scene of an accident

Officer Howard is completing a report on the incident. Which one of the following expresses the above information MOST clearly and accurately?

- A. A red Chevrolet, license plate 727PQA, hit John Lawrence. It left the scene of the accident at 11:15 A.M. at the intersection of Brown and Front Streets.
- B. At 11:15 A.M., John Lawrence was walking at the intersection of Brown Street and Front Street when he was struck by a red Chevrolet, license plate 727PQA, which left the scene.
- C. It was reported at 11:15 A.M. that John Lawrence was struck at the intersection of Brown Street and Front Street. The red Chevrolet, license plate 727PQA, left the scene.
- D. At the intersection of Brown Street and Front Street, John Lawrence was the victim of a car at 11:15 A.M. which struck him and left the scene. It was a red Chevrolet, license plate 727PQA.

19. Police Officer Donnelly has transported an elderly male to Mt. Hope Hospital after finding him lying on the street. At the hospital, Nurse Baker provided Officer Donnelly with the following information:

Name:	Robert Jones
Address:	1485 E. 97th St.
Date of Birth:	May 13, 1935
Age:	73 years old

Type of Ailment: Heart condition

Officer Donnelly is completing an Aided Report.
Which one of the following expresses the above information MOST clearly and accurately?

- A. Mr. Robert Jones, who is 73 years old, born on May 13, 1935, collapsed on the street. Mr. Jones, who resides at 1485 E. 97th Street, suffers from a heart condition.
- B. Mr. Robert Jones had a heart condition and collapsed today on the street, and resides at 1485 E. 97th Street. He was 73 years old and born on May 13, 1935.
- C. Mr. Robert Jones, who resides at 1485 E. 97th Street, was born on May 13, 1935, and is 73 years old, was found lying on the street from a heart condition.
- D. Mr. Robert Jones, born on May 13, 1935, suffers from a heart condition at age 73 and was found lying on the street residing at 1485 E. 97th Street.

20. Police officers on patrol are often called to a scene where a response from the Fire Department might be necessary.
In which one of the following situations would a request to the Fire Department to respond be MOST critical?

10 (#2)

- A. A film crew has started a small fire in order to shoot a scene on an October evening.
- B. Two manhole covers blow off on a September afternoon.
- C. Homeless persons are gathered around a trash can fire on a February morning.
- D. A fire hydrant has been opened by people in the neighborhood on a July afternoon.

21. Police Officer Johnson arrives at the National Savings Bank five minutes after it has been robbed at gunpoint.
    The following are details provided by eyewitnesses: <u>Suspect</u>
    Sex: Male
    Ethnicity: White
    Height: 5'10" to 6'2"
    Weight: 180 lbs. to 190 lbs.
    Hair Color: Blonde
    Clothing: Black jacket, blue dungarees
    Weapon: .45 caliber revolver
    Officer Johnson is completing a report on the incident.
    Which one of the following expresses the above information MOST clearly and accurately?
    A white male

    - A. weighing 180-190 lbs. robbed the National Savings Bank. He was white with a black jacket with blonde hair, is 5'10" to 6'2", and blue dungarees. The robber was armed with a .45 caliber revolver.
    - B. weighing around 180 or 190 lbs. was wearing a black jacket and blue dungarees. He had blonde hair and had a .45 caliber revolver, and was 5'10" to 6'2". He robbed the National Savings Bank.
    - C. who was 5'10" to 6'2" and was weighing 180 to 190 lbs., and has blonde hair and wearing blue dungarees and a black jacket with a revolver, robbed the National Savings Bank.
    - D. armed with a .45 caliber revolver robbed the National Savings Bank. The robber was described as being between 180-190 lbs., 5'10" to 6'2", with blonde hair. He was wearing a black jacket and blue dungarees.

22. While on patrol, Police Officer Rogers is approached by Terry Conyers, a young woman whose pocketbook has been stolen. Ms. Conyers tells Officer Rogers that the following items were in her pocketbook at the time it was taken:
    4 Traveler's checks, each valued at $20.00
    3 Traveler's checks, each valued at $25.00
    Cash of $212.00
    1 wedding band valued at $450.00
    Officer Rogers is preparing a Complaint Report on the robbery.
    Which one of the following is the TOTAL value of the property and cash taken from Ms. Conyers?

    A. $707   B. $807   C. $817   D. $837

23. While on patrol, Police Officer Scott is dispatched to respond to a reported burglary. Two burglars entered the home of Mr. and Mrs. Walker and stole the following items:
    3 watches valued at $65.00 each
    1 amplifier valued at $340.00
    1 television set valued at $420.00
    Officer Scott is preparing a Complaint Report on the burglary.
    Which one of the following is the TOTAL value of the property stolen?

    A. $707   B. $825   C. $920   D. $955

23._____

24. While on patrol, Police Officer Smith is dispatched to investigate a grand larceny. Deborah Paisley, a businesswoman, reports that her 2000 Porsche was broken into. The following items were taken:
    1 car stereo system valued at $2,950.00
    1 car phone valued at $1,060.00
    Ms. Paisley's attache case valued at $200.00 was also taken from the car in the incident. The attache case contained two new solid gold pens valued at $970.00 each.
    Officer Smith is completing a Complaint Report.
    Which one of the following is the TOTAL dollar value of the property stolen from Ms. Paisley's car?

    A. $5,180   B. $5,980   C. $6,040   D. $6,150

24._____

25. Police Officer Grundig is writing a Complaint Report regarding a burglary and assault case. Officer Grundig has obtained the following facts:
    Place of Occurrence: 2244 Clark Street
    Victim: Mrs. Willis
    Suspect: Mr. Willis, victim's ex-husband
    Complaint: Unlawful entry; head injury inflicted with a bat
    Officer Grundig is completing a report on the incident. Which one of the following expresses the above information MOST clearly and accurately?

    A. He had no permission or authority to do so and it caused her head injuries, when Mr. Willis entered his ex-wife's premises. Mrs. Willis lives at 2244 Clark Street. He hit her with a bat.
    B. Mr. Willis entered 2244 Clark Street, the premises of his ex-wife. He hit her with a bat, without permission and authority to do so. It caused Mrs. Willis to have head injuries.
    C. After Mr. Willis hit his ex-wife, Mrs. Willis, at 2244 Clark Street, the bat caused her to have head injuries. He had no permission nor authority do so so.
    D. Mr. Willis entered his ex-wife's premises at 2244 Clark Street without her permission or authority. He then struck Mrs. Willis with a bat, causing injuries to her head.

25._____

KEY (CORRECT ANSWERS)

1. C
2. A
3. B
4. C
5. A

6. B
7. D
8. A
9. C
10. C

11. B
12. D
13. C
14. D
15. A

16. D
17. C
18. B
19. A
20. B

21. D
22. C
23. D
24. D
25. D

PREPARING WRITTEN MATERIAL
EXAMINATION SECTION
TEST 1

Questions 1-15.

DIRECTIONS: For each of Questions 1 through 15, select from the options given below the MOST applicable choice, and mark your answer accordingly.
    A. The sentence is correct.
    B. The sentence contains a spelling error only.
    C. The sentence contains an English grammar error only.
    D. The sentence contains both a spelling error and an English grammar error.

1. He is a very dependable person whom we expect will be an asset to this division.   1.____

2. An investigator often finds it necessary to be very diplomatic when conducting an interview.   2.____

3. Accurate detail is especially important if court action results from an investigation.   3.____

4. The report was signed by him and I since we conducted the investigation jointly.   4.____

5. Upon receipt of the complaint, an inquiry was begun.   5.____

6. An employee has to organize his time so that he can handle his workload efficiantly.   6.____

7. It was not apparent that anyone was living at the address given by the client.   7.____

8. According to regulations, there is to be at least three attempts made to locate the client.   8.____

9. Neither the inmate nor the correction officer was willing to sign a formal statement.   9.____

10. It is our opinion that one of the persons interviewed were lying.   10.____

11. We interviewed both clients and departmental personel in the course of this investigation.   11.____

12. It is concievable that further research might produce additional evidence.   12.____

13. There are too many occurences of this nature to ignore.   13.____

14. We cannot accede to the candidate's request. 14.____

15. The submission of overdue reports is the reason that there was a delay in completion of this investigation. 15.____

Questions 16-25.

DIRECTIONS: Each of Questions 16 through 25 may be classified under one of the following four categories:
    A. Faulty because of incorrect grammar or sentence structure.
    B. Faulty because of incorrect punctuation.
    C. Faulty because of incorrect spelling.
    D. Correct

Examine each sentence carefully to determine under which of the above four options it is best classified. Then, in the space at the right, write the letter preceding the option which is the BEST of the four suggested above. Each incorrect sentence contains but one type of error. Consider a sentence to be correct if it contains none of the types of errors mentioned, even though there may be other correct ways of expressing the same thought.

16. Although the department's supply of scratch pads and stationary have diminished considerably, the allotment for our division has not been reduced. 16.____

17. You have not told us whom you wish to designate as your secretary. 17.____

18. Upon reading the minutes of the last meeting, the new proposal was taken up for consideration. 18.____

19. Before beginning the discussion, we locked the door as a precautionery measure. 19.____

20. The supervisor remarked, "Only those clerks, who perform routine work, are permitted to take a rest period." 20.____

21. Not only will this duplicating machine make accurate copies, but it will also produce a quantity of work equal to fifteen transcribing typists. 21.____

22. "Mr. Jones," said the supervisor, "we regret our inability to grant you an extention of your leave of absence. 22.____

23. Although the employees find the work monotonous and fatigueing, they rarely complain. 23.____

24. We completed the tabulation of the receipts on time despite the fact that Miss Smith our fastest operator was absent for over a week. 24.____

25. The reaction of the employees who attended the meeting, as well as the reaction of those who did not attend, indicates clearly that the schedule is satisfactory to everyone concerned.

25.____

KEY (CORRECT ANSWERS)

1. D
2. A
3. A
4. C
5. A

6. B
7. B
8. C
9. A
10. C

11. B
12. B
13. B
14. A
15. C

16. A
17. D
18. A
19. C
20. B

21. A
22. C
23. C
24. B
25. D

TEST 2

Questions 1-15.

DIRECTIONS: Questions 1 through 15 consist of two sentences. Some are correct according to ordinary formal English usage. Others are incorrect because they contain errors in English usage, spelling, or punctuation. Consider a sentence correct if it contains no errors in English usage, spelling, or punctuation, even if there may be other ways of writing the sentence correctly. Mark your answer:
    A. If only sentence I is correct.
    B. If only sentence II is correct.
    C. If sentences 1 and II are correct.
    D. If neither sentence I nor II is correct.

1.   I. The influence of recruitment efficiency upon administrative standards is readily apparant.
     II. Rapid and accurate thinking are an essential quality of the police officer.

2.   I. The administrator of a police department is constantly confronted by the demands of subordinates for increased personnel in their respective units.
     II. Since a chief executive must work within well-defined fiscal limits, he must weigh the relative importance of various requests.

3.   I. The two men whom the police arrested for a parking violation were wanted for robbery in three states.
     II. Strong executive control from the top to the bottom of the enterprise is one of the basic principals of police administration.

4.   I. When he gave testimony unfavorable to the defendant loyalty seemed to mean very little.
     II. Having run off the road while passing a car, the patrolman gave the driver a traffic ticket.

5.   I. The judge ruled that the defendant's conversation with his doctor was a privileged communication.
     II. The importance of our training program is widely recognized; however, fiscal difficulties limit the program's effectiveness.

6.   I. Despite an increase in patrol coverage, there were less arrests for crimes against property this year.
     II. The investigators could hardly have expected greater cooperation from the public.

7.   I. Neither the patrolman nor the witness could identify the defendant as the driver of the car.
     II. Each of the officers in the class received their certificates at the completion of the course.

8. I. The new commander made it clear that those kind of procedures would no longer be permitted.
   II. Giving some weight to performance records is more advisable than making promotions solely on the basis of test scores.

   8.____

9. I. A deputy sheriff must ascertain whether the debtor, has any property.
   II. A good deputy sheriff does not cause histerical excitement when he executes a process.

   9.____

10. I. Having learned that he has been assigned a judgment debtor, the deputy sheriff should call upon him.
    II. The deputy sheriff may seize and remove property without requiring a bond.

    10.____

11. I. If legal procedures are not observed, the resulting contract is not enforseable.
    II. If the directions from the creditor's attorney are not in writing, the deputy sheriff should request a letter of instructions from the attorney.

    11.____

12. I. The deputy sheriff may confer with the defendant and enter this defendants' place of business.
    II. A deputy sheriff must ascertain from the creditor's attorney whether the debtor has any property against which he may proceede.

    12.____

13. I. The sheriff has a right to do whatever is necessary for the purpose of executing the order of the court.
    II. The written order of the court gives the sheriff general authority and he is governed in his acts by a very simple principal.

    13.____

14. I. Either the patrolman or his sergeant are always ready to help the public.
    II. The sergeant asked the patrolman when he would finish the report.

    14.____

15. I. The injured man could not hardly talk.
    II. Every officer had ought to had in their reports on time.

    15.____

Questions 16-26.

DIRECTIONS: For each of the sentences given below, numbered 16 through 25, select from the following choices the MOST correct choice and print your choice in the space at the right. Select as your answer:
   A. If the statement contains an unnecessary word or expression
   B. If the statement contains a slang term or expression ordinarily not acceptable in government report writing.
   C. If the statement contains an old-fashioned word or expression, where a concrete, plain term would be more useful.
   D. If the statement contains no major faults.

16. Every one of us should try harder.

    16.____

17. Yours of the first instant has been received.

    17.____

3 (#2)

18. We will have to do a real snow job on him.   18._____

19. I shall contact him next Thursday.   19._____

20. None of us were invited to the meeting with the community.   20._____

21. We got this here job to do.   21._____

22. She could not help but see the mistake in the checkbook.   22._____

23. Don't bug the Director about the report.   23._____

24. I beg to inform you that your letter has been received.   24._____

25. This project is all screwed up.   25._____

KEY (CORRECT ANSWERS)

1.	D		11.	B
2.	C		12.	D
3.	A		13.	A
4.	D		14.	D
5.	B		15.	D
6.	B		16.	D
7.	A		17.	C
8.	D		18.	B
9.	D		19.	D
10.	C		20.	D

21. B
22. D
23. B
24. C
25. B

TEST 3

DIRECTIONS: Questions 1 through 25 are sentences taken from reports. Some are correct according to ordinary English usage. Others are incorrect because they contain errors in English usage, spelling, or punctuation. Consider a sentence correct if it contains no errors in English usage, spelling, or punctuation, even if there may be other ways of writing the sentence correctly. Mark your answer:
    A. If only sentence I is correct
    B. If only sentence II is correct
    C. If sentences I and II are correct
    D. If neither sentence I nor II is correct

1.   I. The Neighborhood Police Team Commander and Team Patrolmen are encouraged to give to the public the widest possible verbal and written disemination of information regarding the existence and purposes of the program.
  II. The police must be vitally interelated with every segment of the public they serve.

2.   I. If social gambling, prostitution, and other vices are to be prohibited, the law makers should provide the manpower and method for enforcement.
  II. In addition to checking on possible crime locations such as hallways, roofs yards and other similar locations, Team Patrolmen are encouraged to make known their presence to members of the community.

3.   I. The Neighborhood Police Team Commander is authorized to secure, the cooperation of local publications, as well as public and private agencies, to further the goals of the program.
  II. Recruitment from social minorities is essential to effective police work among minorities and meaningful relations with them.

4.   I. The Neighborhood Police Team Commander and his men have the responsibility for providing patrol service within the sector territory on a twenty-four hour basis.
  II. While the patrolman was walking his beat at midnight he noticed that the clothing stores' door was partly open.

5.   I. Authority is granted to the Neighborhood Police Team to device tactics for coping with the crime in the sector.
  II. Before leaving the scene of the accident, the patrolman drew a map showing the positions of the automobiles and indicated the time of the accident as 10 M. in the morning.

6.   I. The Neighborhood Police Team Commander and his men must be kept apprised of conditions effecting their sector.
  II. Clear, continuous communication with every segment of the public served based on the realization of mutual need and founded on trust and confidence is the basis for effective law enforcement.

7.   I. The irony is that the police are blamed for the laws they enforce when they are doing their duty.
    II. The Neighborhood Police Team Commander is authorized to prepare and distribute literature with pertinent information telling the public whom to contact for assistance.

7.____

8.   I. The day is not far distant when major parts of the entire police compliment will need extensive college training or degrees.
    II. Although driving under the influence of alcohol is a specific charge in making arrests, drunkeness is basically a health and social problem.

8.____

9.   I. If a deputy sheriff finds that property he has to attach is located on a ship, he should notify his supervisor.
    II. Any contract that tends to interfere with the administration of justice is illegal.

9.____

10.   I. A mandate or official order of the court to the sheriff or other officer directs it to take into possession property of the judgment debtor.
    II. Tenancies from month-to-month, week-to-week, and sometimes year-to-year are termenable.

10.____

11.   I. A civil arrest is an arrest pursuant to an order issued by a court in civil litigation.
    II. In a criminal arrest, a defendant is arrested for a crime he is alleged to have committed.

11.____

12.   I. Having taken a defendant into custody, there is a complete restraint of personal liberty.
    II. Actual force is unnecessary when a deputy sheriff makes an arrest.

12.____

13.   I. When a husband breaches a separation agreement by failing to supply to the wife the amount of money to be paid to her periodically under the agreement, the same legal steps may be taken to enforce his compliance as in any other breach of contract.
    II. Having obtained the writ of attachment, the plaintiff is then in the advantageous position of selling the very property that has been held for him by the sheriff while he was obtaining a judgment.

13.____

14.   I. Being locked in his desk, the investigator felt sure that the records would be safe.
    II. The reason why the witness changed his statement was because he had been threatened.

14.____

15.   I. The investigation had just began then an important witness disappeared.
    II. The check that had been missing was located and returned to its owner, Harry Morgan, a resident of Suffolk County, New York.

15.____

16. I. A supervisor will find that the establishment of standard procedures enables his staff to work more efficiently.
    II. An investigator hadn't ought to give any recommendations in his report if he is in doubt.

    16._____

17. I. Neither the investigator nor his supervisor is ready to interview the witness.
    II. Interviewing has been and always will be an important asset in investigation.

    17._____

18. I. One of the investigator's reports has been forwarded to the wrong person.
    II. The investigator stated that he was not familiar with those kind of cases.

    18._____

19. I. Approaching the victim of the assault, two large bruises were noticed by me.
    II. The prisoner was arrested for assault, resisting arrest, and use of a deadly weapon.

    19._____

20. I. A copy of the orders, which had been prepared by the captain, was given to each patrolman.
    II. It's always necessary to inform an arrested person of his constitutional rights before asking him any questions.

    20._____

21. I. To prevent further bleeding, I applied a tourniquet to the wound.
    II. John Rano a senior officer was on duty at the time of the accident.

    21._____

22. I. Limiting the term "property" to tangible property, in the criminal mischief setting, accords with prior case law holding that only tangible property came within the purview of the offense of malicious mischief.
    II. Thus, a person who intentionally destroys the property of another, but under an honest belief that he has title to such property, cannot be convicted of criminal mischief under the Revised Penal Law.

    22._____

23. I. Very early in it's history, New York enacted statutes from time to time punishing, either as a felony or as a misdemeanor, malicious injuries to various kinds of property: piers, boos, dams, bridges, etc.
    II. The application of the statute is necessarily restricted to trespassory takings with larcenous intent: namely with intent permanently or virtually permanently to "appropriate" property or "deprive" the owner of its use.

    23._____

24. I. Since the former Penal Law did not define the instruments of forgery in a general fashion, its crime of forgery was held to be narrower than the common law offense in this respect and to embrace only those instruments explicitly specified in the substantive provisions.
    II. After entering the barn through an open door for the purpose of stealing, it was closed by the defendants.

    24._____

25. I. The use of fire or explosives to destroy tangible property is proscribed by the criminal mischief provisions of the Revised Penal Law.
    II. The defendant's taking of a taxicab for the immediate purpose of affecting his escape did not constitute grand larceny.

25._____

KEY (CORRECT ANSWERS)

1.	D		11.	C
2.	D		12.	B
3.	B		13.	C
4.	A		14.	D
5.	D		15.	B
6.	D		16.	A
7.	C		17.	C
8.	D		18.	A
9.	C		19.	B
10.	D		20.	C

21.	A
22.	C
23.	B
24.	A
25.	A

TEST 4

Questions 1-4.

DIRECTIONS: Each of the two sentences in Questions 1 through 4 may be correct or may contain errors in punctuation, capitalization, or grammar. Mark your answer:
- A. If there is an error only in sentence I
- B. If there is an error only in sentence II
- C. If there is an error in both sentences I and II
- D. If both sentences are correct.

1. I. It is very annoying to have a pencil sharpener, which is not in working order. 1._____
    II. Patrolman Blake checked the door of Joe's Restaurant and found that the lock has been jammed.

2. I. When you are studying a good textbook is important. 2._____
    II. He said he would divide the money equally between you and me.

3. I. Since he went on the city council a year ago, one of his primary concerns has been safety in the streets. 3._____
    II. After waiting in the doorway for about 15 minutes, a black sedan appeared.

Questions 4-8.

DIRECTIONS: Each of the sentences in Questions 4 through 8 may be classified under one of the following four categories:
- A. Faulty because of incorrect grammar
- B. Faulty because of incorrect punctuation
- C. Faulty because of incorrect capitalization or incorrect spelling
- D. Correct

Examine each sentence carefully to determine under which of the above four options it is BEST classified. Then, in the space at the right, print the capitalized letter preceding the option which is the BEST of the four suggested above. Each faulty sentence contains but one type of error. Consider a sentence to be correct if it contains none of the types of errors mentioned, even though there may be other correct ways of expressing the same thought.

4. They told both he and I that the prisoner had escaped. 4._____

5. Any superior officer, who, disregards the just complaints of his subordinates, is remiss in the performance of his duty. 5._____

6. Only those members of the national organization who resided in the Middle west attended the conference in Chicago. 6._____

7. We told him to give the investigation assignment to whoever was available. 7._____

8. Please do not disappoint and embarass us by not appearing in court. 8._____

149

Questions 9-13

DIRECTIONS: Each of Questions 9 through 13 consists of three sentences lettered A, B, and C. In each of these questions, one of the sentences may contain an error in grammar, sentence structure, or punctuation, or all three sentences may be correct. If one of the sentence in a question contains an error in grammar, sentence structure, or punctuation, print in the space at the right the capital letter preceding the sentence which contains the error. If all three sentences are correct, print the letter D.

9. A. Mr. Smith appears to be less competent than I in performing these duties. 9.____
    B. The supervisor spoke to the employee, who had made the error, but did not reprimand him.
    C. When he found the book lying on the table, he immediately notified the owner.

10. A. Being locked in the desk, we were certain that the papers would not be taken. 10.____
    B. It wasn't I who dictated the telegram; I believe it was Eleanor.
    C. You should interview whoever comes to the office today.

11. A. The clerk was instructed to set the machine on the table before summoning the manager. 11.____
    B. He said that he was not familiar with those kind of activities.
    C. A box of pencils, in addition to erasers and blotters, was included in the shipment of supplies.

12. A. The supervisor remarked, "Assigning an employee to the proper type of work is not always easy." 12.____
    B. The employer found that each of the applicants were qualified to perform the duties of the position.
    C. Any competent student is permitted to take this course if he obtains the consent of the instructor.

13. A. The prize was awarded to the employee whom the judges believed to be most deserving. 13.____
    B. Since the instructor believes his book is the better of the two, he is recommending it for use in the school.
    C. It was obvious to the employees that the completion of the task by the scheduled date would require their working overtime.

Questions 14-20.

DIRECTIONS: In answering Questions 14 through 20, choose the sentence which is BEST from the point of view of English usage suitable for a business report.

14. A. The client's receiving of public assistance checks at two different addresses were disclosed by the investigation.
    B. The investigation disclosed that the client was receiving public assistance checks at two different addresses.
    C. The client was found out by the investigation to be receiving public assistance checks at two different addresses.
    D. The client has been receiving public assistance checks at two different addresses, disclosed the investigation.

14.____

15. A. The investigation of complaints are usually handled by this unit, which deals with internal security problems in the department.
    B. This unit deals with internal security problems in the department usually investigating complaints.
    C. Investigating complaints is this unit's job, being that it handles internal security problems in the department.
    D. This unit deals with internal security problems in the department and usually investigates complaints.

15.____

16. A. The delay in completing this investigation was caused by difficulty in obtaining the required documents from the candidate.
    B. Because of difficulty in obtaining the required documents from the candidate is the reason that there was a delay in completing this investigation.
    C. Having had difficulty in obtaining the required documents from the candidate, there was a delay in completing this investigation.
    D. Difficulty in obtaining the required documents from the candidate had the affect of delaying the completion of this investigation.

16.____

17. A. This report, together with documents supporting our recommendation, are being submitted for your approval.
    B. Documents supporting our recommendation is being submitted with the report for your approval.
    C. This report, together with documents supporting our recommendation, is being submitted for your approval.
    D. The report and documents supporting our recommendation is being submitted for your approval.

17.____

18. A. The chairman himself, rather than his aides, has reviewed the report.
    B. The chairman himself, rather than his aides, have reviewed the report.
    C. The chairmen, not the aide, has reviewed the report.
    D. The aide, not the chairmen, have reviewed the report.

18.____

19. A. Various proposals were submitted but the decision is not been made.
     B. Various proposals has been submitted but the decision has not been made.
     C. Various proposals were submitted but the decision is not been made.
     D. Various proposals have been submitted but the decision has not been made.

20. A. Everyone were rewarded for his successful attempt.
     B. They were successful in their attempts and each of them was rewarded.
     C. Each of them are rewarded for their successful attempts.
     D. The reward for their successful attempts were made to each of them.

21. The following is a paragraph from a request for departmental recognition consisting of five numbered sentences submitted to a Captain for review. These sentences may or may not have errors in spelling, grammar, and punctuation:
     (1) The officers observed the subject Mills surreptitiously remove a wallet from the woman's handbag and entered his automobile. (2) As they approached Mills, he looked in their direction and drove away. (3) The officers pursued in their car. (4) Mills executed a series of complicated manuvers to evade the pursuing officers. (5) At the corner of Broome and Elizabeth Streets, Mills stopped the car, got out, raised his hands and surrendered to the officers.
     Which one of the following BEST classifies the above with regard to spelling, grammar, and punctuation?
     A. 1, 2, and 3 are correct, but 4 and 5 have errors.
     B. 2, 3, and 5 are correct, but 1 and 4 have errors.
     C. 3, 4, and 5 are correct, but 1 and 2 have errors.
     D. 1, 2, 3, and 5 are correct, but 4 has errors.

22. The one of the following sentences which is grammatically PREFERABLE to the others is:
     A. Our engineers will go over your blueprints so that you may have no problems in construction.
     B. For a long time he had been arguing that we, not he, are to blame for the confusion.
     C. I worked on his automobile for two hours and still cannot find out what is wrong with it.
     D. Accustomed to all kinds of hardships, fatigue seldom bothers veteran policemen.

23. The MOST accurate of the following sentences is:
     A. The commissioner, as well as his deputy and various bureau heads, were present.
     B. A new organization of employers and employees have been formed.
     C. One or the other of these men have been selected.
     D. The number of pages in the book is enough to discourage a reader.

24. The MOST accurate of the following sentences is: 24._____
    A. Between you and me, I think he is the better man.
    B. He was believed to be me.
    C. Is it us that you wish to see?
    D. The winners are him and her.

KEY (CORRECT ANSWERS)

1.	C		11.	B
2.	A		12.	B
3.	C		13.	D
4.	A		14.	B
5.	B		15.	D
6.	C		16.	A
7.	D		17.	C
8.	C		18.	A
9.	B		19.	D
10.	A		20.	B

21.	B
22.	A
23.	D
24.	A

PREPARING WRITTEN MATERIAL

EXAMINATION SECTION

TEST 1

DIRECTIONS: Each question or incomplete statement is followed by several suggested answers or completions. Select the one that BEST answers the question or completes the statement. *PRINT THE LETTER OF THE CORRECT ANSWER IN THE SPACE AT THE RIGHT.*

1. The one of the following sentences which is LEAST acceptable from the viewpoint of correct usage is:
   A. The police thought the fugitive to be him.
   B. The criminals set a trap for whoever would fall into it.
   C. It is ten years ago since the fugitive fled from the city.
   D. The lecturer argued that criminals are usually cowards.
   E. The police removed four bucketfuls of earth from the scene of the crime.

1._____

2. The one of the following sentences which is LEAST acceptable from the viewpoint of correct usage is:
   A. The patrolman scrutinized the report with great care.
   B. Approaching the victim of the assault, two bruises were noticed by the patrolman.
   C. As soon as I had broken down the door, I stepped into the room.
   D. I observed the accused loitering near the building, which was closed at the time.
   E. The storekeeper complained that his neighbor was guilty of violating a local ordinance.

2._____

3. The one of the following sentences which is LEAST acceptable from the viewpoint of correct usage is:
   A. I realized immediately that he intended to assault the woman, so I disarmed him.
   B. It was apparent that Mr. Smith's explanation contained many inconsistencies.
   C. Despite the slippery condition of the street, he managed to stop the vehicle before injuring the child.
   D. Not a single one of them wish, despite the damage to property, to make a formal complaint.
   E. The body was found lying on the floor.

3._____

4. The one of the following sentences which contains NO error in usage is:
   A. After the robbers left, the proprietor stood tied in his chair for about two hours before help arrived.
   B. In the cellar I found the watchman's hat and coat.
   C. The persons living in adjacent apartments stated that they had heard no unusual noises.

4._____

155

D. Neither a knife or any firearms were found in the room.
E. Walking down the street, the shouting of the crowd indicated that something was wrong.

5. The one of the following sentences which contains NO error in usage is:
   A. The policeman lay a firm hand on the suspect's shoulder.
   B. It is true that neither strength nor agility are the most important requirement for a good patrolman.
   C. Good citizens constantly strive to do more than merely comply the restraints imposed by society.
   D. No decision was made as to whom the prize should be awarded.
   E. Twenty years is considered a severe sentence for a felony.

6. Which of the following sentences is NOT expressed in standard English usage?
   A. The victim reached a pay-phone booth and manages to call police headquarters.
   B. By the time the call was received, the assailant had left the scene.
   C. The victim has been a respected member of the community for the past eleven years.
   D. Although the lighting was bad and the shadows were deep, the storekeeper caught sight of the attacker.
   E. Additional street lights have since been installed, and the patrols have been strengthened.

7. Which of the following sentences is NOT expressed in standard English usage?
   A. The judge upheld the attorney's right to question the witness about the missing glove.
   B. To be absolutely fair to all parties is the jury's chief responsibility.
   C. Having finished the report, a loud noise in the next room startled the sergeant.
   D. The witness obviously enjoyed having played a part in the proceedings.
   E. The sergeant planned to assign the case to whoever arrived first.

8. In which of the following sentences is a word misused?
   A. As a matter of principle, the captain insisted that the suspect's partner be brought for questioning.
   B. The principle suspect had been detained at the station house for most of the day.
   C. The principal in the crime had no previous criminal record, but his closest associate had been convicted of felonies on two occasions.
   D. The interest payments had been made promptly, but the firm had been drawing upon the principal for these payments.
   E. The accused insisted that his high school principal would furnish him a character reference.

9. Which of the following statements is ambiguous? 9.____
   A. Mr. Sullivan explained why Mr. Johnson had been dismissed from his job.
   B. The storekeeper told the patrolman he had made a mistake.
   C. After waiting three hours, the patients in the doctor's office were sent home.
   D. The janitor's duties were to maintain the building in good shape and to answer tenants' complaints.
   E. The speed limit should, in my opinion, be raised to sixty miles an hour on that stretch of road.

10. In which of the following is the punctuation or capitalization faulty? 10.____
    A. The accident occurred at an intersection in the Kew Gardens section of Queens, near the bus stop.
    B. The sedan, not the convertible, was struck in the side.
    C. Before any of the patrolmen had left the police car received an important message from headquarters.
    D. The dog that had been stolen was returned to his master, John Dempsey, who lived in East Village.
    E. The letter had been sent to 12 Hillside Terrace, Rutland, Vermont 05702.

Questions 11-25.

DIRECTIONS: Questions 11 through 25 are to be answered in accordance with correct English usage; that is, standard English rather than nonstandard or substandard. Nonstandard and substandard English includes words or expressions usually classified as slang, dialect, illiterate, etc., which are not generally accepted as correct in current written communication. Standard English also requires clarity, proper punctuation and capitalization and appropriate use of words. Write the letter of the sentence NOT expressed in standard English usage in the space at the right.

11. A. There were three witnesses to the accident. 11.____
    B. At least three witnesses were found to testify for the plaintiff.
    C. Three of the witnesses who took the stand was uncertain about the defendant's competence to drive.
    D. Only three witnesses came forward to testify for the plaintiff.
    E. The three witnesses to the accident were pedestrians.

12. A. The driver had obviously drunk too many martinis before leaving for home. 12.____
    B. The boy who drowned had swum in these same waters many times before.
    C. The petty thief had stolen a bicycle from a private driveway before he was apprehended.
    D. The detectives had brung in the heroin shipment they intercepted.
    E. The passengers had never ridden in a converted bus before.

13. A. Between you and me, the new platoon plan sounds like a good idea.
    B. Money from an aunt's estate was left to his wife and he.
    C. He and I were assigned to the same patrol for the first time in two months.
    D. Either you or he should check the front door of that store.
    E. The captain himself was not sure of the witness's reliability.

14. A. The alarm had scarcely begun to ring when the explosion occurred.
    B. Before the firemen arrived at the scene, the second story had been destroyed.
    C. Because of the dense smoke and heat, the firemen could hardly approach the now-blazing structure.
    D. According to the patrolman's report, there wasn't nobody in the store when the explosion occurred.
    E. The sergeant's suggestion was not at all unsound, but no one agreed with him.

15. A. The driver and the passenger they were both found to be intoxicated.
    B. The driver and the passenger talked slowly and not too clearly.
    C. Neither the driver nor his passengers were able to give a coherent account of the accident.
    D. In a corner of the room sat the passenger, quietly dozing.
    E. the driver finally told a strange and unbelievable story, which the passenger contradicted.

16. A. Under the circumstances I decided not to continue my examination of the premises.
    B. There are many difficulties now not comparable with those existing in 1960.
    C. Friends of the accused were heard to announce that the witness had better been away on the day of the trial.
    D. The two criminals escaped in the confusion that followed the explosion.
    E. The aged man was struck by the considerateness of the patrolman's offer.

17. A. An assemblage of miscellaneous weapons lay on the table.
    B. Ample opportunities were given to the defendant to obtain counsel.
    C. The speaker often alluded to his past experience with youthful offenders in the armed forces.
    D. The sudden appearance of the truck aroused my suspicions.
    E. Her studying had a good affect on her grades in high school.

18. A. He sat down in the theater and began to watch the movie.
    B. The girl had ridden horses since she was four years old.
    C. Application was made on behalf of the prosecutor to cite the witness for contempt.
    D. The bank robber, with his two accomplices, were caught in the act.
    E. His story is simply not credible.

19. A. The angry boy said that he did not like those kind of friends.
    B. The merchant's financial condition was so precarious that he felt he must avail himself of any offer of assistance.
    C. He is apt to promise more than he can perform.
    D. Looking at the messy kitchen, the housewife felt like crying.
    E. A clerk was left in charge of the stolen property.

20. A. His wounds were aggravated by prolonged exposure to sub-freezing temperatures.
    B. The prosecutor remarked that the witness was not averse to changing his story each time he was interviewed.
    C. The crime pattern indicated that the burglars were adapt in the handling of explosives.
    D. His rigid adherence to a fixed plan brought him into renewed conflict with his subordinates.
    E. He had anticipated that the sentence would be delivered by noon.

21. A. The whole arraignment procedure is badly in need of revision.
    B. After his glasses were broken in the fight, he would of gone to the optometrist if he could.
    C. Neither Tom nor Jack brought his lunch to work.
    D. He stood aside until the quarrel was over.
    E. A statement in the psychiatrist's report disclosed that the probationer vowed to have his revenge.

22. A. His fiery and intemperate speech to the striking employees fatally affected any chance of a future reconciliation.
    B. The wording of the statute has been variously construed.
    C. The defendant's attorney, speaking in the courtroom, called the official a demagogue who contempuously disregarded the judge's orders.
    D. The baseball game is likely to be the most exciting one this year.
    E. The mother divided the cookies among her two children.

23. A. There was only a bed and a dresser in the dingy room.
    B. John was one of the few students that have protested the new rule.
    C. It cannot be argued that the child's testimony is negligible; it is, on the contrary, of the greatest importance.
    D. The basic criterion for clearance was so general that officials resolved any doubts in favor of dismissal.
    E. Having just returned from a long vacation, the officer found the city unbearably hot.

24. A. The librarian ought to give more help to small children.
    B. The small boy was criticized by the teacher because he often wrote careless.
    C. It was generally doubted whether the women would permit the use of her apartment for intelligence operations.
    D. The probationer acts differently every time the officer visits him.
    E. Each of the newly appointed officers has 12 years of service.

25. A. The North is the most industrialized region in the country.
    B. L. Patrick Gray 3d, the bureau's acting director, stated that, while "rehabilitation is fine" for some convicted criminals, "it is a useless gesture for those who resist every such effort."
    C. Careless driving, faulty mechanism, narrow or badly kept roads all play their part in causing accidents.
    D. The childrens' books were left in the bus.
    E. It was a matter of internal security; consequently, he felt no inclination to rescind his previous order.

25.____

KEY (CORRECT ANSWERS)

1.	C		11.	C
2.	B		12.	D
3.	D		13.	B
4.	C		14.	D
5.	E		15.	A
6.	A		16.	C
7.	C		17.	E
8.	B		18.	D
9.	B		19.	A
10.	C		20.	C

21. B
22. E
23. B
24. B
25. D

TEST 2

DIRECTIONS: Each question or incomplete statement is followed by several suggested answers or completions. Select the one that BEST answers the question or completes the statement. *PRINT THE LETTER OF THE CORRECT ANSWER IN THE SPACE AT THE RIGHT.*

Questions 1-6.

DIRECTIONS: Each of Questions 1 through 6 consists of a statement which contains a word (one of those underlined) that is either incorrectly used because it is not in keeping with the meaning the quotation is evidently intended to convey, or is misspelled. There is only one INCORRECT word in each quotation. Of the four underlined words, determine if the first one should be replaced by the word lettered A, the second replaced by the word lettered B, the third replaced by the word lettered C, or the fourth replaced by the word lettered D.

1. Whether one depends on fluorescent or artificial light or both, adequate standards should be maintained by means of systematic tests.
   A. natural   B. safeguards   C. established   D. routine

2. A police officer has to be prepared to assume his knowledge as a social scientist in the community.
   A. forced   B. role   C. philosopher   D. street

3. It is practically impossible to indicate whether a sentence is too long simply by measuring its length.
   A. almost   B. tell   C. very   D. guessing

4. Strong leaders are required to organize a community for delinquency prevention and for dissemination of organized crime and drug addiction.
   A. tactics   B. important   C. control   D. meetings

5. The demonstrators who were taken to the Criminal Courts building in Manhattan (because it was large enough to accommodate them), contended that the arrests were unwarranted.
   A. demonstraters
   C. accomodate
   B. Manhatten
   D. unwarranted

6. They were guaranteed a calm atmosphere, free from harassment, which would be conducive to quiet consideration of the indictments.
   A. guarenteed
   C. harassment
   B. atmspher
   D. inditements

Questions 7-11.

DIRECTIONS: Each of Questions 7 through 11 consists of a statement containing four words in capital letters. One of these words in capital letters is not in keeping with the meaning which the statement is evidently intended to carry. The four words in capital letters in each statement are reprinted after the statement. Print the capital letter preceding the one of the four words which does MOST to spoil the true meaning of the statement in the space at the right.

7. Retirement and pension systems are essential not only to provide employees with with a means of support in the future, but also to prevent longevity and CHARITABLE considerations from UPSETTING the PROMOTIONAL opportunities RETIRED members of the career service. 7.____
   A. charitable   B. upsetting   C. promotional   D. retired

8. Within each major DIVISION in a properly set up public or private organization, provision is made so that each NECESSARY activity is CARED for and lines of authority and responsibility are clear-cut and INFINITE. 8.____
   A. division   B. necessary   C. cared   D. infinite

9. In public service, the scale of salaries paid must be INCIDENTAL to the services rendered, with due CONSIDERATION for the attraction of the desired MANPOWER and for the maintenance of a standard of living COMMENSURATE with the work to be performed. 9.____
   A. incidental   B. consideration
   C. manpower   D. commensurate

10. An understanding of the AIMS of an organization by the staff will AID greatly in increasing the DEMAND of the correspondence work of the office, and will to a large extent DETERMINE the nature of the correspondence. 10.____
    A. aims   B. aid   C. demand   D. determine

11. BECAUSE the Civil Service Commission strongly feels that the MERIT system is a key factor in the MAINTENANCE of democratic government, it has adopted as one of its major DEFENSES the progressive democratization of its own procedures in dealing with candidates for positions in the public service. 11.____
    A. Because   B. merit   C. maintenance   D. defenses

Questions 12-14.

DIRECTIONS: Questions 12 through 14 consist of one sentence each. Each sentence contains an incorrectly used word. First, decide which is the incorrectly used word. Then, from among the options given, decide which word, when substituted for the incorrectly used word, makes the meaning of the sentence clear.
EXAMPLE:
The U.S. national income exhibits a pattern of long term deflection.
   A. reflection   B. subjection   C. rejoicing   D. growth

The word *deflection* in the sentence does not convey the meaning the sentence evidently intended to convey. The word *growth* (Answer D), when substituted for the word *deflection*, makes the meaning of the sentence clear. Accordingly, the answer to the question is D.

12. The study commissioned by the joint committee fell compassionately short of the mark and would have to be redone.
    A. successfully
    B. insignificantly
    C. experimentally
    D. woefully

    12.____

13. He will not idly exploit any violation of the provisions of the order.
    A. tolerate   B. refuse   C. construe   D. guard

    13.____

14. The defendant refused to be virile and bitterly protested service.
    A. irked   B. feasible   C. docile   D. credible

    14.____

Questions 15-25.

DIRECTIONS: Questions 15 through 25 consist of short paragraphs. Each paragraph contains one word which is INCORRECTLY used because it is NOT in keeping with the meaning of the paragraph. Find the word in each paragraph which is INCORRECTLY used and then select as the answer the suggested word which should be substituted for the incorrectly used word.

SAMPLE QUESTION:
In determining who is to do the work in your unit, you will have to decide just who does what from day to day. One of your lowest responsibilities is to assign work so that everybody gets a fair share and that everyone can do his part well.
    A. new   B. old   C. important   D. performance

EXPLANATION:
The word which is NOT in keeping with the meaning of the paragraph is *lowest*. This is the INCORRECTLY used word. The suggested word *important* would be in keeping with the meaning of the paragraph and should be substituted for *lowest*. Therefore, the CORRECT answer is choice C.

15. If really good practice in the elimination of preventable injuries is to be achieved and held in any establishment, top management must refuse full and definite responsibility and must apply a good share of its attention to the task.
    A. accept   B. avoidable   C. duties   D. problem

    15.____

16. Recording the human face for identification is by no means the only service performed by the camera in the field of investigation. When the trial of any issue takes place, a word picture is sought to be distorted to the court of incidents, occurrences, or events which are in dispute.
    A. appeals   B. description   C. portrayed   D. deranged

    16.____

163

17. In the collection of physical evidence, it cannot be emphasized too strongly that a haphazard systematic search at the scene of the crime is vital. Nothing must be overlooked. Often the only leads in a case will come from the results of this search.
    A. important
    B. investigation
    C. proof
    D. thorough

17.____

18. If an investigator has reason to suspect that the witness is mentally stable, or a habitual drunkard, he should leave no stone unturned in his investigation to determine if the witness was under the influence of liquor or drugs, or was mentally unbalanced either at the time of the occurrence to which he testified or at the time of the trial.
    A. accused
    B. clue
    C. deranged
    D. question

18.____

19. The use of records is a valuable step in crime investigation and is the main reason every department should maintain accurate reports. Crimes are not committed through the use of departmental records alone but from the use of all records, of almost every type, wherever they may be found and whenever they give any incidental information regarding the criminal.
    A. accidental
    B. necessary
    C. reported
    D. solved

19.____

20. In the years since passage of the Harrison Narcotic Act of 1914, making the possession of opium amphetamines illegal in most circumstances, drug use has become a subject of considerable scientific interest and investigation. There is at present a voluminous literature on drug use of various kinds.
    A. ingestion
    B. derivatives
    C. addiction
    D. opiates

20.____

21. Of course, the fact that criminal laws are extremely patterned in definition does not mean that the majority of persons who violate them are dealt with as criminals. Quite the contrary, for a great many forbidden acts are voluntarily engaged in within situations of privacy and go unobserved and unreported.
    A. symbolic
    B. casual
    C. scientific
    D. broad-gauged

21.____

22. The most punitive way to study punishment is to focus attention on the pattern of punitive action: to study how a penalty is applied, too study what is done to or taken from an offender.
    A. characteristic
    B. degrading
    C. objective
    D. distinguished

22.____

23. The most common forms of punishment in times past have been death, physical torture, mutilation, branding, public humiliation, fines, forfeits of property, banishment, transportation, and imprisonment. Although this list is by no means differentiated, practically every form of punishment has had several variations and applications.
    A. specific
    B. simple
    C. exhaustive
    D. characteristic

23.____

24. There is another important line of inference between ordinary and professional   24.____
criminals, and that is the source from which they are recruited. The
professional criminal seems to be drawn from legitimate employment and, in
many instances, from parallel vocations or pursuits.
   A. demarcation   B. justification   C. superiority   D. reference

25. He took the position that the success of the program was insidious on getting   25.____
additional revenue.
   A. reputed   B. contingent   C. failure   D. indeterminate

KEY (CORRECT ANSWERS)

1.	A		11.	D
2.	B		12.	D
3.	B		13.	A
4.	C		14.	C
5.	D		15.	A
6.	C		16.	C
7.	D		17.	D
8.	D		18.	C
9.	A		19.	D
10.	C		20.	B

21. D
22. C
23. C
24. A
25. B

TEST 3

DIRECTIONS: Each question or incomplete statement is followed by several suggested answers or completions. Select the one that BEST answers the question or completes the statement. *PRINT THE LETTER OF THE CORRECT ANSWER IN THE SPACE AT THE RIGHT.*

Questions 1-5.

DIRECTIONS: Questions 1 through 5 are to be answered on the basis of the following.

You are a supervising officer in an investigative unit. Earlier in the day, you directed Detectives Tom Dixon and Sal Mayo to investigate a reported assault and robbery in a liquor store within your area of jurisdiction.

Detective Dixon has submitted to you a preliminary investigative report containing the following information:

- At 1630 hours on 2/20, arrived at Joe's Liquor Store at 350 SW Avenue with Detective Mayo to investigate A & R.
- At store interviewed Rob Ladd, store manager, who stated that he and Joe Brown (store owner) had been stuck up about ten minutes prior to our arrival.
- Ladd described the robbers as male whites in their late teens or early twenties. Further stated that one of the robbers displayed what appeared to be an automatic pistol as he entered the store, and said, *Give us the money or we'll kill you.* Ladd stated that Brown then reached under the counter where he kept a loaded .38 caliber pistol. Several shots followed, and Ladd threw himself to the floor.
- The robbers fled, and Ladd didn't know if any money had been taken.
- At this point, Ladd realized that Brown was unconscious on the floor and bleeding from a head wound.
- Ambulance called by Ladd, and Brown was removed by same to General Hospital.
- Personally interviewed John White, 382 Dartmouth Place, who stated he was inside store at the time of occurrence. White states that he hid behind a wine display upon hearing someone say, *Give us the money.* He then heard shots and saw two young men run from the store to a yellow car parked at the curb. White was unable to further describe auto. States the taller of the two men drove the car away while the other sat on passenger side in front.
- Recovered three spent .38 caliber bullets from premises and delivered them to Crime Lab.
- To General Hospital at 1800 hours but unable to interview Brown, who was under sedation and suffering from shock and a laceration of the head.
- Alarm #12487 transmitted for car and occupants.
- Case Active.

Based solely on the contents of the preliminary investigation submitted by Detective Dixon, select one sentence from the following groups of sentences which is MOST accurate and is grammatically correct.

1. A. Both robbers were armed.
    B. Each of the robbers were described as a male white.
    C. Neither robber was armed.
    D. Mr. Ladd stated that one of the robbers was armed.

2. A. Mr. Brown fired three shots from his revolver.
    B. Mr. Brown was shot in the head by one of the robbers.
    C. Mr. Brown suffered a gunshot wound of the head during the course of the robbery.
    D. Mr. Brown was taken to General Hospital by ambulance.

3. A. Shots were fired after one of the robbers said, *Give us the money or we'll kill you.*
    B. After one of the robbers demanded the money from Mr. Brown, he fired a shot.
    C. The preliminary investigation indicated that although Mr. Brown did not have a license for the gun, he was justified in using deadly physical force.
    D. Mr. Brown was interviewed at General Hospital.

4. A. Each of the witnesses were customers in the store at the time of occurrence.
    B. Neither of the witnesses interviewed was the owner of the liquor store.
    C. Neither of the witnesses interviewed were the owner of the store.
    D. Neither of the witnesses was employed by Mr. Brown.

5. A. Mr. Brown arrived at General Hospital at about 5:00 P.M.
    B. Neither of the robbers was injured during the robbery.
    C. The robbery occurred at 3:30 P.M. on February 10.
    D. One of the witnesses called the ambulance.

Questions 6-10.

DIRECTIONS: Each of Questions 6 through 10 consists of information given in outline form and four sentences labeled A, B, C, and D. For each question, choose the one sentence which CORRECTLY expresses the information given in outline form and which also displays PROPER English usage.

6. Client's Name: Joanna Jones
    Number of Children: 3
    Client's Income: None
    Client's Marital Status: Single

    A. Joanna Jones is an unmarried client with three children who have no income.
    B. Joanna Jones, who is single and has no income, a client she has three children.
    C. Joanna Jones, whose three children are clients, is single and has no income.
    D. Joanna Jones, who has three children, is an unmarried client with no income.

7. Client's Name: Bertha Smith
    Number of Children: 2
    Client's Rent: $1050 per month
    Number of Rooms: 4

    A. Bertha Smith, a client, pays $1050 per month for her four rooms with two children.
    B. Client Bertha Smith has two children and pays $1050 per month for four rooms.
    C. Client Bertha Smith is paying $1050 per month for two children with four rooms.
    D. For four rooms and two children client Bertha Smith pays $1050 per month.

7.____

8. Name of Employee: Cynthia Dawes
    Number of Cases Assigned: 9
    Date Cases were Assigned: 12/16
    Number of Assigned Cases Completed: 8

    A. On December 16, employee Cynthia Dawes was assigned nine cases; she has completed eight of these cases.
    B. Cynthia Dawes, employee on December 16, assigned nine cases, completed eight.
    C. Being employed on December 16, Cynthia Dawes completed eight of nine assigned cases.
    D. Employee Cynthia Dawes, she was assigned nine cases and completed eight, on December 16.

8.____

9. Place of Audit: Broadway Center
    Names of Auditors: Paul Cahn, Raymond Perez
    Date of Audit: 11/20
    Number of Cases Audited: 41

    A. On November 20, at the Broadway Center 41 cases was audited by auditors Paul Cahn and Raymond Perez.
    B. Auditors Raymond Perez and Paul Cahn has audited 41 cases at the Broadway Center on November 20.
    C. At the Broadway Center, on November 20, auditors Paul Cahn and Raymond Perez audited 41 cases.
    D. Auditors Paul Cahn and Raymond Perez at the Broadway Center, on November 20, is auditing 41 cases.

9.____

10. Name of Client: Barbra Levine
    Client's Monthly Income: $2100
    Client's Monthly Expenses: $4520

    A. Barbra Levine is a client, her monthly income is $2100 and her monthly expenses is $4520.
    B. Barbra Levine's monthly income is $2100 and she is a client, with whose monthly expenses are $4520.

10.____

4 (#3)

C. Barbra Levine is a client whose monthly income is $2100 and whose monthly expenses are $4520.
D. Barbra Levine, a client, is with a monthly income which is $2100 and monthly expenses which are $4520.

Questions 11-13.

DIRECTIONS: Questions 11 through 13 involve several statements of fact presented in a very simple way. These statements of fact are followed by 4 choices which attempt to incorporate all of the facts into one logical statement which is properly constructed and grammatically correct.

11. I. Mr. Brown was sweeping the sidewalk in front of his house.
    II. He was sweeping it because it was dirty.
    III. He swept the refuse into the street.
    IV. Police Officer gave him a ticket.

    Which one of the following BEST presents the information given above?
    A. Because his sidewalk was dirty, Mr. Brown received a ticket from Officer Green when he swept the refuse into the street.
    B. Police Officer Green gave Mr. Brown a ticket because his sidewalk was dirty and he swept the refuse into the street.
    C. Police Officer Green gave Mr. Brown a ticket for sweeping refuse into the street because his sidewalk was dirty.
    D. Mr. Brown, who was sweeping refuse from his dirty sidewalk into the street, was given a ticket by Police Officer Green.

11.____

12. I. Sergeant Smith radioed for help.
    II. The sergeant did so because the crowd was getting larger.
    III. It was 10:00 A.M. when he made his call.
    IV. Sergeant Smith was not in uniform at the time of occurrence.

    Which one of the following BEST presents the information given above?
    A. Sergeant Smith, although not on duty at the time, radioed for help at 10 o'clock because the crowd was getting uglier.
    B. Although not in uniform, Sergeant Smith called for help at 10:00 A.M. because the crowd was getting uglier.
    C. Sergeant Smith radioed for help at 10:00 A.M. because the crowd was getting larger.
    D. Although he was not in uniform, Sergeant Smith radioed for help at 10:00 A.M. because the crowd was getting larger.

12.____

13. I. The payroll office is open on Fridays.
    II. Paychecks are distributed from 9:00 A.M. to 12 Noon.
    III. The office is open on Fridays because that's the only day the payroll staff is available.
    IV. It is open for the specified hours in order to permit employees to cash checks at the bank during lunch hour.

13.____

The choice below which MOST clearly and accurately presents the above idea is:
  A. Because the payroll office is open on Fridays from 9:00 A.M. to 12 Noon, employees can cash their checks when the payroll staff is available.
  B. Because the payroll staff is only available on Fridays until noon, employees can cash their checks during their lunch hour.
  C. Because the payroll staff is available only on Fridays, the office is open from 9:00 A.M. to 12 Noon to allow employees to cash their checks.
  D. Because of payroll staff availability, the payroll office is open on Fridays. It is open from 9:00 A.M. to 12 Noon so that distributed paychecks can be cashed at the bank while employees are on their lunch hour.

Questions 14-16.

DIRECTIONS: In each of Questions 14 through 6, the four sentences are from a paragraph in a report. They are not in the right order. Which of the following arrangements is the BEST one?

14. I. An executive may answer a letter by writing his reply on the face of the letter itself instead of having a return letter typed.
     II. This procedure is efficient because it saves the executive's time, the typist's time, and saves office file space.
     III. Copying machines are used in small offices as well as large offices to save time and money in making brief replies to business letters.
     IV. A copy is made on a copy machine to go into the company files, while the original is mailed back to the sender.

   The CORRECT answer is:
     A. I, II, IV, III   B. I, IV, II, III   C. III, I, IV, II   D. III, IV, II, I

14.____

15. I. Most organizations favor one of the types but always include the others to a lesser degree.
     II. However, we can detect a definite trend toward greater use of symbolic control.
     III. We suggest that our local police agencies are today primarily utilizing material control.
     IV. Control can be classified into three types: physical, material, and symbolic.

   The CORRECT answer is:
     A. IV, II, III, I   B. II, I, IV, III   C. III, IV, II, I   D. IV, I, III, II

15.____

16. I. They can and do take advantage of ancient political and geographical boundaries, which often give them sanctuary from effective policy activity.
     II. This country is essentially a country of small police forces, each operating independently within the limits of its jurisdiction.
     III. The boundaries that define and limit police operations do not hinder the movement of criminals, of course.
     IV. The machinery of law enforcement in America is fragmented, complicated, and frequently overlapping.

16.____

The CORRECT answer is:
A. III, I, IV   B. II, IV, I, III   C. IV, II, III, I   D. IV, III, II, I

17. Examine the following sentence, and then choose from below the words which should be inserted in the blank spaces to produce the best sentence.
    The unit has exceeded _____ goals and the employees are satisfied with _____ accomplishments.
    A. their, it's   B. it's; it's   C. its, there   D. its, their

17.____

18. Examine the following sentence, and then choose from below the words which should be inserted in the blank spaces to produce the best sentence.
    Research indicates that employees who _____ no opportunity for close social relationships often find their work unsatisfying, and this _____ of satisfaction often reflects itself in low production.
    A. have; lack   B. have; excess   C. has; lack   D. has; excess

18.____

19. Words in a sentence must be arranged properly to make sure that the intended meaning of the sentence is clear.
    The sentence below that does NOT make sense because a clause has been separated from the word on which its meaning depends is:
    A. To be a good writer, clarity is necessary.
    B. To be a good writer, you must write clearly.
    C. You must write clearly to be a good writer.
    D. Clarity is necessary to good writing.

19.____

Questions 20-21.

DIRECTIONS: Each of Questions 20 and 21 consists of a statement which contains a word (one of those underlined) that is either incorrectly used because it is not in keeping with the meaning the quotation is evidently intended to convey, or is misspelled. There is only one INCORRECT word in each quotation. Of the four underlined words, determine if the first one should be replaced by the word lettered A, the second one replaced by the word lettered B, the third one replaced by the word lettered C, or the fourth one replaced by the word lettered D.

20. The alleged killer was occasionally permitted to excercise in the corridor.
    A. alledged   B. ocasionally   C. permited   D. exercise

20.____

21. Defense counsel stated, in affect, that their conduct was permissible under the First Amendment.
    A. council   B. effect   C. there   D. permissable

21.____

Question 22.

DIRECTIONS: Question 22 consists of one sentence. This sentence contains an incorrectly used word. First, decide which is the incorrectly used word. Then, from among the options given, decide which word, when substituted for the incorrectly used word, makes the meaning of the sentence clear.

22. As today's violence has no single cause, so its causes have no single scheme. 22.____
    A. deference   B. cure   C. flaw   D. relevance

23. In the sentence, *A man in a light-grey suit waited thirty-five minutes in the ante-room for the all-important document*, the word IMPROPERLY hyphenated is 23.____
    A. light-grey
    B. thirty-five
    C. ante-room
    D. all-important

24. In the sentence, *The candidate wants to file his application for preference before it is too late*, the word *before* is used as a(n) 24.____
    A. preposition
    B. subordinating conjunction
    C. pronoun
    D. adverb

25. In the sentence, *The perpetrators ran from the scene*, the word *from* is a 25.____
    A. preposition   B. pronoun   C. verb   D. conjunction

KEY (CORRECT ANSWERS)

1. D
2. D
3. A
4. B
5. D

6. D
7. B
8. A
9. C
10. C

11. D
12. D
13. D
14. C
15. D

16. C
17. D
18. A
19. A
20. D

21. B
22. B
23. C
24. B
25. A

PREPARING WRITTEN MATERIAL

PARAGRAPH REARRANGEMENT
COMMENTARY

The sentences that follow are in scrambled order. You are to rearrange them in proper order and indicate the letter choice containing the correct answer at the space at the right.

Each group of sentences in this section is actually a paragraph presented in scrambled order. Each sentence in the group has a place in that paragraph; no sentence is to be left out. You are to read each group of sentences and decide upon the best order in which to put the sentences so as to form a well-organized paragraph.

The questions in this section measure the ability to solve a problem when all the facts relevant to its solution are not given.

More specifically, certain positions of responsibility and authority require the employee to discover connection between events sometimes, apparently, unrelated. In order to do this, the employee will find it necessary to correctly infer that unspecified events have probably occurred or are likely to occur. This ability becomes especially important when action must be taken on incomplete information.

Accordingly, these questions require competitors to choose among several suggested alternatives, each of which presents a different sequential arrangement of the events. Competitors must choose the MOST logical of the suggested sequences.

In order to do so, they may be required to draw on general knowledge to infer missing concepts or events that are essential to sequencing the given events. Competitors should be careful to infer only what is essential to the sequence. The plausibility of the wrong alternatives will always require the inclusion of unlikely events or of additional chains of events which are NOT essential to sequencing the given events.

It's very important to remember that you are looking for the best of the four possible choices, and that the best choice of all may not even be one of the answers you're given to choose from.

There is no one right way to solve these problems. Many people have found it helpful to first write out the order of the sentences, as they would have arranged them, on their scrap paper before looking at the possible answers. If their optimum answer is there, this can save them some time. If it isn't, this method can still give insight into solving the problem. Others find it most helpful to just go through each of the possible choices, contrasting each as they go along. You should use whatever method feels comfortable and works for you.

While most of these types of questions are not that difficult, we've added a higher percentage of the difficult type, just to give you more practice. Usually there are only one or two questions on this section that contain such subtle distinctions that you're unable to answer confidently. And you then may find yourself stuck deciding between two possible choices, neither of which you're sure about.

PREPARING WRITTEN MATERIAL
PARAGRAPH REARRANGEMENT
EXAMINATION SECTION
TEST 1

DIRECTIONS: The sentences that follow are in scrambled order. You are to rearrange them in proper order and indicate the letter choice containing the CORRECT answer. *PRINT THE LETTER OF THE CORRECT ANSWER IN THE SPACE AT THE RIGHT.*

1. Police Officer Jenner responds to the scene of a burglary at 2106 La Vista Boulevard. He is approached by an elderly man named Richard Jenkins, whose account of the incident includes the following five sentences:
   I. I saw that the lock on my apartment door had been smashed and the door was open.
   II. My apartment was a shambles; my belongings were everywhere and my television set was missing.
   III. As I walked down the hallway toward the bedroom, I heard someone opening a window.
   IV. I left work at 5:30 P.M. and took the bus home.
   V. At that time, I called the police.
   The MOST logical order for the above sentence to appear in the report is
   A. I, V, IV, II, III   B. IV, I, II, III, V   C. I, V, II, III, IV   D. IV, III, II, V, I

   1.____

2. Police Officer LaJolla is writing an Incident Report in which back-up assistance was required. The report will contain the following five sentences:
   I. The radio dispatcher asked what my location was and he then dispatched patrol cars for back-up assistance.
   II. At approximately 9:30 P.M., while I was walking my assigned footpost, a gunman fired three shots at me.
   III. I quickly turned around and saw a white male, approximately 5'10", with black hair, wearing blue jeans, a yellow T-shirt, and white sneaker, running across the avenue carrying a handgun.
   IV. When the back-up officers arrived, we searched the area but could not find the suspect.
   V. I advised the radio dispatcher that a gunman had just fired a gun at me, and then I gave the dispatcher a description of the man
   The MOST logical order for the above sentences to appear in the report is:
   A. III, V, II, IV, I   B. II, III, V, I, IV   C. III, II, IV, I, V   D. II, V, I, III, IV

   2.____

3. Police Officer Durant is completing a report of a robbery and assault. The report will contain the following five sentences:
   I. I went to Mount Snow Hospital to interview a man who was attacked and robbed of his wallet earlier that night.
   II. An ambulance arrived at 82nd Street and 3rd Avenue and took an intoxicated, wounded man to Mount Snow Hospital
   III. Two youths attacked the man and stole his wallet.

   3.____

IV. A well-dressed man left Hanratty's Bar very drunk, with his wallet hanging out of his back pocket.
V. A passerby dialed 911 and requested police and ambulance assistance.
The MOST logical order for the above sentences to appear in the report is
    A. I, II, IV, III, V   B. IV, III, V, II, I   C. IV, V, II, III, I   D. V, IV, III, II, I

4. Police Officer Boswell is preparing a report of an armed robbery and assault which will contain the following five sentences:
    I. Both men approached the bartender and one of them drew a gun.
    II. The bartender immediately went to grab the phone at the bar.
    III. One of the men leaped over the counter and smashed a bottle over the bartender's head.
    IV. Two men in a blue Buick drove up to the bar and went inside.
    V. I found the cash register empty and the bartender unconscious on the floor, with the phone still dangling off the hook.
    The MOST logical order for the above sentences to appear in the report is
        A. IV, I, II, II, V   B. V, IV, III, I, II   C. IV, III, II, V, I   D. II, I, III, IV, V

4.____

5. Police Officer Mitzler is preparing a report of a bank robbery, which will contain the following five sentences:
    I. The teller complied with the instructions on the note, but also hit the silent alarm.
    II. The perpetrator then fled south on Broadway.
    III. A suspicious male entered the bank at approximately 10:45 A.M.
    IV. At this time, an undetermined amount of money has been taken.
    V. He approached the teller on the far right side and handed her a note.
    The MOST logical order for the above sentences to appear in the report is:
        A. III, V, I, II, IV   B. I, III, V, II, IV   C. III, V, IV, I, II   D. III, V, II, IV, I

5.____

6. A Police Officer is preparing an Accident Report for an accident which occurred at the intersection of East 119th Street and Lexington Avenue. The report will include the following five sentences:
    I. On September 18, while driving ten children to school, a school bus driver passed out.
    II. Upon arriving at the scene, I notified the dispatcher to send an ambulance.
    III. I notified the parents of each child once I got to the station house.
    IV. He said the school bus, while traveling west on East 119th Street, struck a parked Ford which was on the southwest corner of East 119th Street.
    V. A witness by the name of John Ramos came up to me to describe what happened.
    The MOST logical order for the above sentences to appear in the Accident Report is:
        A. I, II, V, III, IV   B. I, II, V, IV, III   C. II, V, I, III, IV   D. II, V, I, IV, III

6.____

7. A Police Officer is preparing a report concerning a dispute. The report will contain the following five sentences:
    I. The passenger got out of the back of the taxi and leaned through the front window to complain to the driver about the fare.

7.____

II. The driver of the taxi caught up with the passenger and knocked him to the ground; the passenger then kicked the driver and a scuffle ensued.
III. The taxi drew up in front of the high-rise building and stopped.
IV. The driver got out of the taxi and followed the passenger into the lobby of the apartment building.
V. The doorman tried but was unable to break up the fight, at which point he called the precinct.

The MOST logical order for the above sentences to appear in the report is
    A. III, I, IV, II, V   B. III, IV, I, II, V   C. III, IV, II, V, I   D. V, I, III, IV, II

8. Police Officer Morrow is writing an Incident Report. The report will include the following four sentences:
   I. The man reached into his pocket and pulled out a gun.
   II. While on foot patrol, I identified a suspect, who was wanted for six robberies in the area, from a wanted picture I was carrying.
   III. I drew my weapon and fired six rounds at the suspect, killing him instantly.
   IV. I called for back-up assistance and told the man to put his hands up.

   The MOST logical order for the above sentences to appear in the report is
       A. II, III, IV, I   B. IV, I, III, II   C. IV, I, II, III   D. II, IV, I, III

9. Sergeant Allen responds to a call at 16 Grove Street regarding a missing child. At the scene, the Sergeant is met by Police Officer Samuels, who gives a brief account of the incident consisting of the following five sentences:
   I. I transmitted the description and waited for you to arrive before I began searching the area.
   II. Mrs. Banks, the mother, reports that she last saw her daughter Julie about 7:30 A.M. when she took her to school.
   III. About 6 P.M., my partner and I arrived at this location to investigate a report of a missing 8-year-old girl.
   IV. When Mrs. Banks left her, Julie was wearing a red and white striped T-shirt, blue jeans, and white sneakers.
   V. Mrs. Banks dropped her off in front of the playground of P.S. 11.

   The MOST logical order for the above sentences to appear in the report is
       A. III, V, IV, II, I   B. III, II, V, IV, I   C. III, IV, I, II, V   D. III, II, IV, I, V

10. Police Officer Franco is completing a report of an assault. The report will contain the following five sentences:
    I. In the park I observed an elderly man lying on the ground, bleeding from a back wound.
    II. I applied first aid to control the bleeding and radioed for an ambulance to respond.
    III. The elderly man stated that he was sitting on the park bench when he was attacked from behind by two males.
    IV. I received a report of a man's screams coming from inside the park, and I went to investigate.
    V. The old man could not give a description of his attackers.

    The MOST logical order for the above sentences to appear in the report is
        A. IV, I, II, III, V   B. V, III, I, IV, II   C. IV, III, V, II, I   D. II, I, V, IV, III

11. Police Officer Williams is completing a Crime Report. The report contains the following five sentences:
    I. As Police Officer Hanson and I approached the store, we noticed that the front door was broken.
    II. After determining that the burglars had fled, we notified the precinct of the burglary.
    III. I walked through the front door as Police Officer Hanson walked around to the back.
    IV. At approximately midnight, an alarm was heard at the Apex Jewelry Store.
    V. We searched the store and found no one.
    The MOST logical order for the above sentences to appear in the report is
    A. I, IV, II, III, V   B. I, IV, III, V, II   C. IV, I, III, II, V   D. IV, I, III, V, II

12. Police Officer Clay is giving a report to the news media regarding someone who has jumped from the Empire State Building. His report will include the following five sentences:
    I. I responded to the 86th floor, where I found the person at the edge of the roof.
    II. A security guard at the building had reported that a man was on the roof at the 86th floor.
    III. At 5:30 P.M., the person jumped from the building.
    IV. I received a call from the radio dispatcher at 4:50 P.M. to respond to the Empire State Building.
    V. I tried to talk to the person and convince him not to jump.
    The MOST logical order for the above sentences to appear in the report is
    A. I, II, IV, III, V   B. III, IV, I, II, V   C. II, IV, I, III, V   D. IV, II, I, V, III

13. The following five sentences are part of a report of a burglary written by Police Officer Reed:
    I. When I arrived at 2400 1st Avenue, I noticed that the door was slightly open.
    II. I yelled out, *Police, don't move!*
    III. As I entered the apartment, I saw a man with a TV set passing through a window to another man standing on a fire escape.
    IV. While on foot patrol, I was informed by the radio dispatcher that a burglary was in progress at 2400 1st Avenue.
    V. However, the burglars quickly ran down the fire escape.
    The MOST logical order for the above sentences to appear in the report is
    A. I, III, IV, V, II   B. IV, I, III, V, II   C. IV, I, III, II, V   D. I, IV, III, II, V

14. Police Officer Jenkins is preparing a report for Lost or Stolen Property. The report will include the following five sentences:
    I. On the stairs, Mr. Harris slipped on a wet leaf and fell on the landing.
    II. It wasn't until he got to the token booth that Mr. Harris realized his wallet was no longer in his back pants pocket.
    III. A boy wearing a football jersey helped him up and brushed off the back of Mr. Harris' pants.
    IV. Mr. Harris states he was walking up the stairs to the elevated subway at Queensborough Plaza.
    V. Before Mr. Harris could thank him, the boy was running down the stairs to the street.

The MOST logical order for the above sentences to appear in the report is
A. IV, III, V, I, II   B. IV, I, III, V, II   C. I, IV, II, III, V   D. I, II, IV, III, V

15. Police Officer Hubbard is completing a report of a missing person. The report will contain the following five sentences:
    I. I visited the store at 7:55 P.M. and asked the employees if they had seen a girl fitting the description I had been given.
    II. She gave me a description and said she had gone into the local grocery store at about 6:15 P.M.
    III. I asked the woman for a description of her daughter.
    IV. The distraught woman called the precinct to report that her daughter, aged 12, had not returned from an errand.
    V. The storekeeper said a girl matching the description had been in the store earlier, but he could not give an exact time.
    The MOST logical order for the above sentences to appear in the report is
    A. I, III, II, V, IV   B. IV, III, II, I, V   C. V, I, II, III, IV   D. III, I, II, IV, V

16. A police officer is completing an entry in his Daily Activity Log regarding traffic summonses which he issued. The following five sentences will be included in the entry:
    I. I was on routine patrol parked 16 yards west of 170th Street and Clay Avenue.
    II. The summonses were issued for unlicensed operator and disobeying a steady red light.
    III. At 8 A.M. hours, I observed an auto traveling westbound on 170th Street not stop for a steady red light at the intersection of Clay Avenue and 170th Street.
    IV. I stopped the driver of the auto and determined that he did not have a valid driver's license.
    V. After a brief conversation, I informed the motorist that he was receiving two summonses.
    The MOST logical order for the above sentences to appear in the report is
    A. I, III, IV, V, II   B. III, IV, II, V, I   C. V, II, I, III, IV   D. IV, V, II, I, III

17. The following sentences appeared on an Incident Report:
    I. Three teenagers who had been ejected from the theater were yelling at patrons who were now entering.
    II. Police Officer Dixon told the teenagers to leave the area.
    III. The teenager said that they were told by the manager to leave the theater because they were talking during the movie.
    IV. The theater manager called the precinct at 10:20 P.M. to report a disturbance outside the theater.
    V. A patrol car responded to the theater at 10:42 P.M. and two police officers went over to the teenagers.
    The MOST logical order for the above sentences to appear in the Incident Report is
    A. I, V, IV, III, II   B. IV, I, V, III, II   C. IV, I, III, V, II   D. IV, III, I, V, II

18. Activity Log entries are completed by police officers. Police Officer Samuels has written an entry concerning vandalism and part of it contains the following five sentences:
    I. The man, in his early twenties, ran down the block and around the corner.
    II. A man passing the store threw a brick through a window of the store.
    III. I arrived on the scene and began to question the witnesses about the incident.
    IV. Malcolm Holmes, the owner of the Fast Service Shoe Repair Store, was working in the back of the store at approximately 3 P.M.
    V. After the man fled, Mr. Holmes called the police.
    The MOST logical order for the above sentences to appear in the Activity Log is
       A. IV, II, I, V, III   B. II, IV, I, III, V   C. II, I, IV, III, V   D. IV, II, V, III, I

19. Police Officer Buckley is preparing a report concerning a dispute in a restaurant. The report will contain the following five sentences:
    I. The manager, Charles Chin, and a customer, Edward Green, were standing near the register arguing over the bill.
    II. The manager refused to press any charges providing Green pay the check and leave.
    III. While on foot patrol, I was informed by a passerby of a disturbance in the Dragon Flame Restaurant.
    IV. Green paid the $15.00 check and left the restaurant.
    V. According to witnesses, the customer punched the owner in the face when Chin asked him for the amount due.
    The MOST logical order for the above sentences to appear in the report is
       A. III, I, V, II, IV   B. I, II, III, IV, V   C. V, I, III, II, IV   D. III, V, II, IV, I

20. Police Officer Wilkins is preparing a report for leaving the scene of an accident. The report will include the following five sentences:
    I. The Dodge struck the right rear fender of Mrs. Smith's 2010 Ford and continued on its way.
    II. Mrs. Smith stated she was making a left turn from 40th Street onto Third Avenue.
    III. As the car passed, Mrs. Smith noticed the dangling rear license plate #412AEJ.
    IV. Mrs. Smith complained to police of back pains and was removed by ambulance to Bellevue Hospital.
    V. An old green Dodge traveling up Third Avenue went through the red light at 40th Street and Third Avenue.
    The MOST logical order for the above sentences to appear in the report is
       A. V, III, I, II, IV   B. I, III, II, V, IV   C. IV, V, I, II, III   D. II, V, I, III, IV

21. Detective Simon is completing a Crime Report. The report contains the following five sentences:
    I. Police Officer Chin, while on foot patrol, heard the yelling and ran in the direction of the man.
    II. The man, carrying a large hunting knife, left the High Sierra Sporting Goods Store at approximately 10:30 A.M.

III. When the man heard Police Officer Chin, he stopped, dropped the knife, and began to cry.
IV. As Police Officer Chin approached the man, he drew his gun and yelled, *Police, freeze.*
V. After the man left the store, he began yelling, over and over, *I am going to kill myself!*

The MOST logical order for the above sentences to appear in the report is
   A. V, II, I, IV, III   B. II, V, I, IV, III   C. II, V, IV, I, III   D. II, I, V, IV, III

22. Police Officer Miller is preparing a Complaint Report which will include the following five sentences:
    I. From across the lot, he yelled to the boys to get away from his car.
    II. When he came out of the store, he noticed two teenage boys trying to break into his car.
    III. The boys fled as Mr. Johnson ran to his car.
    IV. Mr. Johnson stated that he parked his car in the municipal lot behind Tams Department Store.
    V. Mr. Johnson saw that the door lock had been broken, but nothing was missing from inside the auto.

    The MOST logical order for the above sentences to appear in the report is
       A. IV, I, II, V, III   B. II, III, I, V, IV   C. IV, II, I, III, V   D. I, II, III, V, IV

23. Police Officer O'Hara completes a Universal Summons for a motorist who has just passed a red traffic light. The Universal Summons includes the following five sentences:
    I. As the car passed the light, I followed in the patrol car.
    II. After the driver stopped the car, he stated that the light was yellow, not red.
    III. A blue Cadillac sedan passed the red light on the corner of 79th Street and 3rd Avenue at 11:25 P.M.
    IV. As a result, the driver was informed that he did pass a red light and that his brake lights were not working.
    V. The driver in the Cadillac stopped his car as soon as he saw the patrol car, and I noticed that the brake lights were not working.

    The MOST logical order for the above sentences to appear in the Universal Summons is
       A. I, III, V, II, IV   B. III, I, V, II, IV   C. III, I, V, IV, II   D. I, III, IV, II, V

24. Detective Egan is preparing a follow-up report regarding a homicide on 170th Street and College Avenue. An unknown male was found at the scene. The report will contain the following five sentences:
    I. Police Officer Gregory wrote down the names, addresses, and phone numbers of the witnesses.
    II. A 911 operator received a call of a man shot and dispatched Police Officers Worth and Gregory to the scene.
    III. They discovered an unidentified male dead on the street.
    IV. Police Officer Worth notified the Precinct Detective Unit immediately.
    V. At approximately 9:00 A.M., an unidentified male shot another male in the chest during an argument.

The MOST logical order for the above sentences to appear in the report is
A. V, II, III, IV, I   B. II, III, V, IV, I   C. IV, I, V, II, III   D. V, III, II, IV, I

25. Police Officer Tracey is preparing a Robbery Report which will include the following five sentences:
   I. I ran around the corner and observe a man pointing a gun at a taxidriver.
   II. I informed the man I was a police officer and that he should not move.
   III. I was on the corner of 125th Street and Park Avenue when I heard a scream coming from around the corner.
   IV. The man turned around and fired one shot at me.
   V. I fired once, shooting him in the arm and causing him to fall to the ground.
   The MOST logical order for the above sentences to appear in the report is
   A. I, III, IV, II, V   B. IV, V, II, I, III   C. III, I, II, IV, V   D. III, I, V, II, IV

KEY (CORRECT ANSWERS)

1.	B		11.	D
2.	B		12.	D
3.	B		13.	C
4.	A		14.	B
5.	A		15.	B
6.	B		16.	A
7.	A		17.	B
8.	D		18.	A
9.	B		19.	A
10.	A		20.	D

21.	B
22.	C
23.	B
24.	A
25.	C

TEST 2

DIRECTIONS: The sentences that follow are in scrambled order. You are to rearrange them in proper order and indicate the letter choice containing the CORRECT answer. *PRINT THE LETTER OF THE CORRECT ANSWER IN THE SPACE AT THE RIGHT*

1. Police Officer Weiker is completing a Complaint Report which will contain the following five sentences:
   I. Mr. Texlor was informed that the owner of the van would receive a parking ticket and that the van would be towed away.
   II. The police tow truck arrived approximately one half hour after Mr. Texlor complained.
   III. While on foot patrol on West End Avenue, I saw the owner of Rand's Restaurant arrive to open his business.
   IV. Mr. Texlor, the owner, called to me and complained that he could not receive deliveries because a van was blocking his driveway.
   V. The van's owner later reported to the precinct that his van had been stolen, and he was then informed that it had been towed.
   The MOST logical order for the above sentences to appear in the report is
   A. III, V, I, II, IV   B. III, IV, I, II, V   C. IV, III, I, II, V   D. IV, III, II, I, V

   1.____

2. Police Officer Ames is completing an entry in his Activity Log. The entry contains the following five sentences:
   I. Mr. Sands gave me a complete description of the robber.
   II. Alvin Sands, owner of the Star Delicatessen, called the precinct to report he had just been robbed.
   III. I then notified all police patrol vehicles to look for a white male in his early twenties wearing brown pants and shirt, a black leather jacket, and black and white sneakers.
   IV. I arrived on the scene after being notified by the precinct that a robbery had just occurred at the Star Delicatessen.
   V. Twenty minutes later, a man fitting the description was arrested by a police officer on patrol six blocks from the delicatessen.
   The MOST logical order for the above sentences to appear in the Activity Log is
   A. II, I, IV, III, V   B. II IV, III, I, V   C. II, IV, I, III, V   D. II, IV, I, V, III

   2.____

3. Police Officer Benson is completing a Complaint Report concerning a stolen taxicab, which will include the following five sentences:
   I. Police Officer Benson noticed that a cab was parked next to a fire hydrant.
   II. Dawson *borrowed* the cab for transportation purposes since he was in a hurry.
   III. Ed Dawson got into his car and tried to start it, but the battery was dead.
   IV. When he reached his destination, he parked the cab by a fire hydrant and placed the keys under the seat.
   V. He looked around and saw an empty cab with the engine running.
   The MOST logical order for the above sentences to appear in the report is
   A. I, III, II, IV, V   B. III, I, II, V, IV   C. III, V, II, IV, I   D. V, II, IV, III, I

   3.____

183

4. Police Officer Hatfield is reviewing his Activity Log entry prior to completing a report. The entry contains the following five sentences:
   I. When I arrived at Zand's Jewelry Store, I noticed that the door was slightly open.
   II. I told the burglar I was a police officer and that he should stand still or he would be shot.
   III. As I entered the store, I saw a man wearing a ski mask attempting to open the safe in the back of the store.
   IV. On December 16, 2020, at 1:38 A.M., I was informed that a burglary was in progress at Zand's Jewelry Store on East 59th Street.
   V. The burglar quickly pulled a knife from his pocket when he saw me.
   The MOST logical order for the above sentences to appear in the report is
      A. IV, I, III, V, II   B. I, IV, III, V, II   C. IV, III, II, V, I   D. I, III, IV, V, II

5. Police Officer Lorenz is completing a report of a murder. The report will contain the following five statements made by a witness:
   I. I was awakened by the sound of a gunshot coming from the apartment next door and I decided to check.
   II. I entered the apartment and looked into the kitchen and the bathroom.
   III. I found Mr. Hubbard's body slumped in the bathtub.
   IV. The door to the apartment was open, but I didn't see anyone.
   V. He had been shot in the head.
   The MOST logical order for the above sentences to appear in the report is
      A. I, III, II, IV, V   B. I, IV, II, III, V   C. IV, II, I, III, V   D. III, I, II, IV, V

6. Police Officer Baldwin is preparing an accident report which will include the following five sentences:
   I. The old man lay on the ground for a few minutes, but was not physically hurt.
   II. Charlie Watson, a construction worker, was repairing some brick work at the top of a building at 54th Street and Madison Avenue.
   III. Steven Green, his partner, warned him that this could be dangerous, but Watson ignored him.
   IV. A few minutes later, one of the bricks thrown by Watson smashed to the ground in front of an old man, who fainted out of fright.
   V. Mr. Watson began throwing some of the bricks over the side of the building.
   The MOST logical order for the above sentences to appear in the report is
      A. II, V, III, IV, I   B. I, IV, II, V, III   C. III, II, IV, V, I   D. II, III, I, IV, V

7. Police Officer Porter is completing an Incident Report concerning her rescue of a woman being held hostage by a former boyfriend. Her report will contain the following five sentences:
   I. I saw a man holding .25 caliber gun to a woman's head, but he did not see me.
   II. I then broke a window and gained access to the house.
   III. As I approached the house on foot, a gunshot rang out and I heard a woman scream.
   IV. A decoy van brought me as close as possible to the house where the woman was being held hostage.

V. I ordered the man to drop his gun, and he released the woman and was taken into custody.

The MOST logical order for the above sentences to appear in the report is
   A. I, III, II, IV, V   B. IV, III, II, I, V   C. III, II, I, IV, V   D. V, I, II, III, IV

8. Police Officer Byrnes is preparing a crime report concerning a robbery. The report will consist of the following five sentences:
    I. Mr. White, following the man's instructions, opened the car's hood, at which time the man got out of the auto, drew a revolver, and ordered White to give him all the money in his pockets.
    II. Investigation has determined there were no witnesses to this incident.
    III. The man asked White to check the oil and fill the tank.
    IV. Mr. White, a gas attendant, states that he was working alone at the gas station when a black male pulled up to the gas pump in a white Mercury.
    V. White was then bound and gagged by the male and locked in the gas station's rest room.

    The MOST logical order for the above sentences to appear in the report is
       A. IV, I, III, II, V   B. III, I, II, V, IV   C. IV, III, I, V, II   D. I, III, IV, II, V

9. Police Officer Gale is preparing a report of a crime committed against Mr. Weston. The report will consist of the following five sentences:
    I. The man, who had a gun, told Mr. Weston not to scream for help and ordered him back into the apartment.
    II. With Mr. Weston disposed of in this fashion, the man proceeded to ransack the apartment.
    III. Opening the door to see who was there, Mr. Weston was confronted by a tall white male wearing a dark blue jacket and white pants.
    IV. Mr. Weston was at home alone in his living room when the doorbell rang.
    V. Once inside, the man bound and gagged Mr. Weston and locked him in the bathroom.

    The MOST logical order for the above sentences to appear in the report is
       A. III, V, II, I, IV   B. IV, III, I, V, II   C. III, V, IV, II, I   D. IV, III, V, I, II

10. A police officer is completing a report of a robbery, which will contain the following five sentences:
    I. Two police officers were about to enter the Red Rose Coffee Shop on 47th Street and 8th Avenue.
    II. They then noticed a male running up the street carrying a brown paper bag.
    III. They heard a woman standing outside the Broadway Boutique yelling that her store had just been robbed by a young man, and she was pointing up the street.
    IV. They caught up with him and made an arrest.
    V. The police officers pursued the male, who ran past them on 8th Avenue.

    The MOST logical order for the above sentences to appear in the report is
       A. I, III, II, V, IV   B. III, I, II, V, IV   C. IV, V, I, II, III   D. I, V, IV, III, II

11. Police Officer Capalbo is preparing a report of a bank robbery. The report will contain the following five statements made by a witness:
    I. Initialing, all I could see were two men, dressed in maintenance uniforms, sitting in the area reserved for bank officers.
    II. I was passing the bank at 8 P.M. and noticed that all the lights were out, except in the rear section.
    III. Then I noticed two other men in the bank, coming from the direction of the vault, carrying a large metal box.
    IV. At this point, I decided to call the police.
    V. I knocked on the window to get the attention of the men in the maintenance uniforms, and they chased the two men carrying the box down a flight of steps.
    The MOST logical order for the above sentences to appear in the report is
    A. IV, I, II, V, III   B. I, III, II, V, IV   C. II, I, III, V, IV   D. II, III, I, V, IV

12. Police Officer Roberts is preparing a crime report concerning an assault and a stolen car. The report will contain the following five sentences:
    I. Upon leaving the store to return to his car, Winters noticed that a male unknown to him was sitting in his car.
    II. The man then re-entered Winters' car and drove away, fleeing north on 2nd Avenue.
    III. Mr. Winters stated that he parked his car in front of 235 East 25th Street and left the engine running while he went into the butcher shop at that location.
    IV. Mr. Robert Gering, a witness, stated that the male is known in the neighborhood as Bobby Rae and is believed to reside at 323 East 114th Street.
    V. When Winters approached the car and ordered the man to get out, the man got out of the auto and struck Winters with his fists, knocking him to the ground.
    The MOST logical order for the above sentences to appear in the report is
    A. III, II, V, I, IV   B. III, I, V, II, IV   C. I, IV, V, II, III   D. III, II, I, V, IV

13. Police Officer Robinson is preparing a crime report concerning the robbery of Mr. Edwards' store. The report will consist of the following five sentences:
    I. When the last customer left the store, the two men drew revolvers and ordered Mr. Edwards to give them all the money in the cash register.
    II. The men proceeded to the back of the store as if they were going to do some shopping.
    III. Janet Morley, a neighborhood resident, later reported that she saw the men enter a green Ford station wagon and flee northbound on Albany Avenue.
    IV. Edwards complied after which the gunmen ran from the store.
    V. Mr. Edwards states that he was stocking merchandise behind the store counter when two white males entered the store.
    The MOST logical order for the above sentences to appear in the report is
    A. V, II, III, I, IV   B. V, II, I, IV, III   C. II, I, V, IV, III   D. III, V, II, I, IV

14. Police Officer Wendell is preparing an accident report for a 6-car accident that occurred at the intersection of Bath Avenue and Bay Parkway. The report will consist of the following five sentences:
    I. A 2016 Volkswagen Beetle, traveling east on Bath Avenue, swerved to the left to avoid the Impala, and struck a 2014 Ford station wagon which was traveling west on Bath Avenue.
    II. The Seville then mounted the curb on the northeast corner of Bath Avenue and Bay Parkway and struck a light pole.
    III. A 2013 Buick Lesabre, traveling northbound on Bay Parkway directly behind the Impala, struck the Impala, pushing it into the intersection of Bath Avenue and Bay Parkway.
    IV. A 2015 Chevy Impala, traveling northbound on Bay Parkway, had stopped for a red light at Bath Avenue.
    V. A 2017 Toyota, traveling westbound on Bath Avenue, swerved to the right to avoid hitting the Ford station wagon, and struck a 2017 Cadillac Seville double-parked near the corner.
    The MOST logical order for the above sentences to appear in the report is
    A. IV, III, V, II, I   B. III, IV, V, II, I   C. IV, III, I, V, II   D. III, IV, V, I, II

15. The following five sentences are part of an Activity Log entry Police Officer Rogers made regarding an explosion:
    I. I quickly treated the pedestrian for the injury.
    II. The explosion caused a glass window in an office building to shatter.
    III. After the pedestrian was treated, a call was placed to the precinct requesting additional police officers to evacuate the area.
    IV. After all the glass settled to the ground, I saw a pedestrian who was bleeding from the arm.
    V. While on foot patrol near 5th Avenue and 53rd Street, I heard a loud explosion.
    The MOST logical order for the above sentences to appear in the report is
    A. II, V, IV, I, III   B. V, II, IV, III, I   C. V, II, I, IV, III   D. V, II, IV, I, III

16. Police Officer David is completing a report regarding illegal activity near the entrance to Madison Square Garden during a recent rock concert. The report will obtain the following five sentences:
    I. As I came closer to the man, he placed what appeared to be tickets in his pocket and began to walk away.
    II. After the man stopped, I questioned him about *scalping* tickets.
    III. While on assignment near the Madison Square Garden entrance, I observed a man apparently selling tickets.
    IV. I stopped the man by stating that I was a police officer.
    V. The man was then given a summons, and he left the area.
    The MOST logical order for the above sentences to appear in the report is
    A. I, III, IV, II, V   B. III, I, IV, V, II   C. III, IV, I, II, V   D. III, I, IV, II, V

17. Police Officer Sampson is preparing a report containing a dispute in a bar. The report will contain the following five sentences:
   I. John Evans, the bartender, ordered the two men out of the bar.
   II. Two men dressed in dungarees entered the C and D Bar at 5:30 P.M.
   III. The two men refused to leave and began to beat up Evans.
   IV. A customer in the bar saw me on patrol and yelled to me to come separate the three men.
   V. The two men became very drunk and loud within a short time.
   The MOST logical order for the above sentences to appear in the report is
   A. II, I, V, III, IV   B. II, III, IV, V, I   C. III, I, II, V, IV   D. II, V, I, III, IV

18. A police officer is completing a report concerning the response to a crime in progress. The report will include the following five sentences:
   I. The officers saw two armed men run out of the liquor store and into a waiting car.
   II. Police Officers Lunty and Duren received the call and responded to the liquor store.
   III. The robbers gave up without a struggle.
   IV. Lunty and Duren blocked the getaway car with their patrol car.
   V. A call came into the precinct concerning a robbery in progress at Jane's Liquor Store.
   The MOST logical order for the above sentence to appear in the report is
   A. V, II, I, IV, III   B. II, V, I, III, IV   C. V, I, IV, II, III   D. I, V, II, III, IV

19. Police Officers Jenkins is preparing a Crime Report which will consist of the following five sentences:
   I. After making inquirie in the vicinity, Smith found out that his next door neighbor, Viola Jones, had seen two local teenagers, Michael Heinz and Vincent Gaynor, smash his car's windshields with a crowbar.
   II. Jones told Smith that the teenagers live at 8700 19th Avenue.
   III. Mr. Smith heard a loud crash at approximately 11:00 P.M., looked out of his apartment window, and saw two white males running away from his car.
   IV. Smith then reported the incident to the precinct, and Heinz and Gaynor were arrested at the address given.
   V. Leaving his apartment to investigate further, Smith discovered that his car's front and rear windshields had been smashed.
   The MOST logical order for the above sentences to appear in the report is
   A. III, IV, V, I, II   B. III, V, I, II, IV   C. III, I, V, II, IV   D. V, III, I, II, IV

20. Sergeant Nancy Winston is reviewing a Gun Control Report which will contain the following five sentences:
   I. The man fell to the floor when hit in the chest with three bullets from 22 caliber gun.
   II. Merriam's 22 caliber gun was seized, and he was given a summons for not having a pistol permit.
   III. Christopher Merriam, the owner of A-Z Grocery, shot a man who attempted to rob him.
   IV. Police Officer Franks responded and asked Merriam for his pistol permit, which he could not produce.

V. Merriam phoned the police to report he had just shot a man who had attempted to rob him.

The MOST logical order for the above sentences to appear in the report is
   A. III, I, V, IV, II   B. I, III, V, IV, II   C. III, I, V, II, IV   D. I, III, II, V, IV

21. Detective John Manville is completing a report for his superior regarding the murder of an unknown male who was shot in Central Park. The report will contain the following five sentences:
   I. Police Officers Langston and Cavers responded to the scene.
   II. I received the assignment to investigate the murder in Central Park from Detective Sergeant Rogers.
   III. Langston notified the Detective Bureau after questioning Jason.
   IV. An unknown male, apparently murdered, was discovered in Central Park by Howard Jason, a park employee, who immediately called the police.
   V. Langston and Cavers questioned Jason.

The MOST logical order for the above sentences to appear in the report is
   A. I, IV, V, III, II   B. IV, I, V, II, III   C. IV, I, V, III, II   D. IV, V, I, III, II

21.____

22. A police officer is completing a report concerning the arrest of a juvenile. The report will contain the following five sentences:
   I. Sanders then telephoned Jay's parents from the precinct to inform them of their son's arrest.
   II. The store owner resisted, and Jay then shot him and ran from the store.
   III. Jay was transported directly to the precinct by Officer Sanders.
   IV. James Jay, a juvenile, walked into a candy store and announced a hold-up.
   V. Police Officer Sanders, while on patrol, arrested Jay a block from the candy store.

The MOST logical order for the above sentences to appear in the report is
   A. IV, V, II, I, III   B. IV, II, V, III, I   C. II, IV, V, III, I   D. V, IV, II, I, III

22.____

23. Police Officer Olsen prepared a crime report for a robbery which contained the following five sentences:
   I. Mr. Gordon was approached by this individual who then produced a gun and demanded the money from the cash register.
   II. The man then fled from the scene on foot, southbound on 5th Avenue.
   III. Mr. Gordon was working at the deli counter when a white male, 5'6", 150-160 lbs., wearing a green jacket and blue pants, entered the store.
   IV. Mr. Gordon complied with the man's demands and handed him the daily receipts.
   V. Further investigation has determined there are no other witnesses to this robbery.

The MOST logical order for the above sentences to appear in the report is
   A. I, III, IV, V, II   B. I, IV, II, III, V   C. III, IV, I, V, II   D. III, I, IV, II, V

23.____

24. Police Officer Bryant responded to 285 E. 31st Street to take a crime report of a burglary of Mr. Bond's home. The report will contain a brief description of the incident, consisting of the following five sentences:
   I. When Mr. Bond attempted to stop the burglar by grabbing him, he was pushed to the floor.
   II. The burglar had apparently gained access to the home by forcing open the 2nd floor bedroom window facing the fire escape.
   III. Mr. Bond sustained a head injury in the scuffle, and the burglar exited the home through the front door.
   IV. Finding nothing in the dresser, the burglar proceeded downstairs to the first floor, where he was confronted by Mr. Bond who was reading in the dining room.
   V. Once inside, he searched the drawers of the bedroom dresser.
   The MOST logical order for the above sentences to appear in the report is
   A. V, IV, I, II, III   B. II, V, IV, I, III   C. II, IV, V, III, I   D. III, II, I, V, IV

25. Police Officer Derringer responded to a call of a rape-homicide case in his patrol area and was ordered to prepare an incident report, which will contain the following five sentences:
   I. He pushed Miss Scott to the ground and forcibly raped her.
   II. Mary Scott was approached from behind by a white male, 5'7", 150-160 lbs. wearing dark pants and a white jacket.
   III. As Robinson approached the male, he ordered him to stop.
   IV. Screaming for help, Miss Scott alerted one John Robinson, a local grocer, who chased her assailant as he fled the scene.
   V. The male turned and fired two shots at Robinson, who fell to the ground mortally wounded.
   The MOST logical order for the above sentences to appear in the report is
   A. IV, III, I, II, V   B. II, IV, III, V, I   C. II, IV, I, V, III   D. II, I, IV, III, V

KEY (CORRECT ANSWERS)

1. B
2. C
3. C
4. A
5. B

6. A
7. B
8. C
9. B
10. A

11. C
12. B
13. B
14. C
15. D

16. D
17. D
18. A
19. B
20. A

21. C
22. B
23. D
24. B
25. D
